2020
Prophecies
and
Predictions

Visions of the Near and Far Future

Betsey Lewis

Copyright © 2019 by Betsey Lewis. All rights reserved.
ISBN: 978 -170703488-
8
Update April 3, 2020
Cover Design by Betsey Lewis
website: **www.betseylewis.com**

Library of Congress Cataloging in-Publication-Data
2020 Prophecies and Predictions: Visions of the Near and Far Future

TABLE OF CONTENTS

Other Books by Betsey Lewis
Available on Amazon

Star Beings: Their Mission and
Prophecy

Ancient Serpent Gods: The Alien Connection to Reptilian
Dinosaurs

Earth Energy:
Return to Ancient Wisdom

Angels, Aliens and Prophecy II

Communicating with the Other Side: True Experiences of a
Psychic Medium

ACKNOWLEDGMENT

With gratitude to the countless souls who continue to bring about positive changes to our world such as Indigenous leaders Corbin Harney and Ed McGaa "Eagle Man," now working from the Other Side. My heartfelt thanks to my Spirit Guides who have guided and saved my life countless times, especially my Spirit Sister Guide, Kathy.

Chapter One
PROPHECIES AND PREDICTIONS

Many people mistakenly think that prediction and prophecy mean the same thing. They both indeed foretell the future but there is a difference! A prediction is a forecast made by those who calculate the parameters of the subject involved and after evaluating all the odds they can predict the future.

Prophecy is another story. The ancient Pharaohs of Egypt used to say "So shall it be written and so shall it be done." Once written a prophecy is to be fulfilled without exceptions, in other words, it was a preordained event. A prophecy has all the ingredients except the element of time. Without the element of time, a prophecy is hard to pinpoint. Nevertheless, we believe that in the last century or so there have been prophetic visions given by famous seers, but it is debatable whether or not their prophecies were fulfilled. It's all in the interpretation.

Such is the case of the 16th-century French prophet and astrologer Nostradamus and his written visions of the future set in coded quatrains.

Nostradamus's predictions tended to be about general types of events, like natural disasters and conflict-related events that tend to occur regularly as time goes on. Some people believe that his prophecies have included actual events, such as the death of Henry II, the French Revolution, the rise of Napoleon, John F. Kennedy's assassination, the rise of Adolf Hitler, and the 9/11 attacks. One must question if Nostradamus's Hister referred to Hitler. Hister is close to the name Hitler, but it is also the Latin name for the Danube (especially its lower course), or the people living along its banks. Most scholars believe Hister referred to the Danube River.

The late sleeping prophet Edgar Cayce (1877-1945) had misses on his channeled prophecies but fared far better diagnosing illnesses for 1,385 people from 1943 to 1944. It is estimated that Cayce gave a total of 13,000 to 14,000 readings during his lifetime. Perhaps one of his biggest failed predictions was that the Earth's poles would shift around in the late 1990s or near the turn of the 21st century. Yet, Cayce diagnosed thousands of people in his deep trance state and healed many people from all types of illnesses.

When the massive 8.8 magnitude earthquake struck Chile on Saturday, February 10, 2010, it shifted the Earth's axis, creating shorter days, scientists at NASA revealed. Each day should be 1.26 microseconds shorter, according to preliminary calculations. A microsecond is one-millionth of a second. It has been suggested that after NASA revealed this huge earthquake had shifted the Earth's axis and shortened the day, many people wondered if Edgar Cayce's prediction might have been this earthquake instead of a total pole shift. We can only speculate.

Cayce asked this question, "What great change or the beginning of what change, if any, is to take place in the Earth in the year 2000 to 2001 A.D.?" Cayce replied, "When there is the shifting of the poles; or a new cycle begins."

The Maya also saw a new era beginning in the first years of the new millennium but, according to their artifacts, it began when the present age of "Movement" ended on December 21, 2012 A.D.

Astronomers believe the axis wobble (like a spinning top slowing) has occurred for ages and causes the North Pole to point to different Pole Stars or North Stars. How often this occurs is unclear. According to leading scientific teams at major research centers, axis shifts have only occurred every few million or billion years and taken millions of years to be completed. According to other worthy sources (e.g., Encyclopedia Britannica and The Learning Channel), the wobble changes the Pole Star about every 24,000 to 26,000 years.

Cayce stated that the ancient Egyptians knew of these shifts and the Great Pyramid of Giza was built to point to the Axis or Pole Star.

During one of his Cayce's readings, he spoke of a change in the Pole Star. He explained that the Great Pyramid of Giza represented the various ages we have been going through. He said, "At the correct time accurate imaginary lines can be drawn from the opening of the Great Pyramid to the second star in the great Dipper, called Polaris or the North Star." He must be using the word "great" as an adjective of importance because Polaris is in the Little Dipper, but it is, as Cayce said, "The second star."

The north pole of Earth's spinning axis points to a star considered the Pole Star. According to Edgar Cayce, we are about to see a change in our Pole Star, from Polaris to Vega. In Ancient Egypt, the Pole Star was Thuban. This marks a move into a new era—a new age.

In Cayce's own words: "This indicates it is the system toward which the soul takes its flight after having completed its sojourn through this solar system. The Dipper is gradually changing, and when this change becomes noticeable-as might be calculated from the Pyramid, there will be the beginning of the change in the races [he's speaking of root races, not color races]. There will come a greater influx of souls from the Atlantean, Lemurian, La, Ur, or Da civilizations."

He then explained that the Great Pyramid was built in this manner by Ra and Hermes and many others who "sought to bring to man a better understanding of the close relationship between the Creative Forces and that created, between man and man, and man and his Maker."

Cayce then cautioned us that "only those who have been called may truly understand. Who then has been called? Whosoever will make him or herself a channel may be raised to a blessing...."

Let's examine the relationship of the entrance to the Great Pyramid and the shifting Pole Stars. During the age of ancient Egypt, Thuban was the North Star, i.e., at midnight above the North Pole. Thuban would have been the northernmost star. Of course, today the North Star is Polaris. However, Vega will be our North Star in the future. But this would require our planet to roll over dramatically!

Viewing from the North Pole: The shift from Thuban to Polaris would have been about 26°. The shift from Polaris to Vega would be about 51°, a much more significant pole shift.

If one draws an imaginary line from the entrance of the Great Pyramid on the Spring Equinox (about March 22-25) in 4000+ B.C., 2000 A.D., and 10000 A.D., it points directly to the northern star of each age: Thuban, Polaris, and Vega, respectively. Hermes, Ra, and all the others involved sure knew what they were doing when they built that magnificent monument.

At the Spring Equinox during ancient Egyptian times, Thuban was the Pole Star of the Pyramid.

Since Polaris indicates "the system towards which the soul takes flight," could the change to Vega indicate a new flight pattern? Vega is a blue-white star and the fifth brightest star in the sky. It is in the constellation Lyra, the Harp or Lyre of the musician Orpheus. It was said that when Orpheus played this instrument, neither mortal nor god could turn away (Orpheus also introduced reincarnation into Greek mythology, a key concept in Cayce's teachings as well). Interestingly, Vega marks the approximate direction toward which our sun and all its planets are traveling through space.

At the Spring Equinox during our present time, Polaris is the Pole Star of the Pyramid. To have shifted from Thuban as the Pole Star to Polaris, the Earth would have shifted its northern axis pole about 26°, not a drastic shift. However, in order to shift from Polaris as the Pole Star to Vega, the Earth will need to shift its northern axis pole a whopping 51° degrees! But, if it is done gradually, over a very long time, as Cayce indicated, then we should not expect a dramatic pole shift in the next few years. But what if there is an unknown factor like Nibiru aka Planet X lurking in our solar system that plays havoc with all the planets when it passes by? And if Nibiru, a failed star or brown dwarf, really exists Caltech scientists Konstantin Batygin and Mike Brown claimed in 2016 that they had found the elusive Planet X or Planet 9 as the suggested. They discovered the planet's existence through mathematical modeling and computer simulations but have not yet observed the object.

Brown noted that the putative ninth planet—at 5,000 times the mass of Pluto—is sufficiently large that there should be no debate about whether it is a true planet. Unlike the class of smaller objects now known as dwarf planets, Planet Nine gravitationally dominates its neighborhood of the solar system. It dominates a region larger than any of the other known planets—a fact that Brown said makes it "the most planet-y of the planets in the whole solar system."

Astronomers believe that most solar systems have two suns, and some believe our solar system once had two suns. A brown dwarf would make sense and might explain cataclysmic Earth changes that have occurred for 4.543 billion years that Earth was born.

As many of you know, Cayce said that during this new age we will regain the powers we had in our earliest incarnations into this world during the Age of Atlantis and Lemuria or Mu. This was before our souls became encased in physical matter as we are today and back when we had godly powers to solve our material needs more easily. Of course, Cayce warned that we did not handle these powers well, leading to the destruction of these ancient lands.

When asked what the New Age means to humanity, Edgar Cayce replied: "the full consciousness of the ability to communicate with the Creative Forces and be aware of the relationships to the Creative Forces and the uses of same in material environs. This awareness during the era or age in the Age of Atlantis and Lemuria or Mu brought what? Destruction to man, and his beginning of the needs of the journey up through that of selfishness.

Why did Edgar Cayce get some predictions right and others wrong? Or perhaps his shift will come in the far future with Vega is the North Star. Did he see an alternate or parallel reality world where such an event occurred but not in our present-day world?

Some ideas about the quantum world appear to suggest there are many versions of you spread out across many parallel universes. Now, two scientists have formulated a proof that attempts to show this is true. The proof involves a fundamental construct in quantum mechanics called Bell's theorem. This theorem deals with situations where particles interact with each other, become entangled, and then go their separate ways. It is what's called a "no-go theorem", one designed to show that some assumption about how the world works is not true.

In 1954, a young Princeton University doctoral candidate named Hugh Everett III came up with a radical idea that there exist parallel universes, exactly like our universe. These universes are all related to ours; indeed, they branch off from ours, and our universe is branched off of others. Within these parallel universes, our wars have had different outcomes than the ones we know. Species that are extinct in our universe have evolved and adapted in others. In other universes, we humans may have become extinct.

This is mind-boggling and yet, it is still understandable. Notions of parallel universes or dimensions that resemble our own have appeared in works of science fiction and have been used as explanations for metaphysics. But why would a young up-and-coming physicist possibly risk his future career by posing a theory about parallel universes?

With his Many-Worlds theory, Everett was attempting to answer a rather sticky question related to quantum physics: Why does quantum matter behave erratically? The quantum level is the smallest one science has detected so far. The study of quantum physics began in 1900 when the physicist Max Planck first introduced the concept to the scientific world. Planck's study of radiation yielded some unusual findings that contradicted classical physical laws. These findings suggested that there are other laws at work in the universe, operating on a deeper level than the one we know.

Young Hugh Everett agreed with much of what the highly respected physicist Niels Bohr had suggested about the quantum world. He agreed with the idea of superposition, as well as with the notion of wave functions. But Everett disagreed with Bohr in one vital respect.

To Everett, measuring a quantum object does not force it into one comprehensible state or another. Instead, a measurement taken of a quantum object causes an actual split in the universe. The universe is literally duplicated, splitting into one universe for each possible outcome from the measurement. For example, say an object's wave function is both a particle and a wave. When a physicist measures the particle, there are two possible outcomes: It will either be measured as a particle or a wave. This distinction makes Everett's *Many-Worlds theory* a competitor of the Copenhagen interpretation as an explanation for quantum mechanics.

When a physicist measures the object, the universe splits into two distinct universes to accommodate each of the possible outcomes. So a scientist in one universe finds that the object has been measured in a waveform. The same scientist in the other universe measures the object as a particle. This also explains how one particle can be measured in more than one state.

As unsettling as it may sound, Everett's *Many-Worlds* interpretation has implications beyond the quantum level. If an action has more than one possible outcome, then—if Everett's theory is correct—the universe splits when that action is taken. This holds true even when a person chooses not to take action.

This means that if you have ever found yourself in a situation where death was a possible outcome, then in a universe parallel to ours, you are dead. This is just one reason that some find the Many-Worlds interpretation disturbing.

Another disturbing aspect of the *Many-Worlds* interpretation is that it undermines our concept of time as linear. Imagine a timeline showing the history of the Vietnam War. Rather than a straight line showing noteworthy events progressing onward, a timeline based on the Many-Worlds interpretation would show each possible outcome of each action taken. From there, each possible outcome of the actions taken (as a result of the original outcome) would be further chronicled.

But a person cannot be aware of his other selves or even his death—that exist in parallel universes. So how could we ever know if the *Many-Worlds theory* is correct? Assurance that the interpretation is theoretically possible came in the late 1990s from a thought experiment—an imagined experiment used to theoretically prove or disprove an idea called quantum suicide.

This thought experiment renewed interest in Everett's theory, which was for many years considered rubbish. Since Many-Worlds theory was proven possible, physicists and mathematicians have aimed to investigate the implications of the theory in depth. But the Many-Worlds interpretation is not the only theory that seeks to explain the universe. Nor is it the only one that suggests there are universes parallel to our own.

Following his famous *Theory of Relativity*, Albert Einstein spent the rest of his life looking for the one final level that would answer all physical questions. Physicists refer to this phantom theory as the Theory of Everything. Quantum physicists believe that they are on the trail of finding that final theory. But another field of physics believes that the quantum level is not the smallest, so it, therefore, could not provide the *Theory of Everything*.

These physicists turn instead to a theoretical subquantum level called string theory for the answers to all of life. What's amazing is that through their theoretical investigation, these physicists, like Everett, have also concluded that there are parallel universes.

Like the *Many-Worlds theory*, string theory demonstrates that parallel universes exist. According to the theory, our universe is like a bubble that exists alongside similar parallel universes. Unlike the Many-Worlds theory, string theory supposes that these universes can come into contact with one another. String theory says that gravity can flow between these parallel universes. When these universes interact, a Big Bang like the one that created our universe occurs.

While physicists have managed to create machines that can detect quantum matter, the subquantum strings are yet to be observed, which makes them and the theory on which they're built entirely theoretical. It has been discredited by some, although others believe it is correct.

So do parallel universes exist? According to the Many-Worlds theorists, we can't truly be certain, even though we are not aware of them. The string theory has already been tested at least once–with negative results. Dr. Michio Kaku still believes parallel dimensions do exist.

Einstein didn't live long enough to see his quest for the Theory of Everything taken up by others. Then again, if Many Worlds theory is correct, Einstein's still alive in a parallel universe. Perhaps in another alternate universe, physicists have already found the Theory of Everything.

Block Theory

The block universe theory says that our universe may be looked at as a giant four-dimensional block of spacetime, containing all the things that ever happen, explained Dr. Kristie Miller, the joint director for the Centre for Time at the University of Sydney.

In the block universe, there is no "now" or present. All moments that exist are just relative to each other within the three spatial dimensions and one time dimension. Your sense of the present is just reflecting where in the block universe you are at that instance. The "past" is just a slice of the universe at an earlier location while the "future" is at a later location.

So, is time just an elaborate mind trick? And more importantly— is time travel possible?

Dr. Miller's answer to that is "yes." "Of course, just hypothetically, since we'd need to figure out first how to travel at "some reasonable percentage of the speed of light". Going to the past would entail using wormholes, like "short cuts through space-time."

Now, if you did manage to get back in time, you won't be able to change it. This is because your past is always simultaneously someone else's future. So if you travel to the past, you're just making that future the way it is. What's more, perhaps the past has already been altered by time travelers.

How would we be able to tell if it hasn't? "For all we know, the reason the past is the way it is, is in part due to the presence of time travelers," added Miller.

By that logic, what you do tomorrow will make it the way it is, with you fulfilling a certain destiny in time, which is in itself more of an illusion than a fundamental property of nature.

While the debate of time continues, the block universe theory is one of the most promising that can reconcile the cosmological view of time with our everyday experience. What may be certain time is much more than what it appears to be. Unraveling its mysteries is integral to understanding the human experience.

James Gates, Ph.D., Professor of Theoretical Physics, who researches supersymmetry and superstring theory at the University of Maryland, College Park, believes that we possibly live inside of a Matrix.

If this is the case, we might have something in common with The Matrix science-fiction films, which depict a world where everything human beings experience is the product of a virtual-reality-generating computer network." In 2017, theoretical physicists published in Physical Review Letters "substantial evidence" that we are living in a holographic universe. Studying our universe's cosmic microwave background leftover from the singularity moment when the universe erupted in the Big Bang— the scientists can detect large amounts of what they call "imprints of information" embedded in the white noise or microwaves left over from the moment the universe exploded into this dimension and kept growing.

Perhaps our world is Maya, the Vedic term for illusion or magic.

How does time travel and alternate/parallel worlds theory explain what many have experienced in The Mandela Effect? South African anti-apartheid political leader Nelson Mandela, who this theory is named after, died in 2013. However, countless people distinctly remember him dying in prison in the 1980s. But his death isn't the only example of a Mandela Effect.

We have been wrong about so many dates, details, and more. Keep going for more commonly misremembered moments in history. In perhaps the most memorable moment during the 1989 Tiananmen Square protects in China, recollections of the event vary. Some say the unidentified man known as "Tank Man" was run over and killed, but other videos show him moving away from the scene. I remember he was killed.

Author and Psi Researcher Starfire Tor lectures on her theory of Time Shifts, Core Matrix, Co-Existing Time Lines and Unified Field Theory of Psi. She believes that a Time Shift, also known as an "Event Horizon Shift" or "Reality Shift" is defined as an alternation of our reality/space-time continuum. In other words, realities can change from one event to another and back again.

When such an event takes place we sometimes sense something is different, but can't put our finger on it. Our brain accepts the new event and new reality.

There are many examples of this throughout history. In 1901, two English women were visiting the Palace of Versailles in Paris. Being adventurous, the women followed an old path and suddenly found people dressed from the 19th century and speaking in a different dialect. The women decided to return and followed a man in the direction they had seen before. Suddenly they found themselves transported forward in time again and in the middle of a wedding from their present time.

Starfire Tor claims to have had her own personal experiences which she says was captured while filming a music video in Southern California. During one of the scenes, she was asked to ride her horse away from the camera and crew, gallop over a short field and around an oak tree. The ride would take less than a minute. As soon as the director said "action" she began riding, leaving the crew behind her. After rounding the tree she halted the horse and looked back, and to her utter amazement, no one was there. Feeling disoriented, she rode her horseback to where the main set was located and found the crew waiting. No one seemed to remember the incident except Starfire.

The following day the location photographs were delivered. Although the photographs showed Starfire on her horse and her crew, there was one glaring anomaly. On the left side of the photo was something that looked like an otherworldly portal or doorway. Starfire believes she went through a time vortex or stargate that day, and she has the photograph to prove it.

I had a time displacement (TD) experience in 1965 on a summer day in Idaho. My mom, a smoker, often gave me a cigarette to light for her (no, I'm not a smoker). On this particular day, while working at our lake resort concession stand, I removed a cigarette from the pack and lit it. As I pulled it away from my mouth, I was shocked to see a perfect letter "B" on the filter tip. A chill went through me, sensing I had sent a message to myself from the future. Why would I think this? Mom and I talked about the incident for many years, and we both sensed that time travel was involved that day where I sent a message to the past me from a future timeline. What a mind-blowing thought!

Another possible time shift or "TD" (time displacement) occurrence for me happened in 1978. I had recently moved to Portland, Oregon, and decided to visit my father and stepmother in Salem on a Friday afternoon, a distance of 47 miles, approximately an hour drive from South Portland. I phoned my father to let him know I was on my way at 4:00 p.m. and I'd see him by five, but as soon as I arrived my father had a confused look on his face, "Where have you been?" he questioned.

"Driving to see you," I replied.

He then pointed to the clock—it was a little after six. An extra hour had passed without me having any recall of anything unusual that day. Where did I go during that extra hour? I have no recollection of missing any time. I don't recall any heavy traffic at that time to account for the anomaly.

I've also experienced TD while residing in Tucson, Arizona, in 2001. No matter where I went in the city, I felt that many of the people looked eerily familiar, yet we had never met. This was the first time I'd been to Tucson, at least in this lifetime. Had I dreamed of them or leaped into the future?

So what does time travel and multiverses have to do with psychics and prophets? Everything! Here is an analogy of time. Suppose you are on a river and beyond you is the past and up ahead lies the future, but there is a caveat. There are tributaries in this imaginary river and countless tributaries head (the future). So which future will be the one that becomes your reality in the present? That depends on the person in the boat and the mind-set and thoughts this person has about the future. Does the person believe he or she is the master of their fate or do they believe they have no control over events?

The future has infinite possibilities. When a psychic makes a prediction, they are predicting a possible future for that person, but free-will can change any outcome. Does that make sense?

Does that mean that destiny doesn't exist and nothing is predetermined or fated to happen? Yes and no. Certain events (mostly natural events) are inevitable and while anything involving humans can be manipulated by mass consciousness.

For instance, Apollo 13 appeared to be doomed on April 13, 1970, when astronauts John Swigert Jr., Jack Lovell, and Fred Haise discovered an oxygen tank exploded while traveling 200,000 miles from Earth. The explosion crippled the service module upon which the Command Module depended. A miracle happened on that day. Events became worse with an electrical problem and the realization that the astronauts had less oxygen than they thought.

First, Astronaut Ken Mattingly was grounded from the mission when he contacted German measles. But that turned out to be a blessing in disguise. With NASA engineers and Mattingly's skills, they invented a new gadget with only the ship's limited resources.

But something else remarkable happened during that time—from Wall Street, the Pope and to the Wailing Wall in Jerusalem people came together and prayed for the astronaut's safe return to Earth. Seven days later, on April 17, 1970, the Apollo 13 capsule splashed down safely in the South Pacific Ocean, southwest of American Samoa and was recovered by the USS Iwo Jima. All the men were in good condition except for Haise who suffered from a serious urinary tract infection due to dehydration.

If you still don't accept that human consciousness can alter events through intent and prayer, consider what happened on September 11, 2001, after the first plane hit the World Trade Center Buildings. Two National Oceanic and Atmospheric Administration (NOAA) space weather satellites known as GOES-8 AND GOES-9, which monitor the Earth's geomagnetic field, picked up a huge spike in Earth's magnetic field during the attacks and several days after. It was theorized the spike indicated there were unbelievable stress waves created that day by mass human emotion on the planet. GOES-8, while orbiting 22,300 miles around the equator on that day, detected the first surge that topped out at nearly 50 units (or nanoteslas), higher than any reading previously recorded. The time was 9:00 am Eastern standard time. 15 minutes after the first plane hit the World Trade Center and 15 minutes before the second impact.

September 11, 2001, was a prime event that changed the course of human history. There are stories of those who worked at the Trade Tower building that were given warnings not to go into work or were miraculously delayed from getting to work. Did some foresee this event? Hundreds did have a foreboding of something happening. I dreamed one year before the event of a huge tree. The dream was like watching a movie where this huge tree had apples and was beautiful and green. Suddenly the leaves began to wither and the apples drop. Then the entire tree was sucked into the ground and vanished. The dream was a symbol but at the time I didn't understand the symbology until after 9-11. The apple tree in my dream represented New York City, nicknamed "The Big Apple" in the 1920s.

My premonition was showing me that by the way it was pulled straight down into the ground that the World Trade Buildings were downed not by planes, but by an implosion by explosives. There's so much more I could add to what happened on that day, but most people would not believe my visions of the events that lead to the attack and the well-known people involved.

Now that I have explained timelines, time travel, multiverses, perhaps you understand why a good psychic isn't always right. Time is malleable and can be altered by thought, action, and prayer. This is why psychics and prophets never get it right all the time. If there was one psychic in the world who was perfectly accurate, I can guarantee they would be working in some top-secret military think-tank and never see the light of day!

Remember the name of the game here is state of mind. How you feel about reality and how you program reality with your thoughts and actions each day is how you are going to respond to it or how it is going to present itself to you. Dream of the impossible, because everything is possible if you believe! You can do it! You can do whatever you want to do. You will transform the world no matter what state the world is in.

Remember, when you learn the rules of the game of life—you are a result of thought, and that is a law within our universe. All you need to do is think of how you want to be and how you want the world to be and so you and the world shall be.

"For where two or three gather in my name, there am I with them."

Chapter Two
BORN A PSYCHIC

Most people have a preconceived notion that only special people have psychic abilities but that belief is far from the truth. Most of you reading this have experienced an intuitive feeling or psychic moment in your life—whether it was a dream or a warning that comes out of the blue and saves you from harm, or a gut feeling about a car turning into your lane that prevents an accident. Ancient humans had to survive by trusting their intuitive instinct or perish without the aid of modern technology so they turned to shamans or medicine people who could see into the future.

I inherited my psychic ability from two generations of psychic women—my mother and my great aunt. But there might have been more family members with this gift that I unaware of. I am a psychic-clairvoyant and part-time medium. I can psychically see into the past, present, and future. Some of my premonitions come to me as lucid dreams, symbolic dreams, a vision and what I call "the knowing." The knowing feeling tells me that I am 100% right. I know exactly will happen as if I had jumped into the future for an instant. Sometimes I will touch an object and get a feeling about it and its owner.

My husband and I were at a casino in Nevada a few years ago and I sensed without a doubt that a quarter slot machine would pay off if I tried it. I walked over to the machine put one quarter in and won $100. That is what instant knowing. Unfortunately, it hasn't worked for lottery games.

Also, I am a medium who gets messages from those who have passed on. For me, I have found that those who have passed on have their schedule and show up when they need to convey an important message. The dead don't follow you around night and day as some mediums would have you think. They have a life on the Other Side too.

My deceased family members have contacted me often, especially my sister Kathy who passed away in 2003. She has given me many messages and she has demonstrated remarkable feats of spirit energy—turning a stereo/radio off and on, turning on the television late at night, causing lights to turn off and on, and scaring our cat half to death one night until I explained to him that it was Kathy. She has levitated utensils, caused our car's horn to sound in the garage, and then stop, and made a sapling tree shutter back and forth as if an invisible hand moved it. She created a perfect happy face on the bottom of a glass coaster from water condensation after my husband and I discussed happy faces used everywhere.

I was born in March on the seventh day at 7:48 in the morning— under the astrological sign of Pisces. Seven is a very spiritual number and as Pisces, I feel my psychic gifts were enhanced by my birth on the 7th day and at 7:48 am. My great grandmother traveled to Israel during the late 1800s and retrieved a bottle of the Holy Water from the River Jordan and had me christened with it. The River Jordan is where John the Baptist supposedly baptized Jesus.

My mother first noticed that I had a gift for communicating the unseen world at age three. I described my two invisible playmates and often told her they gave me secrets, although I don't recall them now or the messages given to me. I refused to divulge any of the messages. Growing up I sensed that I had been given an urgent message, but erased from my memory for a later time.

At age seven, I was followed home from first grade by a gigantic silver disk in the sky. I had lost sometime during the walk home because I arrived home one hour later from a walk that usually took 10 minutes. My mother was fearful and started looking for me. Oddly, other children in the neighborhood had witnessed this UFO, yet it was never reported in the Southern Idaho news.

Shortly after this UFO encounter, I began to experience recurring and very lucid dreams of catastrophic Earth changes— tsunami waves hitting coasts worldwide, violent earthquakes and volcanoes awakening. It was as if I was viewing a television monitor of a violent Earth. I have found that anytime I have repeating dreams it's a warning of a future event. The events I was privy too at age seven are happening in this timeline.

I was lucky to have a psychically gifted mother who also believed in the supernatural, UFOs, reincarnation and helped me to enhance my gift through playing cards. She would hold a deck of cards so I couldn't see the color or suit. Then she would have me guess what card she held. I became proficient at the game. And we both like to guess who was calling on our rotary phone (this was long before caller ID). We usually got it right!

Mom also had the gift of telepathy and together we could communicate without talking. She described her astral travel where she would leave her physical body and materialize in other places. Friends often commented that they saw her miles away from home.

Mom recalled a past life in ancient China as a worker who helped build the Great Wall of China. She described how she died as an old man, a convict, and was buried inside a section of the wall, a fact that was not known during the 1950s. According to texts, Emperor Qin Shi Huang ordered the construction of the Great Wall around 221 B.C., and the labor force that built the wall was made up largely of soldiers and convicts. It is said that as many as 400,000 people died during the wall's construction; many of these workers were buried within the wall itself.

Hours before my mother passed away in Southern California her astral body came to comfort me while I was grocery shopping. Something told me to look down at my hand. In an instant, my mother's hand had transformed became my left hand and I knew it was her way of telling me goodbye. She died later that night of a massive heart attack and never regained consciousness. Often people visit their loved ones before they pass either in a dream or an astral visit to say goodbye one last time.

My childhood wasn't all fun and games. My parents fought all the time and some of their arguments became physical. Often my younger sister and I were pulled out of schools to escape with Mom to a friend's house or relative's house in a nearby town. During that time, I discovered my empathic gift and felt my mother's pain and fear. Empaths can sense emotional energy both from the people around them and the environment they happen to be in. I am also clairsentient, meaning that I can physically tune in to the emotional experiences of another person or place.

Such people follow the path of emotion and the heart. And so having this ability is a double-edged sword. Science says empaths don't exist—but I can tell you such people exist –I exist. So to that end, I found it hard to exist with parents that were angry, dysfunctional and unhappy.

One profound example of this happened is the time I spent with a former boyfriend in San Francisco who had suffered two strokes. His paralyzes had caused him to lose a lot of his mobility with his left arm and leg, but he still could speak clearly. I stayed with him for a few days, but I realized that I had to leave.

My empathic ability happened after a friend's husband threatened me one night after I visited their home. I sensed his violent anger and had closed the door on my Ford Blazer too quickly and received a gash over my left eye that required several stitches. Months later, my friend divorced him. Within a year, her husband was imprisoned for threatening a young boy with a gun on a bike path.

I quickly learned that it was important to put a protective invisible shield around my physical body, even if I don't know where the unwanted emotions or negativity originate from. Many empaths, like me, try to avoid hospitals and have an intense dislike for doctor's offices or crowded gatherings. It's psychic overload for me to be around certain sick people, angry people, emotionally disturbed people or those in great pain even when my nature is to reach out and help them. Those wonderful and caring people who do psychic healing always protect themselves. Perhaps that is why Edgar Cayce died two months before his sixty-eighth birthday from the thousands of life readings he gave through the years and the illnesses he diagnosed.

My first spirit encounter happened after my paternal grandfather died suddenly of a massive heart attack while walking up a hill to his gold mine on the Idaho/Nevada border. At age eight, this was my first experience with a family member dying and I was devastated.

Shortly after his death, poltergeist activity began in our newly built home in Twin Falls, Idaho. Our black Labrador dog barked incessantly at unseen things and Mom often heard loud footsteps crossing the living room floor while she doing laundry. She ran upstairs and was shocked no one was there. She was frightened.

I prayed to see Grandfather one more time and say goodbye, and he obliged me late one night with a ghostly visitation. It was late night when I woke to see a white gauzy figure of a man standing beside my bed who I thought at first was my father. I tried to call out but I couldn't find my voice and quickly pulled the covers over my head until morning.

I explained my paranormal encounter to Mom, and she calmed my fears and explained it was Grandfather appearing to me as a younger and much thinner man. Spirits often materialize during a time they looked their best—thirties to early forties. His spirit form never returned, probably due to my fear. But I still sensed him near, watching over me, calling me his "little kooks." Obviously, he sensed that I was different than most children my age.

One year later, my grandfather returned to save my life.

A big snowstorm had hit Southern Idaho and a plow had pushed the snow near our house into a big pile. Alone, I built a snow cave on the side of the road. I had hollowed out the heavy wet snow and crawled inside when suddenly the snow cave collapsed on me, and I couldn't move. I was trapped and running out of air. My only thought was I was going to suffocate in the snow cave and no one would know I was there until the snow melted days later.

Just as I thought that I was pulled up from the heavy snow that entrapped me, only to find no one there, at least physically. My grandfather reached out from beyond to save my life that day. And my spirit guides have saved my life countless times through the years in incredible situations where I should have died. They must know that I have much to accomplish on Earth before I die.

By the time I was twelve, my mother had me giving psychic readings for friends and family members. One summer day I had a premonition that my sister was going to die young. To clear her karma, I told her that if she needed to walk backward for a day and that would enable her to live a long life. I didn't prevent the inevitable. Kathy's life was cut short by cancer at the age of fifty while living in Argentina.

Oddly, the year before she died, my Spirit Guides urged me to move from Tucson, Arizona to Southern California and be with her. Whenever I get these messages to move, I listen. That is why I recently moved from Idaho to the desert in Southern Nevada, sensing there was an important reason to be here at this time. Believe me, I love the mountains, lakes, and rivers of Idaho where I was born, and so I could never imagine living in Southern Nevada until recently. I sense that major Earth changes will increase and the Southwest will be a far better place to live in the future.

Shortly after Kathy's death, her spirit began visiting my husband and me to prove to me that she was watching over us. She made a sapling tree with her wind chimes move back and forth without the aid of wind or an earthquake. Through the years she has made kitchen utensils levitate, she has turned on the television set in the middle of the night and she often turned a radio/stereo off and on.

One morning, I said a prayer to her out loud that it was okay for her to move on. Moments later, the radio bean playing Never Can Say Goodbye by The Jackson Five and then turned off by itself. My husband was standing in the kitchen and heard the radio turn off. He laughed and said, "Guess she told you that she's never going to say goodbye."

Kathy scared our cat one night in the hallway just above family photos, included one of her. Comet hissed and his back arched as he starred at an invisible presence. I picked him up and told him it was Kathy watching over him and it was as if he understood. He calmed down. One year later Comet died, and I knew Kathy, a great animal lover, was there to welcome him over.

She is my spirit guide since her death in 2003 and she visits me often during psychic readings and in dreams. Her voice comes to me like a soft whisper, a gut feeling or just an instant knowing. Often our spirit guides change through the years when needed.

Recently, she woke my husband and me from a sound sleep in the middle of the night by making our fire alarms blare. As soon as I said Kathy, it stopped. She can be a bit mischievous, but I had asked her to let me know if she had moved with us to the Southwest. And her answer was a resounding "yes."

It was 1981, shortly after renowned author and MUFON investigator Ann Druffel regressed Mother and me back to our UFO encounter that I volunteered to work for Stephan A. Schwartz and his Mobius Group in Los Angeles where Ann was assisting in various investigations. The Mobius Group was unique and enlisted an international association of scientists from many disciplines, including one of the most extensively tested team of psychics ever assembled.

I periodically would answer the phones for Stephan. One day a group of psychics (Stephan didn't know I was a psychic) gathered to remote view two hunters who had vanished in the Canadian wilderness. The psychics all believed the two men were alive, but my mom and I envisioned they had died from hypothermia in the frigid weather. I might have mentioned to Stephan that we sensed the men had died, but I don't think we were taken seriously with such renowned psychics working on this missing person's case. Days later, the bodies of the two men were found near the river.

Both Mother and I had a vision that was so strange, but wondrous. It happened in Sherman Oaks, California on August 7, 1985 (note the day was the 7th, my angelic number). It was a hot day with wispy cirrus clouds shedding ice trails across the sky like angel's wings.

Mom and I had been grocery shopping and I had just turned into the driveway when something told me to look up.

A brilliant rainbow band (not a rainbow arch) was at the one o'clock position in the sky facing north. For days, I had been thinking about the death of my father in January and the recent death of my stepfather, Maurice Blatty, eldest brother of bestselling author and screenplay writer William Peter Blatty, known for his horror novel The Exorcist. Seeing this strange brilliant rainbow was like an answer to my prayer that they were watching over us.

The rainbow band is known as a full spectrum colored-band produced as the sun hits the flat ice crystals in these high clouds. The phenomenon is known as a circumhorizontal arc, essentially an ice halo or partial halo by the refraction of the sunlight off of the ice crystals.

But there was something odd about the rainbow band. Four luminous colors held our attention, and stranger yet was the cigar-shaped cloud behind the brilliant rainbow. The rainbow band consisted of red at the top, then gold, purple and brilliant indigo at the bottom—four distinctive colors. Even stranger was the hole in the purple band that looked like a heavenly eye looking down on us.

Mom and I watched in awe as each color dripped down into the colors below, one by one as if the phenomenon might fade, but then suddenly each color became brilliant again. I ran into the house and called a friend who worked in downtown Los Angeles and asked him if he could see the rainbow band. He returned to the phone and said he couldn't see anything usual in the sky. I returned to where Mom stood as we watched spellbound as the colors melted into each other again and turned radiant one by one.

This pattern continued three more times.

Thirty minutes had passed and the cigar-shaped cloud and the rainbow band remained in the same position. Then slowly the four colors began to fade into each other and abruptly the iridescent indigo band at the bottom of the band dripped down on the right side, turned into a luminous white band, and shot off like a laser toward the east along with the cigar-shaped cloud.

We were stunned! I remember mumbling, "What in the world?"

The Los Angeles area is one of the hot spots for UFO sightings dating back to the 1940s. As far as I know, the sighting was never reported to media, but I contacted UCLA Department of Meteorology and spoke to a professor, asking if he had ever heard of such a weird sky anomaly. He suggested the sighting was a fire rainbow as I first thought. Sounds logical, right? However, he agreed the duration of the sighting was highly unusual and he couldn't offer any explanation for the cigar-shaped cloud and luminous white band that shot off to the East.

I continued to ponder why this vision was shown to only me and my mom. Then it dawned on me the four colors in my vision represented the Four Directions. There is a Hopi legend that Creator gathered the people of the Earth together on an island that is now beneath the water and he told them, "I am going to send you in the four directions, and over time, I am going to change you into four colors." The merging of colors in my vision represented the four races on Earth.

The vision also represented the precious Rainbows, the new children coming into our Earthly plane in the past few years to selected spiritual parents. These children are telepathic and linked to the Star Beings and have alien DNA. They remember who they are and their mission here, and have committed to return during these troubled times to change the planetary vibration. Only those parents who understand the spiritual and psychic responsibility will have these special children. These children will bring new sciences, music, and spiritual concepts for a new world.

Can you imagine what transformational changes the world will experience when we realize we're not alone in the Universe? History and religions will be revamped, and our once-myopic beliefs of the Universe will be changed forever. The Rainbows, the new Earthkeepers, will exist in peace and harmony.

Below are a few of the amazing predictions I have made through the years that have proven accurate.

• On June 1, 1969, I was given a symbolic dream of a gypsy holding my hand and carving a cross on the palm of my hand, blood dripping from my hand. I sensed the dream was a warning that someone was going to be assassinated.

- On the night of June 5, Senator Robert Kennedy was walking through the Ambassador Hotel in the kitchen area after addressing supporters in the ballroom. A 24-year-old Palestinian named Sirhan Sirhan opened fire with a 22- caliber revolver, hitting Kennedy three times and five other people were wounded. Senator Kennedy died the next day never gaining consciousness. One year later, I had a conversation with a CBS reporter when I worked at the Newsroom on Sunset near Vine. She told me that she witnessed another man come up behind Kennedy and shoot him. I was flabbergasted. I asked why she didn't report this and she answered, "Are you kidding? Do you know how many people mysteriously died after witnessing the JFK assassination?"

- I was shown a vivid dream of a huge earthquake three nights in a row before the 6.5 magnitude earthquake struck on Feb. 9, 1971, at 6 am Pacific time, near San Fernando, California. I lived in Los Angeles at the time and worked at a brokerage firm in Beverly Hills. On the fourth day, I woke early and was dressed earlier than usual when the earthquake struck.

- Weeks before the eruption of Mount St. Helens in Washington State on May 18, 1980, I had a peculiar dream of a mountain growing in size, its side bulging as if it was pregnant. Then I heard an explosion that shook the ground and the mountain exploded. The eruption was the most significant volcanic eruption to occur in the contiguous 48 U.S. states since the much smaller 1915 eruption of Lassen Peak in California. Fifty-seven people died in the horrific volcanic explosion. Mount St. Helens is still an active volcano and part of the Cascadia Subduction Zone. Scientists say that another volcanic eruption is inevitable.

- A few days before October 6, 1981, I dreamed that I was in a movie theater when a man behind me began shouting and shooting an automatic rifle, killing a man on stage. He died instantly. In the dream, I felt the hate permeating from the assassin. Then on October 6, 1982, Egypt's President Anwar Sadat was assassinated while attending a victory parade held in Cairo to celebrate Egypt's crossing of the Suez Canal. Islambouli emptied his assault rifle into Sadat while in the front of the grandstand. Eleven others were killed that day.
- A year before 9-11-2001 I was shown a symbolic dream of the NYC Trade Tower buildings collapsing in the form of a giant apple tree losing its apples. The giant tree leaves withered in my dream and the apples and leaves began to fall as the entire tree was pulled straight down into the ground and vanished. Today, I know the buildings were downed by explosives, not planes!
- The week before December 26, 2004, I sensed a huge earthquake in the South Pacific. I had a vision pulled out of place wrong place. On December 26 a magnitude 9.1 megathrust earthquake hit and caused a devastating tsunami hitting Sumatra, Indonesia. It is estimated that 230,000 souls lost their lives. Interestingly, the full moon occurred on December 25, one day before the earthquake.
- I visualized a huge earthquake and tsunami several days before Japan's 9.0 earthquake and tsunami struck on March 11, 2011. It is estimated that twenty thousand people died that day.
- I predicted former President George H.W. Bush's death a few months after his wife died on April 17, 2018. He passed on Nov. 30, 2018.

- For the past few years, I predicted in several books that leaders and the famous would Fall from Grace from sexual allegations and sexual abuse. The list continues to grow—sex trafficker Jeffrey Epstein, Today Show's Matt Lauer, Former President Bill Clinton's involvement with Jeffrey Epstein, England's Prince Andrew, CBS Chief Executive Les Moonves, Astrophysicist Neil deGrasse Tyson, Newscaster Tom Brokaw, Actors Sylvester Stallone, Morgan Freeman, Athletic coaches, and Catholic Priests and Nuns. There are many more that will fall in 2020, and investigations will show that some very famous people who have died were pedophiles.

- Predicted Prince Harry would marry Meghan Markle and their firstborn would be a boy.

- Predicted Donald Trump would be elected President in 2016, seven months before the Presidential election while other psychics predicted Hillary Clinton's win. Even the news media claimed all polls showed Hillary winning.

- I woke early on December 14, 2012, with a horrific foreboding feeling I couldn't shake and didn't understand. That morning, 20-year- old Adam Lanza walked into the Sandy Hook School in Newtown, Connecticut and killed 20 children and 6 adults.

- As Hurricane Maria was forming in the Atlantic in September of 2017, I warned my followers on my Earth News blog that it would be devastating to the Caribbean. Maria in Puerto Rico emailed me and asked about her Island. I warned her that it would be a Category 5 Hurricane and to do whatever she and her family could to stay safe. In 2018, she emailed this: "I would like to say Thank You. You saved the lives of my family last year when you warned me Hurricane Maria was going to hit Puerto Rico. We prepared as best we could. And again I thank you for saving our lives." —Maria, Puerto Rico, May 4, 2018

- On June 27, 2019, at 3 am Mountain time, I woke from a lucid dream about a huge earthquake near the West Coast and posted it on my Earth News blog, sensing it would happen somewhere in Southern California. As my dream premonition warned, a magnitude 7.1 earthquake struck on July 5, 2019, near eastern California's Searles Valley that resulted from shallow strike-slip faulting in the North America plate crust.
- I have accurately predicted solar flares and predicted earthquakes and volcanic eruptions based on geomagnetic storms, solar eclipses, and the full moon.
- My spirit guides also warn me about my pets dying and family members passing. Whenever a move is in my future, my guides always prepare me.

At times I can visualize what happened to a missing child or a missing person, but I can honestly say I'd rather not remote view or envision what happened to them. It's usually involved murder.

Several years ago, a young boy in Boise, Idaho disappeared. The boy's mother and her boyfriend seemed distraught and organized friends to search for him with the local police. But I sensed it was an act and they were responsible for his death. Locals rallied around the couple and searched along the river for the missing boy. Days later, the boy's body was discovered floating in the river with signs of abuse. The mother and boyfriend were arrested shortly after. This story upset me greatly that such an innocent soul had been abused and killed.

Psychics can't always be forewarned of major disasters. Sometimes I can foresee an event and warn people on my website, but rarely do people take predictions seriously, except a few. Some events are not meant to be foreseen. Each soul plans his or her own death and the manner it will happen. Some prefer to go with a large group, such as an airplane crash or even the events of 9-11. Even a pandemic that kills millions like the 1917-1918 Spanish Flu. We are only physical containers that house souls and we reincarnate time after time for the fun of it and to learn powerful lessons of love, compassion, and forgiveness.

Once I tried to prevent a premonition from happening. My husband and I invited several friends for dinner one night. After dinner, we sat on our new sofa in the living room. In my vision, I saw my friend's dog cause her to spill red wine on our light-colored sofa and area rug. So I thought that if I exchanged her stemmed glass that I would prevent the premonition. Wrong!

It happened but not in the way I had envisioned. Instead of the dog jumping on my friend's lap, he jumped on my husband's lap and caused him to spill his wine everywhere. All I did was prolong the inevitable. The future had been changed but ever so slightly that the outcome was still the same—red wine staining the sofa and carpet.

Does that mean we can't stop an event from happening? If certain events already too far into the probable timeline, it usually can't be altered. Certain events are meant to happen no matter how hard we try to stop it.

Here's another example of trying to alter a destiny event. Dennis Carver and his wife, Lorraine, decided to attend the Harvest music festival in Las Vegas, Nevada on the night of October 1, 2017. That was the night a shooter opened fire on the crowd of concert-goers on the Las Vegas Strip, killing 58 people and wounding 413.

As round after round of gunshots were unloaded into the crowd, the couple ran for their lives—and miraculously survived. But then two weeks after making it out of the massacre, Dennis, 52, and Lora, 53, died in a car crash less than a mile from their Riverside, California home on October 16 when their Mercedes smashed into a metal gate and brick pillars outside their community.

The Carvers somehow escaped one destiny in Las Vegas that horrible night, but it seemed that a cosmic oversight had been made and Death caught up with them. When the Las Vegas massacre didn't take their lives, another scenario opened up. Instead of dying by gunshots, they died in a car accident. Both were horrible events, but one event would have been caused by an outside source and dying in a car crash didn't include an outside source.

My spirit guides say that we choose how we will die before coming into this Earthly plane. Great numbers of people often decide to leave with a soul group, others prefer to go with their spouse and still, others prefer to die alone. That's free-will.

I sense the Carvers viewed what their life would be before they were born into this present life and decided that the only way they could die together was in some horrific way. However, accidents do happen from time to time. We can only speculate that this might have been the only opportunity or window for them to go together. There are countless stories of a husband or wife dying only for the spouse to follow them with days or months.

This happened with actresses Debbie Reynolds and her daughter Carrie Fisher. Carrie Fisher died at age 60 on December 27, 2016, and her mother actress Debbie Reynolds died at age 84, the next day, December 28, 2016. They were soul friends and had many lifetimes together.

What about catastrophic events—can they be stopped or altered before they happen?

Let's theorize the events of 9-11 were planned in 1980, so the Family of Dark had twenty-one years to plan the downing of the World Trade Buildings on a Master Number day 11, which would give the event incredible power of becoming a Prime Event that would change the course of history. They knew how humans operate. Those who orchestrated the downing of the Trade Tower Buildings understood the supernatural power of numbers and knew number 11 symbolizes the potential to push the limitations of the human experience into the stratosphere. This is the ultimate symbolic power of the 11. But they were not going to use it for the highest good, but instead, their plan was pure evil. They also knew that if planes hit the towers they could cover their tracks and claim the towers fell from the plane's impact instead of explosives which caused the buildings to fall straight down without toppling.

The Family of Dark knew that humans would project anger, hate, and confusion into the ethers after the 9-11 events, and this would help their cause to control us to a greater degree. In a way, the freewill aspect is what has been exploited in our world as the basis for the evil planner's ability to manipulate humanity to be the vehicle of their power. They have worked out a way to create a downward spiral for all of us into heavier energy rather than lifting of vibration as it should have been.

My precognitive symbolic dream one year before September 11, 2001, was of a giant apple tree (New York City is the Big Apple) and I noticed the tree had lots of apples and leaves (souls). Suddenly the giant apple tree began to drop its apples and the leaves began to wither and fall, and the entire tree was pulled straight down into the ground and vanished. Shortly after 9-11 happened and the Trade Tower building fell, I knew it had been downed by explosives and not commercial planes. Later, I had visions of what happened to the people inside the planes, but I will not reveal what I was shown.

The Harmonic Convergence was a positive Primary Event that brought millions of people together on the weekend of August 16-17, 1987, to meditate for global peace. José Argüelles and his wife Lloydine Burris Argüelles via the Planet Art Network organized this first global prayer/meditation event without the internet, which was not available then.

The Harmonic Convergence celebrations took place at 200 sites across the United States, most notably at Mount Shasta, Central Park, Chaco Canyon and Sedona, Arizona. Fifty other celebrations occurred at sites worldwide including Ayer's Rock, Mount Fuji, Stonehenge and the Great Pyramid of Egypt. Participants danced, drummed, chanted and meditated together with celebrities including Shirley MacLaine, John Denver and Timothy Leary taking part in the celebrations. Johnny Carson even had his studio audience chant "OM" on the day of the convergence.

The idea of it was to raise the consciousness of the planet to bring about an age of peace as we moved into the Age of Aquarius, the age of brotherhood. It's hard to say whether the Harmonic Convergence staved off the Apocalypse or spared humanity from decades of war, but many believe that the positive mass consciousness allowed the Berlin Wall to fall in November of 1991, four years after the Harmonic Convergence.

Jose Argüelles died in 2011 at the age of 72, but I had the honor of interviewing him from Australia when he agreed to be a guest on my Rainbow Vision Talk Show in 2009. That interview is available on YouTube.

The splitting of the atom was also a Primary Event. Primary events can be huge events or small private events, and they alter the course of history drastically. So, to anchor a new timeline into the planet, there has to be a mass event taking place.

What then anchored the primary event into our timeline? It's called the mass consciousness of humans. There are beings now that are reconstructing the fabric of time where everything will change on Earth. This will change all of time as we know it. There are whole universes like ours being worked on and cleaned up. We think we have pollution on Earth, but there are whole universes like this being worked on and cleaned up. Can you imagine an entire universe polluted with chaos because all the timelines are not connected? Just imagine that one day you go to the store and when you return to your home it is gone because it slipped through a hole or stargate. Another reality now exists there.

Parallel universes and multiverses exist and not all the laws that we have existed in those worlds. The next thought is why do bad things happen to good people? Where is God and why doesn't he/she stop the insanity here, the killing, the wars, the disease and on and on.

Betty Andreasson Luca and her husband, Bob Luca, renowned for their alien encounters, were regressed under hypnosis. Author and investigator Raymond Fowler wrote about their astounding encounters through the years in his books *Watchers I* and *The Watchers I*, Bob was given this information by the alien beings about the need for evil in our world.

"Evil on this earthly plane is the negative aspect. Evil on the larger plane is part of the overall plan that gives us all a chance to advance and rise above it. Everyone in the earthly plane can do evil. Those that don't—those that fight evil, those that learn and overcome evil, and those who have advanced—have gained tremendously in the next realm. Everything in nature...has a plus and a minus, a light and dark, a negative and positive, a good and bad. It must be, for without some content of evil, there can be no good. There can be no growth."

The hypnotist was flabbergasted by Bob's remark and made the rhetorical question, "We need evil for good?"

Bob replied, "We do not need evil for good. We need choice. The Creator gave us choice [free-will]. We cannot use that choice unless we have two choices to make. Evil or good. It is so simple. It's beautiful. But there must be evil to be the choice. It's simple. I don't know how to explain it. Evil on this plane must exist."

Again, the hypnotist wanted clarification of Bob's words and asked, "I'm feeling that as we evolve as a civilization—won't there be more good, more kindness?"

"That would only be due to those who are advancing. And, yes eventually there will be. But, there will be some very distressing times before that happens," Bob said. "As the population of this planet increases, there will be those that have. There will be those who are greedy. There will be those that have not and are starving or will starve. There will be much dissension. There will be more conflict. The world, this plane, is not perfect. There will be evil."

"Always?"

"There will come a time when evil will be wiped away. That time is not close at hand. When that time comes, our growth will not cease. Rather, we will advance into further planes of existence. Right now, the type of society that you speak of is not impossible."

"Because?" the hypnotist continued to question. "Because the people of this plane as a whole are not very advanced spiritually. Technology is advancing. Spirituality, unfortunately, is not keeping pace. Man is developing many things that are harmful to him, which he does not understand. Man needs spiritual growth badly." Bob continued. "You see, the body, the shell—the real you is the light person inside—the motivation, the light force, the part that does not die, and the part that goes on and on. That's the light person. That's the real you! That part [human soul] advances in stages. Our existence here...that we know of now, is only one step of many in a long, learning process This process, the human mind is unable to comprehend just as it is unable to comprehend the endlessness of the universe in space. It is a never-ending process. It will always be and has always been." He continued, "Life is wonderfully fair. Those of us in this plane just don't understand it. When you see a small child that becomes ill and dies, people weep, they cry, they grieve. They grieve for themselves. The child does not need to be here any longer. The child has already advanced, much as you would skip a grade in school. It is not a bad thing. People that are sick, or injured...their faith is being tested. Their reactions recorded. This determines whether or not they need more teaching. It determines how they advance spiritually. Can they go to the next step? Is there more they must learn?" Bob went on to say that we never die, only the physical body dies. Life is stages, like a never-ending school"

The hypnotists then asked about the future, and Bob replied, "The future is not to be known to us, as it is something that can be given at times when it's deemed proper, but it is not our decision to determine when that time will be. It is the decision of the Elders [advanced spiritual beings], those who watch over, make that decision and...help us if necessary. An example would be...to give a personal warning that would enable them to avoid a bad situation. On occasions like that, people are given a glimpse into the future event...on the scale of an earthquake or a volcanic eruption. The person that is given this information may have it known, and often they are not believed.

"But people miss the point. Oftentimes, these people are given that information because, at that time, there may be thousands of people involved. The message may be to only one or two people— to listen, to believe and for that reason, all through the course of their life, by not being in that place at that time or whatever...they may complete their life cycle in the manner that they are supposed to...Accidents do happen, but yet those who have a destiny to fulfill—if they're not to leave this plane before this destiny is fulfilled. They will be given help to avoid a bad situation—like not boarding an airplane that they sense might crash or not being in a town where an earthquake is about to happen or not taking a boat or cruise because of a premonition something bad will happen. In these cases, a glimpse of the future is given for a specific person, not for all because it wasn't their time to die.

Bob Luca went on to discuss how we are all monitored. "Nothing that you do in your life escapes them [the Star Beings]. It's just like a recorder. Your life, your existence on the Earth plane is all recorded from the time you are born until the time you die; everything is there. How you react, what you do during your life. Even your innermost thoughts, feelings, and emotions. They're all recorded. It's all part of the process. This process determines how rapidly you will advance and hat your next step or phase will be, what teaching you need to receive, what hardship you must undergo to deepen your understanding. It's all recorded."

General George S. Patton who commanded the U.S. Seventh Army in the Mediterranean theater of World War II, and the U.S. Third Army in France and Germany following D-Day, the Allied invasion of Normandy in June 1944, defied death many times during the war, never fearing for his life because he knew he had a mission to complete. He believed that he was born in that timeline to fight in a great war as he had done in previous lifetimes as a warrior or soldier. While traveling through Europe he often walked in open fields, recalling a vivid past life where he fought ancient wars.

On December 8, 1945, Patton's chief staff, Major General Hobart Gay, invited him on a pheasant hunting trip. He commented on how awful war is and such a waste, and moments later his car collided with an American army truck at low speed. Major Gay and others were slightly injured, but Patton hit his head on the glass partition in the back seat. He began bleeding from a gash to the head and complained that he was paralyzed and having trouble breathing. At the Heidelberg Hospital, it was discovered that Patton had a compression fracture and dislocation of the cervical third and fourth vertebrae, resulting in a broken neck and cervical spinal cord injury that rendered him paralyzed from the neck down.

Patton spent most of the next 12 days in spinal traction to decrease the pressure on his spine. He was told that he had no chance to ever ride a horse or resume a normal life, and he commented to the staff, "This is a hell of a way to die." And he died in his sleep at 18:00 on December 21, 1945.

After we fulfill our earthly mission in life, it's time to move on to the next great adventure.

Chapter Three
ANCIENT PROPHECY

Why do humans want to know the future? Even if we knew what was going to happen tomorrow or months or years from now, how could we live a normal life knowing something horrible might be around the corner? We believe our lives and the planet we live on is part of a divine plan. For centuries prophets and seers have offered us a chance to glimpse the future and to possibly change it. It seems that we have more control over the future than we think.

What is Prophecy? It is defined as "foreseeing war and ruin." We live in a precarious world where World War III could come at any minute. Each day we see frightening images on the news of terrorism, poverty, starvation, mass shooting, natural disasters, and human disasters, and yet we still want to know what the future holds.

What if the past could be altered to change the present and future? According to quantum physics, this theory isn't so far – fetched.

The prophets have given us frightening scenarios of the future, and at the moment much of what they have described hasn't come to pass. Does that mean they were wrong? As I explained in the beginning of the book, either prime events created a new future timeline in which we live and the prophecy won't happen or these predictions were delayed for a future time.

One of the most famous books of dire prophecy is Revelations book in the Holy Bible. The Book of Revelations in the New Testament, also known as the Apocalypse of John, is filled with calamitous predictions of the end times. The word "Revelation" comes from the Greek term *apokalypsis*, meaning "unveiling" or "revelation." Unveiled in the book are the invisible forces and spiritual powers at work in the world and in the heavenly realms, including forces at war against the church [Catholic Church?].

The visions came to the Apostle John which unfolded before him like a science fiction novel, and much of what he warned about, he tried to describe in his vernacular during the time. Many of his descriptions are numbers and symbols used during his time in Asia Minor because they were familiar with the Old Testament prophetic writings of Isaiah, Ezekiel, Daniel and other Jewish texts, including the Dead Sea Scrolls. Was he warning us of Armageddon created by human folly, such as World War III, or did he foresee some natural cataclysmic event such as an asteroid striking Earth and wiping out most of humanity and life, the way scientists believe happened to the dinosaur that existed for 160 million years and then suddenly vanished?

Interpretation or deciphering esoteric prophecies can be a tricky business. Many skeptics believe that the Bible has been drastically changed over the centuries. In reality, the Bible has been translated into many languages, first Latin, then English and other languages. However, the ancient manuscripts (written in Hebrew, Aramaic, and Greek) have been reliably copied over the centuries—with very few alterations and that includes both the Old and New Testaments.

Before the discovery of the Dead Sea Scrolls the earliest Hebrew copy of the Old Testament was Masoretic text, dating to around 800 A.D. The Dead Sea Scrolls date to the time of Jesus and was copied by the Qumran community, a Jewish sect living around the Dead Sea. There is also the Septuagint which is a Greek translation of the Old Testament dating in the second century B.C. When we compared both the Old and New Testaments they are ninety-five percent identical with only minor variations and a few discrepancies.

Most Bibles include the options as footnotes when there are discrepancies. How could there be such amazing accuracy over a period of 1,400 years of copying? Two reasons: The scribes that did the copying had meticulous methods for checking their copies for errors. 2) The Holy Spirit made sure we would have an accurate copy of God's word so we would not be deceived. Several religions claim the Bible has been tampered with and this has proven false by the extensive, historical manuscript evidence.

How did the prophets see into future—numerology, astrology, scrying into black mirrors or water, remote viewing, visions given by angelic beings or other-worldly beings? Did extraterrestrials and angels show the children of Fatima visions of the future that were too frightening for the Catholic Church to reveal? Even Black Elk's vision appears to be extraterrestrial in origin, especially a little known story of his UFO experience while attending a sweat lodge ceremony.

Is there a Golden Age awaiting us in the future or a Mad-Max scenario of chaos and destruction?

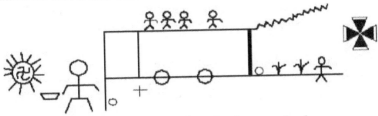

The diagram above shows the Hopi petroglyphs on an ancient sacred rock called Prophecy Rock in Arizona. It shows the large human figure on the left is the Great Spirit. The bow in his left hand represents his instructions to the Hopi to lay down their weapons. The vertical line to the right of the Great Spirit is a time scale in thousands of years. The point at which the Great Spirit touches the line is the time of his return.

The "life path" established by the Great Spirit divides into the lower, narrow path of continuous Life in harmony with nature and the wide upper road of white man's scientific achievements. The bar between the paths, above the cross, is the coming of white men; the Cross is that of Christianity. The circle below the cross represents the continuous Path of Life.

The two circles on the lower Path of Life are the "great shaking of the Earth" (World Wars One and Two). The swastika in the sun and the Celtic cross represent the two helpers of Pahana, the True White Brother. The short line that returns to the straight Path of Life is the last chance for people to turn back to nature before the upper road disintegrates and dissipates. The small circle above the Path of Life, after the last chance, is the Great Purification, after which corn will grow in abundance again when the Great Spirit returns. And the Path of Life continues forever.

The Hopi shield in the lower right corner symbolizes the Earth and the Four-Corners area where the Hopi have been reserved. The arms of the cross also represent the four directions in which they migrated according to the instructions of the Great Spirit. The dots represent the four colors of Hopi corn and the four racial colors of humanity.

Another ancient Hopi Indian prophecy states, "When the Blue Star Kachina makes its appearance in the heavens, the Fifth World will emerge." This will be the Day of Purification. The Hopi name for the star Sirius is Blue Star Kachina. It will come when the Saquasohuh (Blue Star) Kachina dances in the plaza and removes its mask.

Could the Blue Star be Planet X aka Nibiru, a failed star or brown dwarf, believed to travel through our solar system every 3,600 years and create havoc on all the planets?

The Bible has a great deal to say about what is going to happen in the future. And one of its most amazing, stunning, and awesome prophecies contains predictions and descriptions of what could be a nuclear war. Today, India, Pakistan, Iran and North Korea all have the potential to flood the world market with plutonium, highly enriched uranium. We know that North Korea has a military nuclear weapons program and, as of early 2019, is estimated to have an arsenal of approximately 30– 60 nuclear weapons. North Korea has also stockpiled a significant quantity of chemical and biological weapons. The People's Republic of China has also developed weapons of mass destruction, including chemical and nuclear weapons. The first of China's nuclear weapons tests took place in 1964, and its first hydrogen bomb test occurred in 1967.

Since science gave mankind nuclear weapons, the thought of a Third World War and the devastating effects it would have on mankind can never completely be pushed out of our minds. We build our lives happily fulfilling long term dreams, and that's okay, but then sometimes we are reminded that it can all abruptly come to an end.

Our fragile peace on Earth hangs by a thing called MAD [Mutual Assured Destruction]. Between the great nuclear powers of the world, they have this. "You attack me, be assured that I will have enough attacking ability left to destroy you too, and then there's nothing left of both of us. Thus it is MAD for you to come after me, and MAD for me to go after you. Come after my land bases, and I will strike back from some sub which you don't know where it is."

And on such an insurance policy world peace does not seem too reassuring, does it? It's a no-win situation.

Nearly two thousand years ago, John the Apostle was banished to an island as a punishment for sharing his faith in Christ. There, as he communed with God on the island, he had a series of visions that described things that would take place in the last days. The visions he was given are recorded in the Book of Revelation.

Many have tried to defuse the book by turning it into a giant parable in which nothing can be known except that in the end Christ will triumph and all will be well. But such an interpretation makes all the details of the visions meaningless. Some have dared to suggest that John's visions may have been more literal than most have supposed. This more literalistic interpretation just might make sense if John was seeing the terrible results of a nuclear holocaust just before Christ's coming to claim planet Earth.

In Hal Lindsay's book, *There's A New World Coming* (1973), he wrote: "Although it is possible for God to supernaturally pull off every miracle in the Book of Revelation and use unheard of means to do it, I believe that all the enormous ecological catastrophes described in this chapter (Revelation 8) are the direct result of nuclear weapons.

"In actuality, man inflicts these judgments on himself. God simply steps back and removes His restraining influence from man, allowing him to do what comes naturally out of his sinful nature. If the Book of Revelation had never been written, we might well predict these very catastrophes within fifty years or less!"

Hal Lindsey first popularized the theory that the terrible plagues and judgments seen and described by the Apostle John in the book of Revelation might by man's hand from thermonuclear war. Lindsey refers to the fractional orbital bomb, and then goes on to cite nuclear passages in the book of Revelation:

Revelation 6:12:

And I beheld when he opened the sixth seal, and lo, there was a great earthquake; and the sun became as black as sackcloth of hair, and the moon became as blood.

Hal Lindsay wrote, "It [the bomb] consists of a dozen or so nuclear-tipped missiles which can be fired simultaneously from an orbiting space platform. Because the missiles come straight down from the sky, they can strike several cities simultaneously and with virtually no warning. When these missiles streak through the air they'll look like meteors showering the atmosphere!"

Was this how Revelations 6:13 might be fulfilled: *And the stars of heaven fell unto Earth, even as a fig tree casteth her untimely figs when she is shaken of a mighty wind.*

Apostle John's vision goes on to describe the sun becoming black as sackcloth and the moon becoming like blood perfectly describes the phenomena that would result from massive amounts of dust and debris blown into the sky by multiple nuclear bursts.

Revelation 6:14:

And the heaven departed as a scroll when it is rolled together, and every mountain and island were moved out of their places. Here's what happens in a nuclear explosion—the atmosphere rolls back on itself! It's this tremendous rush of air that backs into the vacuum that causes much of the destruction of a nuclear explosion. John's words in this verse could depict a nuclear exchange—and if such an event happened, the entire world would be literally shaken apart!

He didn't use nuclear warheads, ICBMs, or fractional orbital bombs, but he did use words like "hail and fire," "a great mountain burning the fire," and a "great star"...burning like a torch. We would expect this type of language from a First Century man, describing what would have seemed beyond belief about two-thousand years ago.

What if John was describing a real star such as a comet, asteroid or Planet X, a brown dwarf or failed star that is believed to travel through our solar system every 3,600 years causing planetary destruction?

Here's the really interesting news—our sun is a solitary star, but most solar systems are binary, meaning they have two stars. Perhaps millions of years ago our solar system had a binary star system, and one died and became a brown dwarf that was ejected from our solar system and now travels unseen most of the time through our heavens.

Some theorize that Planet X, also known as Nibiru, travels closer to the Earth at times and because of its enormous magnet pull, causes great geological changes. There is no proof from our scientific community or NASA about Planet X, but in the past few years, there have been many YouTube videos posted on what looks like a second sun.

In June 2012, the BBC released a documentary on Nibiru with shocking footage. The Inuit Tribe is an indigenous people who live in the Canadian Arctic, Greenland, Siberia, and Alaska. Their elders wrote to the National Space and Aeronautics Administration (NASA) to tell them that the Earth's axis has shifted. The elders do not believe that carbon emissions from humans are causing the current climate changes.

The Inuit elders have noticed climate change in the melting glaciers, deterioration of sealskin, and burns on seals, and disappearing sea ice. They attribute these changes in climate to changes in the sky. The tribal elders claim that the sun no longer rises where it used to rise. The days heat up more quickly and last longer. The stars and moon are also in different places in the sky and this affects the temperatures. This is a population that relies on the placement of the moon and stars for their survival as they live in total darkness during part of the year.

The elders say they can no longer predict the weather, as they have been able to in the past. They observe that warmer winds are changing the snowbanks, making their ability to navigate overland more difficult. Polar bear populations are increasing, which causes the bears to wander into the Inuit neighborhoods.

Scientists theorized that the Inuits probably saw the effects of the powerful Japanese 9.1 earthquake that unleashed a devastating tsunami on March 11, 2011. They say the earthquake moved the main island of Japan by 8 feet (2.4 meters) and shifted the Earth on its axis by nearly 4 inches (10 centimeters), according to Kenneth Hudnut, a geophysicist with the U.S. Geological Survey (USGS).

There are three possible sources of the death and devastation so pointedly predicted by Scripture. First, it could be that the great and terrible destructions predicted will be brought about supernaturally by God. Secondly, some of the judgments predicted could be describing a cosmic disturbance created by a comet, an asteroid whose path leads it uncomfortably close to the Earth or hits Earth. Global earthquakes and incredible hurricane winds, and tsunamis would sweep across the globe, resulting in famines on an unprecedented scale.

The third and most likely explanation for the terrible judgments, which will cause near extinctions on Earth, has to do with nuclear weapons. Since the end of World War II, nuclear weapons have been proliferating all over the globe and currently in the hands of a tyrant named Kim Jong-un, Supreme Leader of North Korea, who possess 60 nuclear weapons and has enough uranium to produce 6 new nuclear bombs each year.

Nearly every year new nations are added to the list of those countries with nuclear capabilities. Our capacity to destroy all life on Earth has multiplied many times over. The reason we have not seen a nuclear war since 1945 might be attributed only to divine intervention or ET intervention! How long that divine hand or otherworldly hands will continue to restrain us, only God knows.

There are stories of U.S. missiles that have been deactivated by a UFO hovering over a missile silo, and also, there are stories of UFOs that tried to launch a nuclear missile in Russia.

In Revelations, the most frightening prophecy is in Chapter 8 where John has a vision of fire and desolation pouring out during the opening of the seventh seal. It begins: *And when he had opened the seventh seal, there was silence in heaven about the space of half an hour. And I saw the seven angels which stood before God, and to them were given seven trumpets.*

In verse three, it tells of an angel who stood at an altar, having a golden censer. *And the angel took the censer, and filled it with fire of the altar, and cast it into the Earth, and there were voice, and thunderings, and lightnings, and an earthquake. (Revelation 8:5).*

Since 2012, or even earlier, mysterious booms and noises have been heard and recorded worldwide, and some of the sounds have been described as a trumpet (Archangel Gabriel's horn blowing), scraping noises and train-like roar. These have been accompanied by strange lights in the sky and earthquakes not recorded by the U.S.G.S. monitors. How did John foresee these apocalyptic visions happening now over two-thousand-years ago?

Verses 6-12: *And the seven angels which had the seven trumpets prepared themselves to sound. The first angel sounded, and there followed hall and "fire mingled with blood, and they were cast upon the Earth: and the third part of trees was burnt up, and all green grass was burnt up. And the second angel sounded, and as it were a great mountain and burning with fire was cast into the sea; [volcanism?]and the third part of the sea became blood. And the third part of the creatures which were in the sea, and had life, died; and the third part of the ships were destroyed. And the third angel sounded, and there fell a great star from heaven, burning as it were a lamp, and it fell upon the third part of the rivers, and upon the fountains of water;[could this be description of an asteroid or bolide meteor?] And the name of the star is called Wormwood: and the third part of the waters became Wormwood, and many men died of the waters because they were made bitter.*

The name Wormwood has been attributed to both a nuclear explosion and Planet X. It is mentioned seven times in the Jewish Bible and always with the implication of bitterness. If we take the meaning literally, the Bible says that Wormwood is a heavenly star, but what kind of star—human-made or natural?

John said that the "sting" of the "locusts" does not kill people, but causes so much pain (for five months!) that "men will seek death, and will not find it; they will desire to die, and death will flee from them" (Revelation 9:6). This could be a description of radiation sickness or sickness from biological weapons. He said that an army of 200 million will "kill a third of mankind" (Revelation 9:15,16). With the world population now at 7.3 billion, this would be more than 2 billion people will die!

Instead of one big cataclysmic event, John might have been describing two events.

So is there any real hard evidence Planet X exists? The answer is yes! On December 30, 1983, U.S. newspapers ran a story of a heavenly body discovered near the constellation Orion. This article ran in the Washington Post:

A heavenly body possibly as large as the giant planet Jupiter and possibly so close to Earth that it would be part of this solar system has been found in the direction of the constellation Orion by an orbiting telescope aboard the U.S. infrared astronomical satellite. So mysterious is the object that astronomers do not know if it is a planet, a giant comet, a nearby "protostar" that never got hot enough to become a star, a distant galaxy so young that it is still in the process of forming its first stars or a galaxy so shrouded in dust that none of the light cast by its stars ever gets through. "All I can tell you is that we don't know what it is," Dr. Gerry Neugebauer, a scientist for California's Jet Propulsion Laboratory and director of the Palomar Observatory for the California Institute of Technology said in an interview.

The most fascinating explanation of this mystery body, which is so cold it casts no light and has never been seen by optical telescopes on Earth or in space, is it's a giant gaseous planet, as large as Jupiter and as close to Earth as 50 billion miles. While that may seem like a great distance in earthbound terms, it is a stone's throw in cosmological terms, so close in fact that it would be the nearest heavenly body to Earth beyond the outermost planet Pluto. "If it is that close, it would be a part of our solar system," said Dr. James Houck of Cornell University's Center for Radio Physics and Space Research and a member of the IRAS science team. "If it is that close, I don't know how the world's planetary scientists would even begin to classify it."

The mystery body was seen twice by the infrared satellite as it scanned the northern sky from last January to November 2016, when the satellite ran out of the supercold helium that allowed its telescope to see the coldest bodies in the heavens. The second observation took place six months after the first and suggested the mystery body had not moved from its spot in the sky near the western edge of the constellation Orion in that time. "This suggests it's not a comet because a comet would not be as large as the one we've observed and a comet would probably have moved," Houck said. "A planet may have moved if it were as close as 50 billion miles but it could still be a more distant planet and not have moved in six months.

Whatever it is, Houck said, the mystery body is so cold its temperature is no more than 40 degrees above "absolute" zero, which is 459 degrees Fahrenheit below zero. The telescope aboard IRAS is cooled so low and is so sensitive it can "see" objects in the heavens that are only 20 degrees above absolute zero. When IRAS scientists first saw the mystery body and calculated that it could be as close as 50 billion miles, there was some speculation that it might be moving toward Earth. "It's not incoming mail," Cal Tech's Neugebauer said. "I want to douse that idea with as much cold water as I can."

In 1992, NASA issued a press release, "Unexplained deviations in the orbits of Uranus and Neptune point to a large outer solar system body of 4 to 8 Earth masses on a highly tilted orbit, beyond 7 billion miles from the Sun." (NASA Press Release, 1992). Another news press release stated, "Astronomers are so sure of the 10th planet they think there is nothing left but to name it" Ray T. Reynolds, NASA (NASA Press Release, 1992). These stories were quickly retracted without any explanation.

It was late December 2015 when I began posting my predictions for 2016 on my website and wrote this: watch for NASA to announce more weird news on planets and astonishing finds in our solar system and beyond. They are going to make some outrageous claims and maybe even an alien disclosure about ancient alien structures in outer space, Mars and the Moon. Are they preparing us for the big disclosure?

Then the most incredible thing happened on January 20, 2016; two Caltech scientists gave a press conference and announced they had discovered a ninth planet in our solar system, 10 times the size of Earth. They announced evidence that a body nearly the size of Neptune—but as yet unseen—orbits the sun every 15,000 years. During the solar system's infancy 4.5 billion years ago, they say, the giant planet was knocked out of the planet-forming region near the sun. Slowed down by gas, the planet settled into a distant elliptical orbit, where it still lurks today.

The claim is the strongest yet in the centuries-long search for a "Planet X" beyond Neptune. The quest has been plagued by far-fetched claims and even outright quackery. But the new evidence comes from a pair of respected planetary scientists, Konstantin Batygin and Mike Brown of the California Institute of Technology (Caltech) in Pasadena, who prepared for the inevitable skepticism with detailed analyses of the orbits of other distant objects and months of computer simulations. "If you say, 'We have evidence for Planet X,' almost any astronomer will say, 'This again? These guys are clearly crazy.' I would, too," Brown says. "Why is this different? This is different because this time we're right." Batygin and Brown inferred its presence from the peculiar clustering of six previously known objects that orbit beyond Neptune. They say there's only a 0.007% chance, or about one in 15,000, that the clustering could be a coincidence. Instead, they say, a planet with the mass of 10 Earths has shepherded the six objects into their strange elliptical orbits, tilted out of the plane of the solar system.

The orbit of the inferred planet is similarly tilted, as well as stretched to distances that will explode previous conceptions of the solar system. Its closest approach to the sun is seven times farther than Neptune, or 200 astronomical units (AUs). (An AU is a distance between Earth and the sun, about 150 million kilometers.) And Planet X could roam as far as 600 to 1200 AU, well beyond the Kuiper belt, the region of small icy worlds that begins at Neptune's edge about 30 AU.

If Planet X is out there, Brown and Batygin say, astronomers ought to find more objects in telltale orbits, shaped by the pull of the hidden giant. But Brown knows that no one will believe in the discovery until Planet X itself appears within a telescope viewfinder. "Until there's a direct detection, it's a hypothesis— even a potentially very good hypothesis," he says. The team has time on the one large telescope in Hawaii that is suited for the search and they hope other astronomers will join in the hunt.

Batygin and Brown published the result today in The Astronomical Journal. Alessandro Morbidelli, a planetary dynamicist at the Nice Observatory in France, performed the peer review for the paper. In a statement, he says Batygin and Brown made a "very solid argument" and that he is "quite convinced by the existence of a distant planet."

Even if Batygin and Brown can convince other astronomers that Planet X exists, they face another challenge: explaining how it ended up so far from the sun. At such distances, the protoplanetary disk of dust and gas was likely to have been too thin to fuel planet growth. And even if Planet X did get a foothold as a planetesimal, it would have moved too slowly in its vast, lazy orbit to hoover up enough material to become a giant.

Instead, Batygin and Brown propose that Planet X formed much closer to the sun, alongside Jupiter, Saturn, Uranus, and Neptune. Computer models have shown that the early solar system was a tumultuous billiard table, with dozens or even hundreds of planetary building blocks the size of Earth bouncing around. Another embryonic giant planet could easily have formed there, only to be booted outward by a gravitational kick from another gas giant.

It's harder to explain why Planet X didn't either loop back around to where it started or leave the solar system entirely. But Batygin says that residual gas in the protoplanetary disk might have exerted enough drag to slow the planet just enough for it to settle into a distant orbit and remain in the solar system. That could have happened if the ejection took place when the solar system was between 3 million and 10 million years old, he says, before all the gas in the disk was lost into space.

So these scientists haven't seen Planet X they claim, but from their calculations—it exists. I find it beyond coincidence that they announced the possible existence of Planet X at this time when our planet is experiencing increased earthquakes, volcanic activity, meteors coming into our atmosphere and mysterious booms heard worldwide. It's interesting that in 1983 NASA seemed to indicate the object they had discovered was 11 times the size of Earth, as large as Jupiter and possibly a brown dwarf or failed star. The Caltech scientists believe they found an elusive ninth planet in our solar system.

I do not doubt that more high strangeness will be forthcoming from the scientific community in 2020 on Planet X.

Why hint at Planet X now? Will scientists tell us that all our Earth changes are due to this huge brown dwarf that has a megalithic magnetic hold on our planet and other planetary bodies in the solar system and we can expect cataclysmic events in the future? I doubt it. There will be more hints forthcoming from the scientific community when they know they can no longer pretend that something is causing all the huge Earth changes and extreme weather.

Previous studies have suggested Planet Nine, which some astronomers refer to as "Planet X," has a mass between five and 15 times that of Earth. In the past few years, our Sun has gone quiet, meaning few sunspots. Could the magnetic pull of this massive failed star cause our star to go quiet as it travels through our solar system?

Strange Fissures and Cracks appear. A few years ago, a giant crack appeared on a Wyoming ranch near the Big Horn Mountain range late September of 2015, and it grew to the size of more than six football fields. Scientists were baffled and wondered if a volcano might be forming in the area. As of this date, it has not.

Then on March 19, 2018, a huge fissure or chasm suddenly developed in the East African Rift Valley in Kenya. This spot, however, is just one of the tens, perhaps hundreds, of other weak spots on the Great Rift Valley, which runs through the continent from the Horn of Africa to Mozambique, scientists say. The story went viral and some claimed Kenya was pulling away from the African continent, but there is no proof that will happen overnight.

Eight months later, before 9.30 am on Sunday, November 11, 2018 (11-11), a series of unusual seismic pulses rippled around the world almost undetected. The waves rang for over 20 minutes, emanating about 15 miles off the shores of Mayotte—a tiny island in the Indian Ocean between Madagascar and Africa.

From here, they reverberated across Africa, setting off geological sensors in Zambia, Kenya, and Ethiopia. It was not only the power of the seismic waves which puzzled scientists when they began to examine the readings, but also the curiously regular shape of the waveform. In a typical earthquake, the rapid crash of a tectonic plate movement sends out what is known as a "wave train," composed of several types of waves moving at different speeds from the epicenter of the quake.

Did the November 11 event trigger the massive earthquake in Alaska on November 30? At 17:29:28 on November 30, 2018, a 7.0 magnitude earthquake shook 13km North off Anchorage, Alaska causing huge destruction to roads and bridges. No deaths were reported.

The sun is currently in a deep solar minimum and it is about to reach a historic milestone. So far this year the sun has been blank (i.e., no visible sunspots) for 266 days and, barring any major surprises, it'll reach 269 days early next week which will be the quietest year in terms of sunspots since 1913 when the sun was spotless for 311 days. In fact, the current stretch of consecutive spotless days has reached 29 and for the year the sun has been blank 77% of the time. The current record-holder in the satellite era for spotless days in a given year is 2008 when the sun was blank for 268 days making the 2008-2009 solar minimum the deepest since 1913. A huge object in our solar system such as a Brown Dwarf/failed star might have a huge magnetic pull on the Sun, it's caused it to go quiet until it passed through our solar system?

Could there be a manmade explanation for all the huge geological changes? Many conspiracy theorists suggest the CERN Hadron Collider in Switzerland and HAARP are responsible for the huge changes taking place on Earth.

The Large Hadron Collider (LHC) is the world's largest and most powerful particle collider, the largest, most complex experimental facility ever built, and the largest single machine in the world. It was built by the European Organization for Nuclear Research (CERN) between 1998 and 2008 in collaboration with over 10,000 scientists and engineers from over 100 countries, including hundreds of universities and laboratories. It resides in a tunnel 17 miles (27 kilometers) in circumference, 574 feet (175 meters) beneath the France-Switzerland border near Geneva, Switzerland. The first experiment took place on March 30, 2010, to February 13, at an initial energy of 3.5 teraelectronvolts (TeV) per beam (7 TeV total), almost 4 times more than the previous world record for a collider.

Stephen Hawking, who was a theoretical physicist, cosmologist, author, and Director of Research at the Centre for Theoretical Cosmology within the University of Cambridge, stated the Higgs boson 'God particle' could destroy the universe, and that space and time could suddenly collapse. We would not see it coming. If scientists put too much energy in the Higgs boson at CERN the universe could end, but physicists say it's unlikely due to such a small collider. But why would scientists want to take that chance?

Although I don't feel Earth will be destroyed by CERN's collider, there's so much more we should be concerned about how— the disappearance of clean water, pollutions of the oceans, rivers, and lakes, the extinction of many species, the pollution of our air and the toxins pouring into the ground daily.

In the past five years, there have been wild theories by conspiracy theorists about secret underground bunkers in the United States. They are said to exist in Nevada, Colorado, part of the Midwest and the Ozarks built by the United States government or military. Former Minnesota governor Jesse Ventura heard about the rumors that the elite are building fortified retreats and underground bunkers in remote areas of the country in preparation for a doomsday event and decided to investigate in 2012 for an episode of truTV Conspiracy Theories episode. He traveled to the Ozarks to investigate the construction of an alleged 75,000 sq. ft., "single-family," fortified mansion owned by a satellite surveillance mogul and government defense contractor. Later, Ventura and his team are guided by a local informant to a massive underground warehouse facility, complete with railroad access, that is located in nearby Springfield, Missouri.

Next Ventura investigated the Denver Airport and a rumored 360,000 square foot underground secret bunker. A construction worker at the site believed the airport is a decoy to hide the construction of the secret bunker estimated to be larger than the Cheyenne Mountain military installation and nuclear bunker located in Colorado Springs, Colorado. Some believe it was built by the New World Order to house the elites in case of economic collapse, civil war, nuclear holocaust, a solar event or any other natural catastrophe. The rumored bunker supposedly sits under the Denver Airport, an airport that was built in the middle of nowhere despite having a perfectly good, functional airport 19 miles closer to the city. In flatlands, they moved about a third of the dirt compared to the earth removal during the Panama Canal construction, but that's still huge. Coincidently, the airport is located 120 miles from Cheyenne Mountain, a well-known underground survival bunker, which is rumored to be linked by a tunnel to the airport 120 miles away.

The Denver Airport was commissioned in 1989 at a cost of 1.7 billion dollars, and finished in 1995, six years later, at 4.8 billion dollars, roughly 3.1 billion over budget. The airport was privately funded, and nobody knows by whom, however, there is a marker stone in the terminal and above the words—New World Airport Commission. Above the name is an emblem of Freemasonry represented by a square and compass emblem. No one seems to know who the New World Airport Commission might be.

For many years visitors to the Denver Airport immediately noticed several mysterious masonic symbols and frightening murals depicting an apocalyptic end for humanity. Jesse Ventura believes the giant murals inside the airport, now removed, held a deeper meaning which can be gleaned by the initiated of the New World Order and Freemasons. One of the murals depicted people living in underground bunkers, mothers weeping and holding their dead babies, and a malevolent soldier holding saber in one hand, killing the Dove of Peace and an AK47 rifle in the other hand. There was also a mural of burning bushes, dead animals, red waters, and children lying dead in coffins. The murals have since been removed from the airport.

Now travelers passing through Denver International Airport are greeted to a comedic animatronic gargoyle that is full of quick adlibs, sarcasm and spooky conspiracy theories. Video footage of the gargoyle entertaining passengers has been viewed by 648,172 people on YouTube as of December 3, 2019. Representatives for the Denver Airport made this statement February of 2019: "DEN is known for the conspiracies about our airport, and we wanted to find a playful way to embrace the conspiracies. We always strive to win the hearts of our passengers by giving them the unexpected," a spokesperson said. "We hope the gargoyle gave them all a good belly laugh, and more reason to want to travel through DEN."

Chapter Four
SAINT MALACHY

Pope Francis, 83-years-old, born on December 17, 1936, in Buenos Aires, Argentina, became the head of the Catholic Church on March 13, 2013, at the age of 76 (7+6= 13), following the resignation of Pope Benedict XVI—a controversial move and the first of its kind in more than 500 years. There is much speculation about the prophecies made in 1139 by Saint Malachy, a medieval Irish priest, and Kabbalist, whose prophecies revealed the long list of illustrious pontiffs who were to rule the Church until the end of time. However, a source close to the Pope claimed in 2013 that he would only serve for seven more years, stating he would follow in the footsteps of his predecessor. Does that mean he will resign in 2020, treading the path for an ancient prophecy to be fulfilled?

Journalist Austen Ivereigh is the former Director for Public Affairs of the previous Archbishop of Westminster, Cardinal Cormac Murphy-O'Connor and works closely with the Vatican. He said in 2013: "I don't think there's ever been any doubt that he will resign in 2020.

"He made clear from the beginning that he regarded Pope Benedict's (XVI) act as a prophetic act of great modesty and he would have absolutely no problem in doing the same. "What was interesting was he said to a Mexican television in 2014 that he believed that he would have a short papacy of about five years. "Now, given that he was elected in March 2013, then in 2017, he would have considered stepping down if nature hadn't intervened. The revelation will no doubt put some Christians on the edge of their seats, as it could fulfill a 900-year-old prophecy made by 12th-century Archbishop Saint Malachy.

In 1139, Malachy went to Rome from Ireland to give an account of his affairs, when he reportedly received a strange vision about the future, including the names of 112 future Popes. His prediction concerning the 111th pope, Pope Benedict XVI, was "Gloria Olivae," which means "the glory of the Olive."

Saint Malachy was born in 1094 A.D. in Armagh, Ireland and long known to have the gift of prophecy, and he even predicted his death on November 2, 1148, in Clairvaux, France. Malachy was canonized the first Irish Saint in the Catholic Church by Pope Clement III in 1190 A.D. It is said the Saint Malachy while on a visit to Rome in 1139 had a vision of all the popes and their reign. He then wrote down on paper a series of Latin phrases describing the popes to come. He grouped each one with an epigrammatic verse, such as the tears of the sun.

The Malachy Prophecies were first published in 1595, by a Benedictine monk and historian Arnold de Wyon, who found them five years earlier in the Vatican archives. Arnold recorded them in the book, entitled: Lignum Vitæ. There is speculation the papers were not authentic, and rumors persist that the papers were actually hidden in the Vatican archives for 400 years.

These short prophetical announcements indicate traits of all future popes starting with Celestine II, who was elected in the year 1130, until the end of the world ending with Pope 112.

Many researchers believe Pope Benedict was Malachy's Pope 111. He was the forerunner to the anti-pope or false pope. According to Daniel 9:27, Revelation 13 and 17:10-18, Satan will incarnate the last pontiff who will deify himself and break Rome's covenant with the Jewish bankers.

Some prophecy scholars claim that Malachy made only 111 predictions and that the Benedictines invented pope 112 in order to dissociate their order from the "Beast" so that John Paul II's successor should be the final pope. However *Gloria olivae* resides still in Rome as Pope Emeritus, His Holiness Benedict XVI, and it appears Malachy's prophecy of popes 111 and 112 are intended to be conjoined in accordance with the two popes mentioned in Revelation 19:20, and 20:10. This scripture seems to be reinforced by the fact that Pope Benedict was the first pope to receive the Ring of St. Peter after it was re-instated by John Paul II who did not wear the ring, and contrary to custom Pope Benedict XVI did not destroy his ring but "disabled the seal" and now wears the ring contemporaneously with Pope Francis I, enjoining both to St. Peter—something that has never happened in the history of the false church, but fulfilling Jesus' prophecy!

The 112th prophecy states: "In the final persecution of the Holy Roman Church there will reign Petrus Romanus, who will feed his flock amid many tribulations; after which the seven-hilled city will be destroyed and the dreadful Judge will judge the people."

The meaning isn't totally clear but could be interpreted to mean the last pope will led the Catholics from unity and the papacy. It may also predict a huge earthquake that will destroy much of Rome. I sense that Pope Francis will either resign or pass away in 2020.

To learn more about Pope Francis and his strange connection to the number 13, which has been linked to the Illuminati, read my book *Mystic Revelations of Thirteen* on Amazon.

Chapter Five
SAINT HILDEGARD

Saint Hildegard of Bingen (1098 to 1179) was a German writer, composer, philosopher, and Christian mystic. On October 7, 2012, Pope Benedict XVI named her Doctor of the Church. Throughout her life, she continued to have many visions, and in 1141, at the age of 42, Hildegard received a Godly vision and was instructed to "write down that which you see and hear."

"The time is coming when princes and peoples will reject the authority of the Pope. Some countries will prefer their own Church rulers to the Pope. The German Empire will be divided.

"Before the comet comes, many nations, the good excepted, will be scourged by want and famine. The great nation in the ocean that is inhabited by people of different tribes and descent will be devastated by earthquakes, storms, and tidal waves. It will be divided and, in great part, submerged. That nation will also have many misfortunes at sea and lose its colonies.

"[After the] great Comet [Planet X?], the great nation will be devastated by earthquakes, storms, and great waves of water, causing much want and plagues. The ocean will also flood many other countries, so that all coastal cities will live in fear, with many destroyed. All sea coast cities will be fearful, and many of them will be destroyed by tidal waves, and most living creatures will be killed, and even those who escape will die from a horrible disease. For in none of those cities does a person live according to the Laws of God.

A powerful wind will rise in the North, carrying heavy fog and the densest dust, and it will fill their throats and eyes so that they will cease their butchery and be stricken with a great fear."

Perhaps lightning striking the roof of St. Peter's Basilica hours after Pope Benedict XVI's shocking announcement of resignation on February 28, 2013, was an omen of the Vatican's future.

Chapter Six
NOSTRADAMUS

Michel de Nostre-Dame, also known as Nostradamus, was an astrologer and physician who was born at St. Remy de Provence in France on December 14, 1503, at high noon and died on July 2, 1566. He was of Jewish descent, but his family later converted to Catholicism by 1512. He was described as a very handsome man with dark curly hair and beard, a noble forehead, a long thin nose, a sensitive mouth, and widely set eyes, dark and burning with intellect. He looked like a prophet.

From childhood, he showed great signs of intelligence and even mastered Latin, Greek, Hebrew, and mathematics. He was also an accomplished astrologer before the age of twenty and some say, an experienced alchemist. He believed in the Copernican theory of the solar system a century before Galileo was persecuted by the church for his theory that the Earth revolves around the Sun.

Nostradamus hid many of his talents. In a preface to his famous prophecies book addressed to his son, Caesar, Nostradamus says that he burnt all his magical and alchemical books, and advised his son to avoid such practices because of the Inquisition at the time. Converted Jews to Catholicism were frequently looked upon with greater suspicion than those who were unconverted.

The Black Plague, or Bubonic Plague, raged during Nostradamus' early adulthood, and he gained a high reputation for his fearless fight to save lives. He is believed to affected many cures. How he cured so many and avoided the Plague himself, was a mystery; even for modern scientists confronting plagues; even modern knowledge of viruses and their behavior is slowly unraveling today when confronting plagues. Distant towns raised subscriptions to bring him to assist in their dying populations. Today, we are still baffled by Nostradamus' ability as a healer and a physician during a dark time in history.

This prophecy may have foretold about the Coronavirus.

2-95: *The populated places will be uninhabitable,*
To have field great division;
Kingdoms delivered to incapable prudent ones,
Then the great brothers death and dissension.

Nostradamus became legendary for his ability to foresee the future, even for his time. Along with astrology, Nostradamus is said to have used a black obsidian mirror as a scrying tool and a bowl of water. His predictions were nebulous and written in quatrains for his Centuries book or sometimes called, *Prophecies Book* in 1555. The prophecies were poor poetry, which is doubtful that was his intention. They are ungrammatical, elliptical to the point of perversity, abstruse, and obscure. The Centuries were grouped together in ten sets of one hundred quatrains that were short and rhymed. They included words in no French dictionary, and refer to persons and places unknown, and were probably full of errors from early type-setters.

Napoleon and Hitler were convinced that they were mentioned specifically and at length in these prophecies, thus confirming them as men of destiny, justifying their actions. Many modern translators have tried to insert their own meaning to fit a certain historical event. He used the name "Hister" in a quatrain and translators turned it into "Hitler".

Catherine de Medici, Frances Queen Mother, was convinced he had accurately predicted her husband's horrible death four years before the event. The quatrain read:

The young lion will overcome the old one,
On-field of battle in single combat:
In a cage of gold, his eyes will be split,

Two ruptures one, then to die, cruel death.

In June of 1559, a tournament lasted several days in Paris to celebrate a peace treaty between France and Spain. King Henry II entered and was to be presented before lords, ladies, including Queen Catherine, Diane de Poitiers, a prominent courtier and lover of King Henry and his favorite, Francis I and Mary Queen of Scots. After several rounds Catherine tried to persuade him not to continue in the joust, fearing he was tired. He didn't listen and insisted on another contest with Count of Montgomery.

Montgomery's lance struck the King's helmet and a long splinter pierced Henry's eye and brain. Bleeding profusely and almost unconscious, he was carried to his apartments. Henry forgave Montgomery, saying it wasn't his fault and he had carried himself bravely and well. The royal doctors removed the splinter from the King's eye and other pieces that had pierced his head and throat while bleeding him until he relapsed into a coma. The King died on July 9 at age 40-years-old, never regaining consciousness.

The following quatrain seemed to predict the near assassination of Pope John Paul II:

Roman pontiff beware of approaching
The city which two rivers water,
Thy blood will come close to spitting there.
Thou and thine when the rose blooms.

Perhaps this is more than coincidence but on May 13, 1981, Pope John Paul II was shot as he entered St. Peter's Square. He was critically wounded by Mehmet Ali Agca, an expert Turkish gunman who was a member of the militant fascist group Grey Wolves. Surgeons had to perform a colostomy rerouting the upper part of the large intestine. He lost nearly three-quarters of his blood from the gunshot wound to his abdomen. Before the operation, he briefly regained consciousness and instructed the doctors not to remove his Brown Scapular during the operation. After his miraculous recovery, the Pope stated that Our Lady of Fatima keep him alive throughout his ordeal, where she had appeared to three Fatima children on the 13th of the month for six consecutive months from May 13, 1917, to October 13, 1917.

Nostradamus accurately foretold of Pope John Paul's assassination attempt by Rome's river Tiber, which is fed by two springs, the event would take place when the rose blooms (May) and the pontiff would survive the assassination attempt.

This quatrain might describe a disastrous earthquake in our century. Could the theatre refer to Los Angeles known for television and movies or did he mean the ancient Roman theatre?

Quatrain 9-83:

The sun in twenty degrees of Taurus, there will be a great earthquake; the great theatre full up will be ruined. Darkness and trouble in the air, on sky and land, when the infidel calls upon God and the Saints.

This next quatrain appears to describe the corruption within the Roman Catholic Church, the prophesized antichrist and the end of the Catholic Church as we know it today.

Quatrain 2-30:

One who the infernal gods of Hannibal (Satan?),
Causes to be reborn, terror to humans:
Nevermore horror journals will tell,
Than before will come Babel to the Romans."

This prophecy might relate to terrorists in Mid-Eastern countries and their terrorism in Europe and worldwide. Fez could relate to mid-eastern countries, and "blade will slice" means to cut down or kill. "Fire their city" could mean bombs or automatic weapons. The last sentence seems to indicate the terrorists will be chased across water and lands until they are killed.

Quatrain 6-80

From Fez, the Kingdom will stretch to those of Europe,
Fire their city, and blade will slice:
The great one of Asia land and sea with great throng
So that blues, sea green, cross to death will be chased.

Dolores Cannon, (1931-2014), author, past-life regressionist and hypnotherapist who specialized in the recovery and cataloging of "Lost Knowledge," wrote three books on Nostradamus's prophecies and their explanation. In *Conversations with Nostradamus* (1989), she said Nostradamus had broken through the barriers of time and space and spoke to her through her hypnotized subjects. Many of the prophecies that Nostradamus revealed were filled with depressing horror and painted a very bleak picture of the future. However, he said, "If I show you the most horrible things you can do to yourself, will you do something to change it?"

This prediction in *Century II-41* by Nostradamus got my attention:

The great star will burn for seven days and the cloud will make the sun appear double. The large mastiff will howl at night when the great pontiff changes his abode.

Pope Francis refused to live in the Vatican like all Pope before him. Instead, he took up residency at the papal apartments. So this prophecy seems to refer to this current timeline. The great star could be referring to Planet X, near the sun, making it appear to be two suns in the sky, and the large mastiff will howl at night (mysterious booms heard worldwide in the past few years) could refer to the signs leading up to the pole shift. In Cannon's book, Nostradamus confirmed the quatrain was about the pole shift.

In Century quatrain 1-17, Nostradamus describes Earth changes and perhaps even a pole shift.

For forty years the rainbow will not be seen. For forty years it will be seen every day.

The dry earth will grow more parched and there will be great floods when it is seen.

Although the channeled information said the meaning of this quatrain is lots of floods and droughts and a drought lasting forty years. I interrupt it as meaning that a shift of the Earth's poles will create erupting volcanoes everywhere and will obscure the rainbow for many years. Survival will be tough on humans, who will need to melt ice from the poles or by purifying water from the sea.

Years ago, I was shown a giant spiral in a dream and sensed I was being shown what time looks like and how events can repeat or be changed on this cosmic spiral. I was surprised to see that Nostradamus said one of the aspects of time is that it moves in a spiral, confirming my dream. At similar positions on each of the loops of the spiral, events have the possibility of being similar.

In *Conversations with Nostradamus* quatrain 9-83, which I listed earlier, according to channeled information from Nostradamus, he says that he was talking about a weapon being tested that can create earthquakes worldwide. He's not sure of the concept, but it is something that is dropped or either something that is projected like a laser ray or something airborne. Some extension of the device is carried in a plane and the plane must fly over the area where the earthquake is to be or at least fly over the area where the earthquake must be triggered, regardless of the area the earthquake ends up affecting. But that will not be the entire device. That will just simply be like the point of the spear, just the operating part of it. The power behind the weapon and the science behind it will be based in a secret underground laboratory elsewhere. Somehow the power of the underground laboratory will be linked to the airborne device in such a way as to be able to channel it to the desired effect of a triggered earthquake.

The sun in twenty degrees of Taurus, there will be a great earthquake; the great theatre full up will be ruined. Darkness and trouble in the air, on sky and land, when the infidel calls upon God and the Saints.

Nostradamus went on to say that the country that develops this device will be able to hold it as a major threat over the heads of all the major nations. Any nation can be intimidated that has any geological faults in their country that are susceptible to earthquakes. He says it will be very similar to the situation immediately after World War II when the United States was the only country with nuclear power. He says the concept of it will be so awe-inspiring and frightening, much the way nuclear power was at first to the world, that it will cause everybody, including the infidels, to call upon the saints for protection.

The sun in twenty degrees of Taurus refers to when the weapon becomes generally known. In 1989 when Cannon's book was published, Nostradamus said the weapon was already being developed.

The High-Frequency Active Auroral Research Program (HAARP) began operation in 1993. Designed and built by BAE Advanced Technologies (BAEAT), its purpose was to analyze the ionosphere and investigate the potential for developing ionospheric enhancement technology for radio communications and surveillance. The HAARP program operated a major sub-arctic facility, named the HAARP Research Station, on an Air Force-owned site near Gakona, Alaska.

For conspiracy theorists HAARP is capable of modifying weather, disabling satellites, exerting mind control over people, and used as a weapon against terrorists. It's even be blamed for creating earthquakes, droughts, storms and floods, the 1996 crash of TWA Flight 800, the 2003 destruction of the space shuttle Columbia.

But as outrageous this conspiracy theory might seem in the scope of natural science, it isn't when you consider that the late great Nikola Tesla, a Serbian American inventor, electrical engineer, mechanical engineer, physicist, and futurist, (1856- 1943), was experimenting with resonance as early as 1893 when he invented and patented the electro-mechanical oscillator, a steam-powered electric generator. Later in life, Tesla claimed one version of the oscillator created an earthquake in New York City in 1898 and was later dubbed "Tesla's earthquake machine." Tesla also claimed he could split the earth in half with the machine if he could get enough power.

In the television show, The Mythbusters, cast members set out to disprove Tesla's invention and made a device powered by electricity rather than steam. It produced vibrations that could be felt hundreds of feet away, but no earthquake shaking on the modern bridge they attached to; they judged that the claim that the device produced an earthquake to be false, which hardly proves or disproves Tesla's claims.

Tesla was a genius, known for these inventions: Tesla coil, alternating current, induction motor, three-phase electric power, remote control, wireless telegraphy, neon lamp and some say he was the originator of the telephone but did not receive credit for his invention and many others.

Later in life, Tesla claimed he had made a teleforce weapon after studying the Van de Graaff generator. The press called it a "peace ray' or "death ray," to be used against ground-based infantry or for antiaircraft purposes. Tesla gives the following description concerning the "particle gun's" operation: [The nozzle would] send concentrated beams of particles through the free air, of such tremendous energy that they will bring down a fleet of 10,000 enemy airplanes at a distance of 200 miles from a defending nation's border and will cause armies to drop dead in their tracks.

On January 7, 1943, Tesla died at age 86, alone in room 3327 at the New Yorker Hotel of coronary thrombosis, according to the medical examiner. Here's the strange part that feeds conspiracy theorists—two days later, the FBI ordered the Alien Property Custodian to seize Tesla's records, even though Tesla had become an American citizen. Tesla's entire estate from the Hotel and other New York City hotels were transported to the Manhattan Storage and Warehouse Company under the Office of Alien Property (OAP) seal. John G. Trump, a professor, and inventor at M.I.T (this was President Trump's uncle and his father's brother), who also served to the National Defense Research Committee, was asked to analyze the Tesla items at OAP. After three days of investigation, Trump reported that there was nothing that would constitute a hazard in unfriendly hands. Was that the truth or a cover-up for Tesla's incredible inventions, including an earthquake machine?

So far, Dolores Cannon's channeled Nostradamus prophecies have not come true. For those who still don't believe Nostradamus was a gifted prophet, think about this: he predicted the exact day of his own death—July 2, 1566—of natural causes.

Chapter Seven
EDGAR CAYCE

Edgar Cayce, (1877-1945) known as the "Sleeping Prophet," one of the world's best-known psychics, gave thousands of readings in a trance-like state about past pole shifts as well as future shifts. The shifting of the Earth's poles, according to Cayce, is accompanied by a change in the consciousness of humanity. In some cases, it appears that Cayce was referring to an actual physical shifting of the Earth's poles. These were sudden movements that created cataclysmic events. However, in other readings, Cayce was likely referring to alterations in the magnetic poles. These could relate to a drifting of the magnetic poles or an actual reversal of the polarity.

When Cayce was asked, "What great change or the beginning of what change, if any, is to take place in the Earth in the year 2000 to 2001 A.D.?" Cayce replied, "There will be upheavals in the Arctic and Antarctic that will cause the eruption of volcanoes in the torrid areas and the pole shift. When there is the shifting of the poles; or a new cycle begins." And when asked what great change or the beginning of what change, if any, is to take place in the Earth in the year 2000 and 2001 A.D., he said, "When there is a shifting of the poles. Or a new cycle begins." Obviously, he missed the prediction, but it's interesting to note our concerns over climate change, the increase in earthquakes and volcanic activity and the receding of Antarctic's glaciers and ice shelves.

Astronomers believe the axis wobble (like a spinning top slowing) has occurred for ages and causes the North Pole to point to different Pole Stars or North Stars. How often this occurs is unclear. According to leading scientific teams at major research centers, axis shifts have only occurred every few million or billion years and taken millions of years to be completed. The flip cycle starts with the magnetic field weakening over the span of a few thousand years, then the poles flip and the field springs back up to full strength again. However, a new study shows that the last time the Earth's poles flipped, it only took 100 years for the reversal to happen. What's more, our planet's magnetic fields appear to be weakening, suggesting a magnetic flip is on its way. Data collected this past summer by the European Space Agency (ESA) satellite suggest the field is weakening 10 times faster than scientists originally thought. They predicted a flip could complete within the next couple thousand years, not unless some outside force triggers it much sooner.

Here's what we do know about the Earth's axis. It spins like a top making a complete revolution every 24 hours. However, just like a spinning top tends to lean, creating a spin axis, the Earth also leans as it spins. The spin axis of the Earth is about 23 degrees off-center. Because they observed the long-term movements in the Earth's crustal plates, scientists have been somewhat skeptical about a sudden shift in the axis of the Earth's spin. Such a sudden change would be catastrophic for all life on Earth. Depending on the degree of shift would determine how catastrophic. Such an event might have explained the sudden extinction event of dinosaurs and other creatures like the Mammoths found piled up in Siberia with flowers in their mouths. Whatever geological event killed them happened extremely fast.

Cayce's readings indicated a sudden physical change in the Earth's rotational axis created by many catastrophic events is shared by researchers and some scientists. Interestingly, the dates suggested by these researchers matched Cayce's dates.

In the 1970s, two Canadians, Rand, and Rose Flenn-Ath began working on the maps Professor and author Charles Hapgood had used in his book, Maps of the Ancient Sea Kings. They concluded that an ice-free Antarctica was accurately depicted in many ancient maps. They also believed that the legend of Atlantis and the continent's sudden catastrophic end was based on a civilization that had once existed in Antarctica.

In an article published on July 25, 1997 issue of Science indicated that sudden shifts in the Earth's crust probably have occurred. Dr. Joseph L. Kirschvink, Professor of Geobiology at California's Caltech, and other esteemed coauthors provided geological evidence in the article that 530,000,000 years ago the crust slid exactly as Hapgood suggested it could, moving the poles to the equator. It was this shift that caused a jump in evolution at the time. Fossil evidence, geologic evidence, radioactive formations, and the knowledge that such shifts have occurred on other planets were cited. The authors collected their data over a 20-year period from various locations on Earth.

Cayce states that the ancient Egyptians knew of these shifts and the Great Pyramid of Giza was built to point to the Axis or Pole Star.

Chapter Eight
BLACK ELK'S VISIONS

In *Mother Earth Spirituality,* Oglala Sioux Ceremonial Leader Ed McGaa "Eagle Man" wrote about Black Elk and his interpretation of Black Elk's visions for us and our planet. "Visions and foretelling prophecies are not uncommon among my people, the Oglala," Ed writes. "The demanding Vision Quest—in which the seeker stays alone, on an isolated mountain top or badlands butte— the Sun Dance ritual and the powerful Yuwipi (Spirit-calling) Ceremony, have resulted in strong foretelling power for our holy men and holy women.

"Long ago, a holy man called Drinks Water envisioned that the animals, primarily the buffalo, would go back into the Earth—that is, they would be killed. He saw that the Sioux would be ruled by a different race of people, who would make the Indians live in square, gray houses on barren land, and that they would starve. His vision was true. History shows that in the 1890s the Sioux were, indeed, forced to live on reservations in square, gray houses and that many starved to death."

Black Elk, also known as Hehaka Sapa and Nicholas Black Elk, was a famous holy man, traditional healer, and visionary of the Oglala Lakota (Sioux) of the northern Great Plains. He was born in December of 1863 on the Little Powder River in Wyoming, west of present-day South Dakota. He was the son of the elder Black Elk, who supported Chief Crazy Horse, the Lakota resistance leader, and White Cow Sees Woman. He had five sisters and one brother.

Black Elk was born in December, probably under the sun sign Sagittarius, an astrological sign often connected to seers and prophets. During his lifetime he witnessed many battles: he was three-years-old when the Fetterman Battle took place in 1866, he was five-years-old during the signing of the 1868 Fort Laramie Treaty, and about 12 years old when the Battle of the Little Big Horn was fought, and General George A. Custer and his soldier perished. He experienced the end of the Sioux wars and the beginning of aggressive federal "Pacification" policies imposed by the U.S. government upon his people.

In 1877, the Lakota people, including Black Elk and his family, fled north into Canada. They followed Chief Sitting Bull, who had become the Lakota resistance leader after the stabbing death of Crazy Horse. Following Chief Sitting bull's surrender and arrest, Black Elk, his family, and other Lakota returned to internment on the Pine Ridge Reservation.

In 1886, Black Elk rejoined Buffalo Bill Cody's Wild West Show. He traveled with the show throughout the United States and Europe. When he finally returned home to the Pine Ridge Reservation, he became their spiritual authority and supported the Ghost Dance movement, based on the belief that the dance would cause white people to leave and the buffalo to return to them, which had been nearly killed to extinction by white soldiers and pioneers. Black Elk was a witness to the Wounded Knee Massacre on December 29, 1890, near Wounded Knee Creek on the Lakota Pine Ridge Indian Reservation in the U.S. state of South Dakota.

According to some eye-witnesses, the U.S. 7th Cavalry Regiment commanded by Major Samuel M. Whiteside intercepted Spotted Elk's band of Miniconjou Lakota and 38 Hunkpapa Lakota near Porcupine Butte and escorted them 5 miles westward to Wound Knee Creek, where they made camp. On December 29, troops went to disarm the Lakota, and one version of the story claimed an Indian rifle accidentally discharged causing the 7th Cavalry to open fire from all sides, killing men, women, and children, as well as some of their own fellow soldiers. By the time the gunfire ended more than 200 men, women and children of the Lakota tribe were dead and 51 were wounded (4 men, 47 women, and children, some of whom died later). Twenty-five soldiers also died that day and 39 were wounded. At least twenty soldiers were awarded the Medal of Honor, but in 2001, the National Congress of American Indians passed two resolutions condemning the awards and called on the U.S. government to rescind the. The site of the battlefield has been designated as a National Historic Landmark.

It is said that Black Elk, on horseback, charged the soldiers and helped to rescue some of the wounded. A bullet grazed his hip.

In 1931, author John G. Neihardt interviewed Black Elk at age 68 about his life and visions in a book titled, *Black Elk Speaks*, published in 1932. Black Elk spoke of a new world.

When Black Elk was nine years old, he became very ill and was unresponsive for several days. During this time he had a powerful vision in which he was visited by the Thunder Beings (Wakinyan), and taken to the Grandfathers—spiritual representatives of the six sacred directions: west, east, north, south, above, and below. These "...spirits were represented as kind and loving, full of years and wisdom, like revered human grandfathers." When he was seventeen, Black Elk told a medicine man, Black Road, about the vision in detail. Black Road and the other medicine men of the village were "astonished by the greatness of the vision."

Part of Black Elk's vision involved the Earth becoming sick. The animals, the winged ones, and the four-legged ones grew frightened and all living things became poor and sickly. The air and the waters dirtied and smelled foul. And then Black Elk saw a blue man creating the sickness on Mother Earth. The powers of the four directions, represented by four horses, charged the blue man but were beaten back. Then the Grandfathers called upon Black Elk who picked up his bow which transformed into a spear. He swooped down on the blue man, killing him. After the blue man was dead, all life came back upon the Earth; all things fresh and healed again.

Ed McGaa also believed that what Black Elk witnessed was the Earth becoming sick and dying.

Black Elk was shown his people over a great period, beginning with the time his people all walked in a sacred manner, following the good red road, camping in a sacred circle. A holy tree stood out sharply within the encampments center. "Behold, a good nation, walking in a sacred manner, in a good land," the people sang. In time, however, the people broke into little groups and denominations, each group following a different path and all around them was fighting and war. The sacred tree withered. Black Elk saw miserable, starving faces of people who were sick and dying.

A red man appeared among the people. His transformation into a buffalo indicated a time of plenty. A sacred herb became four flowers, four blossoms on a single stem. The four-rayed herb—red, yellow, black, and white, became the flowering tree. Black Elk heard a song: A good nation I will make live, this nation above has said, they have given me the power to makeover.

Then Black Elk saw the sacred hoop of his people was only one of many hoops, all joined together to make one great circle, the great hoop of all peoples. In the center of the great hoop stood a powerful, shelter, flowering tree, and under it gathered children of all nations.

At the end of Black Elk's vision, two-spirit men gave him the day-break-star herb of understanding. He dropped the herb down to the world below, and it flowered, spreading its power out into the whole world. In time, he was promised his people would be free and would help spread this power of peace and understanding.

Black Elk lived to be an old man. In his lifetime he witnessed the free spirit of the mystic warriors of the plains become a tethered eagle to a *washichu's*, or white man's, zoo. He and his people became captives of the dark reservation road. Old warriors waited in remoteness, amid poverty and despair, for the promise of yesterday.

In Dr. Ardy Sixkiller Clarke's book, *Encounters with Star People,* she was told a story about Black Elk and a special stone he carried with him all his life after a UFO encounter. The story goes that Black Elk was visiting his cousin Benjamin. He was in the sweat lodge, when according to Benjamin's family; a circular craft came out of the sky and hovered over it. Suddenly a stone penetrated the closed door and landed between Black Elk's feet. He picked up the stone but had to complete the sweat lodge ceremony before he could leave. By the time he was able to leave the lodge, the spacecraft was gone. Another holy man on the reservation remembered Black Elk and how he carried the rock and how he still used the sacred pipe. He said that when he lit his sacred pipe, Black Elk would laugh and call his pipe an antenna for contacting the Star People.

Dr. Clarke's source said, "Black Elk believed the Star People came to Earth hundreds of thousands of years ago from Sirius and the Pleiades. He called them the answers of the people."

From what I've heard indigenous people worldwide have communicated with Star People for eons and continue to connect with them. In Dr. Clarke's travels to South America and speaking to the Maya people, she was told that the Star People have warned them that we are going from the Fourth World into the Fifth World where a great cleansing will take place. The Maya have no fear of these Earth changes because they know how to survive in the natural world unlike people in the Western world who live the cities and have no idea how to survive in nature.

I agree with Ed McGaa that the blue man of Black Elk's vision is symbolic of all those who harm Mother Earth and her creatures and do so knowingly. The blue man, the great violator, symbolizes greed, corruption, dishonesty, and selfishness. Mother Earth, represented by the four directions, has fought back against the one who has made the grass and animals sick and the streams and air unclean. Mother Earth has natural self-healing powers, but without the help of knowledgeable humans, she cannot set herself right. A reversal of the world values, a spiritual concept of the Earth as God-created and sacred, is in order before we two-leggeds can be environmentally effective on a global basis. The blue man will meet his death when takes place.

Ed said this, "Brothers and sisters, we must go back to some of the old ways if we are going to truly save our Mother Earth and bring back the natural beauty that every person seriously needs, especially in this day of vanishing species, vanishing rain forests, overpopulation, poisoned waters, acid rain, a thinning ozone layer, drought, rising temperatures, and weapons of complete annihilation. In conclusion, our survival is dependent on the realization that Mother Earth is a truly holy being, that all things in the world are holy and must not be violated, and that we must share and be generous with one another. Think of your fellow men and women as holy people who were put here by the Great Spirit. Think of being related to all things!"

There will come a time when the birds will fall from the trees, the rivers will be poisoned and the wolves will die in the forests. But then the warriors of the rainbow will appear and save the world.——Cree Indian saying.

Chapter Nine
INDIGENOUS PROPHECIES

From October 11 through October 17, 2004 something extraordinary happened. The Thirteen Indigenous Grandmothers met for the first time in Phoenicia, New York. They traveled from the Amazon rain forest, the Arctic circle of North America, the great forests of the American Northwest, the vast plains of North America, the highlands of Central America, the Black Hills of South Dakota, the mountains of Oaxaca, Mexico, the American Southwest, the mountains of Tibet, and the rain forest of central Africa.

Their calling was for a common vision to form a new global alliance with traditional medicine people and communities throughout the world. They united in New York as one in prayer, education, and healing for Mother Earth and all her inhabitants, for the children of the world and the next seven generations.

Their urgency was for the abuse and disregard of Mother Earth—the unprecedented destruction of the air, waters, and soil; the atrocities of war, the global scourge of poverty; the threat of nuclear weapons and waste permeating the planet; the prevailing culture of materialism; the epidemics that threaten the health of Earth's peoples; the exploitation of indigenous medicines; and the destruction of the indigenous culture and knowledge handed down from generation to generation.

The Grandmothers believe that their ancestral wisdom of prayer, ceremony, peacemaking, and healing are urgently needed now. In the beautifully written book, *Grandmothers Counsel the World—Women Elders Offer Their Vision of Our Planet,* author Carol Schaefer interviewed each of the Thirteen Indigenous Grandmothers from around the world. The wisdom and guidance they imparted is invaluable to ensure that future generations have a thriving and healthy planet.

Grandmother Clara of the Amazon was visited by the Star Beings and was told that 12-21-2012 heralded the "Galactic Dawn"—a mass awakening of humanity to our cosmic origins and intergalactic relationships. "What I see today in the world is a lot of darkness and a few points of light trying to illuminate us as we go through the dark tunnel of our Age. We Grandmothers here are holding each other's hands, illuminating the path so that we can bring health to this Mother Earth and heal the wounds. She is suffering from wounds made by ignorant men, ignorant of the truth of the Light and of the Creator. The message from the Beings of the Stars is that it is necessary for everyone to open their hearts to the truth of the Spirit, of the Spirit World, as it is this truth that will lead us to our salvation," says Grandmother Clara.

As the Earth changes accelerate each year—extreme weather, increased earthquakes and volcanic activity worldwide, and sinkholes forming everywhere, we are moving into a time of the cleansing of accumulated negativity caused by humanity's greed and materialism. We are out of balance say the Grandmothers, but Earth's changes will bring about an awakening of spiritual consciousness in humanity. There is the possibility of a great number of people leaving the planet. During times of crisis, people help each other—that's where the real spirit of humanity shines.

All the Grandmothers agree that we must develop a different relationship with Mother Earth. They say people will need physical, mental, emotional and spiritual strength to change; otherwise, a huge portion of the population will suffer immeasurably. Unfortunately, at this time, most of humanity is materially oriented instead of spiritually oriented.

Nepalese Grandmother Aama Bombo called upon Kali, the female goddess who can take the form of the Destroyer, during her prayer with the Grandmothers in New Mexico. Aama conveyed: "Kali is not happy with what is going on in the world. She sees that humanity is lacking in good values, and she is not happy with the cruelty of the people, who have been killing each other every day just to fulfill their selfish egos. They are poisoning the Motherland and the sky. This has led to the suffocation of all the creatures, who are not allowed a fresh breath. Spirituality and its values have been subordinated to the ego and injustice."

The Grandmothers say we must learn love and compassion again. The people who will survive are those who love and affirm life in every way. But we must be willing to change the way we view the living library of Earth—all creation. The survivors will be those who are open to a whole new level of consciousness and seek true communication with the Earth and Creator.

Grandmother Flordemayo says the Maya are among those whose prophecy reveals a new consciousness coming where the feminine will prevail again. "I come from the Star People of the Pleiades, and I am also a child in Central America. In our oral teachings, we were told that at this particular time it will be the women who lead the nations. I bow to the spirit of women from the beginning of time, the spirit of woman that is within all of us. Male/female, female/male—we all come from that One. We are also told that at this time it is the energy of the stars that will move the nations."

Grandmother Mona believes the Hopi legend of the butterfly can help us through turbulent times of darkness and confusion by revealing to us our path of transformation. These times are necessary for learn and enabling humanity as a whole to transform into a comprehension of the truth of our oneness with each other and with all of Creation. Only by going into darkness and breaking down the old ways can we move from the myopic view of the caterpillar to the greatly expanded view of the butterfly—the only way we will save our planet for the next generations to come.

Yupik Grandmother Rita Blumenstein explains that with every new experience, we have the power to redefine ourselves, so that no matter what our past mistakes, we can always change. "The past is not a burden. It is a scaffold that has brought us to this day. With this understanding, we are free to be who we are. We create our lives out of our past and out of the present. The quicker way to heal is by going forward, however—not by spending a great amount of time and energy dwelling on the past. We are our ancestors when we heal ourselves. We also heal our ancestors, our grandmothers, our grandfathers, and our children. When we heal ourselves, we also heal our Mother Earth, and we heal future generations."

When we transform from caterpillar to butterfly, we will become our true luminous selves and evolve into a higher level in the Cosmos.

Grandmother Julieta of Mexico believes in the power of prayer. "I live in the place of power of prayer. What I see is that unity is what the world must strive for now. In this unity form, everything comes together again. All our relations come together again in circles of people, who are at peace again within themselves and also patient with the ones who have not arrived at such peace yet. These circles need to be formed everywhere, so that we can become one again on the whole planet, in this visible world, and in the invisible world."

Grandmother Flordemayo also believes that it is only by living in the moment that we will save ourselves because when we are living in the moment we feel more alive, more love and community. "If we pray 100 percent at that moment, we can move the consciousness of humanity," she says. "The period of scattered prayers and scattered wishes has ended. We must pray to the spirit of the heavens and the Earth, the spirit of the sacred waters, the spirit of our Mother Earth. We must pray to the spirit of humanity to acknowledge each other as brother and sister, as nations of people that breathe the same air, as nations of people who are being fed by the spirit of ancestors of the sacred waters. If we do not acknowledge this, we will lose our way. So I pray for the moment, I pray to be present without ego, with total passion, with total love to Spirit, because it is the only way."

When the 9/11 attacks happened, Grandmother Flordemayo went into intense prayer and asked the Grandmothers from the Spirit World to give her understanding of the event. In a vision the north wall of her be room seemed to disappear and she was shown angels gathering in a circle. The angels were so big; they might have been ten to eighteen feet tall. They had huge wings that touched the sky and the Earth. In the middle of the circle was a holy man. The angels began singing, in a heaven celestial way.

The vision represented how our planet is protected by angels.

From all that I have learned from the indigenous people of North American and the messages given by the thirteen indigenous Grandmothers, the only thing that separates us from each other is our prejudices and hate. When we learn that we need to come from pure heart as One, and stop destroying our natural resources, killing each other and abusing the creatures of the planet, and when we see everything on Earth as sacred, then spiritual doors of ancient knowledge will become available to us. Our planet will be transformed.

It is this disrespect and greed that has brought us to this dire place in Earth's history. And this disrespect is spreading into us in the form of cancers and many illnesses because we are out of balance—*ayni.*

There was a time, the Grandmothers remind us when all of our ancestors revered the Earth and used a ritual to maintain the Earth's balance. The old people used to tell the people to go to the oceans or the rivers or the streams and call up the water spirits for healing and rebalancing, the Grandmothers say. All of us are connected to the whales, the wolves, the polar bears, to all of creation. We should all be praying that drilling doesn't impact the great caribou migration patterns because we too will be hurt, the Grandmothers say.

They advise us to teach our children a new way, in order to ensure that future generations will experience the beauty and abundance the Creator has given us. We must humbly pray to the rocks, the trees, the sky, the mountains, the sacred waters, the birds, and the animals, to help us to give us their power to help Mother Earth again and all her creatures.

Western Shoshone Nation Spiritual Leader Corbin Harney

It was in the mid-1990s that I had the honor of meeting a great man and spiritual leader, Corbin Harney of the Western Shoshone Nation. Shortly after I introduction in Boise, Idaho Corbin and I began to plan an Earth healing ceremony at Sundance in Utah owned by Corbin's favorite actor Robert Redford. After many letters to Robert Redford, he agreed to the healing ceremony, but a few months later our dream of a ceremony was canceled due to Redford's commitment to the movie, The Horse Whisperer. Corbin and I kept in touch for a few more years, and he always talked about how he almost met Robert Redford.

Corbin died in 2007, at age 87, but he accomplished so much during those years, which included a book, *The Way It Is*, recounting his Earth visions and how he organized peaceful protests against underground nuclear testing in Nevada.

Corbin said, "A few years ago I was praying to the water. I was praying that it would run pure and clear and that it would be able to take care of us for countless generations. The water came to me and spoke to me. It said, 'In a few years I'm going to look like water, but you're not going to be able to use me anymore.'"

At the time of the publication of his book in 1995, Corbin saw his vision coming true. Much of our water throughout the world is already contaminated. Corbin was deeply saddened by the state of the Earth, especially the damage he had seen coming from the underground nuclear testing sixty miles northwest of Las Vegas, Nevada on Western Shoshone land. He "came out from behind the bush," as he said, and in 1985 started to protest the U.S. government's nuclear weapons testing. Along with other Western Shoshone leaders, they crossed the cattle guard into the 1,350-square-mile Test Site. Soon they were joined by more and more people in marches supporting a nuclear test ban.

As an advocate for the well-being of our Mother Earth, Corbin took hundreds of protestors into the sweat lodge to pray. He always encouraged a strong but peaceful demonstration. In addition to U.S. citizens, people around the world began to attend his gatherings. Corbin believed and said this many times, "We all breathe the same air...all over this world. We all drink the same water. We are all warmed by the same sun, and we are all fed nourished by the same Earth. What we do here in Nevada affects the life of everyone on the planet."

What Corbin was saying applies to the Butterfly Effect, which is this idea that a single butterfly flapping its wings on one side of the globe can, in theory, can start a hurricane on the other side of the globe. Everything is connected.

In 1993, Corbin visited Kazakhstan and learned about the water's contamination from dangerous levels of radiation. During his visit, he went to a children's hospital and prayed for the children who were there suffering from birth deformities and painful, terminal illnesses caused by radiation poisoning. "This is really sad," he said. "because these people are going through what is soon coming our way. We've got to wake up and do something about it. The contamination is still going on today, and soon it's going to be too late. How can we live on without water? How can anything live?"

When he spoke at the Glastonbury Festival in England in the spring of 1994 he said, "I was told that raw nuclear waste is being dumped into the Irish Sea covering 300 square miles. This is terrible! The water travels everywhere, and the contamination is already destroying our sea life...and without our sea life, how can we live on? It is time for all of us, wherever we are, to start working together to save our planet here

"Everywhere I go, people say, 'But, what can I do about this? I'm just one person. It's too big to stop because our economy is based largely on things that pollute our Earth."

Corbin responded to these people, "All these things, like nuclear plants and test sites, the mining toxins and chemical plants are all destroying our Earth. We're sucking our mother dry. If we want to have a Mother Earth to leave to our future generations, then we have to stop the way we're doing things now. The only way, as I see it, is to return to a native way of life where we take care of everything that we've got. From the beginning of time, that was the native way.

"In my life as a native of the land, I have tried to preserve our sacred sites and burial grounds. I have tried to keep our culture alive among young people. These things are important. But now the very survival of all life is at stake, and we must save our Earth before we don't have an Earth to live on anymore.

"We, the people today, everywhere across this Mother Earth, need to unite together, no matter what color we are, no matter what language we speak. We need to find ways to get involved to help our Mother. Take pictures and videos to show what's going on. There is power in the people when we unite together. There is an even greater power when we come together to pray for our Mother Earth and all the living things. I always say, 'Don't pray like me; pray your own way, but pray for everything out there.' Everything is alive and we forget that. Prayer is the only way we're going to live on.

"The Spirit came to me and said, 'You're going to have to come out from behind the bush and give us a hand here.' But not just me. Now it's time for all of us to come out from behind the bush. You people, you have a voice. Use that voice! Let's work together to have a beautiful, clean Earth for our future generations."

If Corbin had lived to see the Fukushima disaster and the tons of radiation that poured into the ocean, and that is probably still going into it, he would have been broken-hearted. The very thing he was trying to prevent happened because of our continued disrespect of Mother Earth and nuclear energy is in use and nuclear weapons that have been stockpiled all over the world. Would he have given up the fight to save our planet? I don't think so—Corbin was a fighter and didn't believe in giving up, and I'm sure he'd ask each of us to never give up the good fight for saving Earth and all life.

In 1996, the Comprehensive Nuclear-Test-Ban Treaty (CTBT) was created by which countries agree to bank all nuclear explosions in all environments, for military or civilian purposes. It was adopted by the United Nations General Assembly on September 10, 1996, but it has not entered into force due to the non-ratification of eight specific states. Three countries have tested nuclear weapons since the CTBT opened for signature in 1996. India and Pakistan both carried out two sets of tests in 1998. North Korea carried out three announced tests in 2006, 2009 and 2013.

Mary Summer Rain

Mary Summer Rain, a Native American author, wrote about her blind Chippewa medicine woman teacher, No-Eyes, in a series of books. No-Eyes supposedly taught Mary Summer Rain about ancient truths, but Mary Summer Rain has long had her distractors and those who believe she concocted the entire story. Even if No Eyes didn't exist, Mary Summer Rain has the gift of prophecy.

In her book, *Phoenix Rising,* (1987 first printing) No-Eyes gave a series of warnings of a world that lies ahead if humanity continued to live out of balance with the natural world. The book describes tumultuous times of strong winds, hurricanes, tidal waves, a global collapse in the financial and property markets.

What is so compelling about Mary Summer Rain's books is that she wrote these books years before they were published in the late 1980s, long before any psychic was predicting cataclysmic Earth changes.

No-Eyes discussed the legendary Phoenix and how the bird was symbolic of the changes coming to our planet. She said the Phoenix was going be reborn on Earth when Mother Earth goes into labor. No Eyes said, "Great Phoenix gonna rise up again just like all times ago. He's been forming for years now and he's all ready to break out of Earth Mother's womb. If peoples quiet themselves, they gonna feel the labor contractions of Earth Mother. She be so tired. She gonna give up great Phoenix soon, Summer see."

It seemed No Eyes was using a metaphor for mega Earth changes coming...or was she? Whether or not you believe Mary Summer Rain's story of No-Eyes doesn't matter—only her predictions stand the test of time and are now proving frighteningly accurate.

What appeared to be a huge bird on fire was captured by a webcam on July 23, 2018, flying over Teton National Park near Yellowstone Park. But four days before the Phoenix-looking bird was captured over Teton National Park on a massive fissure opened up near Yellowstone National Park on July 18, 2018.

Firebird photo left is an enlargement of the actual bird on the right captured by webcam over Teton National Park on July 23, 2018

Could such a bird exist? The Phoenix is known through cultures worldwide, including Native Americans and their legends of a powerful bird called the Thunderbird. The Phoenix is described as a huge bird that is associated with the sun. Every five hundred years, according to some popular legends, it dies in flames and is reborn out of its own ashes. It is an omen of things that are about to be destroyed in fiery ashes and then reborn.

No-Eyes envisioned a great earthquake in California. "Summer, peoples already know 'bout big tearing in California [earthquake fault]. That gonna be most bad one. That one be more bad tear. Many places no have tears happen. Many places no have earth rumble, ever. That gonna change. Big noises gonna come from Earth Mother [mysterious booms heard recently worldwide?] — deep down inside. They gonna be coming many more times in new laces, places where no tears ever been before. They [earthquakes] gonna show up in many new land places. They gonna be bigger and bigger as Phoenix rise from birthing place. Earth Mother move much under skin. She gonna make big moves."

Since 2011, author and Earth mysteries investigator Linda Moulton Howe of Earthfiles.com has received a huge amount of reports on bizarre booms, mysterious lights, metallic scraping noises, horn-like sounds, and strange shaking not associated with earthquakes, according the USGS. What is it? Theories suggest sonic booms from meteors, space debris, and maybe even deep core Earth movement. Is this a warning from Earth of a polar shift? Many believe our planet is wobbling and stretching—but what will be the trigger point to shift the Earth's axis? That I can't answer, I just know there will be more warnings. The Indigenous Elders worldwide have been warned by the "Sky People" for years that we are going from the Fourth World into the new Fifth World. There have been more warnings—cracks forming in the earth, sinkholes, increased methane gas, animals and sea creatures suddenly dying worldwide, and extreme weather (some of the weather is being controlled by HAARP and jet chemtrails).

No-Eyes also warned about volcanoes becoming extremely active in the near future. "Many more stuff gonna be coming out. This time many more peoples move away. Hot rocks gonna take many houses. Hot rocks be all over stuff. Earth Mother blow and blow stuff all over."

When Mary summer Rain asked if No-Eyes was talking about Hawaii and Washington State, she answered, "No-Eyes talk 'bout all over."

"But there aren't volcanoes all over."

"Gonna be! No-Eyes say old holes be hot again."

No-Eyes had visions of hurricane winds blowing over the land, which reminded me of my recurring visions of fierce winds at age seven. She went on to say, "Summer, Earth Mother gonna breathe real hard. Phoenix be hard on her. She gonna blow her breath all over. It be fire hot. It gonna dry land up [droughts]. Big part of land gonna be all dry. It gonna be burned crispy." She was saying that the winds would increase and that their intensity would be stronger than normal. And when the winds take the waters over the lands, there will be widespread areas of massive flooding.

The horrible truth is we are seeing droughts worldwide—in Africa, South East Asia, Brazil, California, Texas, Southwest, Northwest and United States Midwest.

No-Eyes began to make short panting breaths. "Earth Mother gonna go like this. She go like that and make fast, powerful breaths. It blow people's cars, it blows people's boats and trains before they know it coming even!" Many people gonna feel stuff. They gonna die when she do that." Mary Summer Rain interpreted the winds to be quick guests that come out of nowhere.

No-Eyes predictions included soil erosion from drought conditions and water under Earth Mother drying. "Landfall into many big holes all over. When water under, earth goes dry, Earthfall into place where water been."

In other words, sinkholes will form and swallow up houses, cars, and people, which has been happening globally. In the Urals of Russia huge sinkholes suddenly opened up, perhaps caused by the permafrost melting and causing methane gas to explode within the Earth. Also, the Midwest had a house swallowed up by a sinkholes with a man inside, who was never found, a massive sinkhole opened up near a Ihop restaurant in Meridian, Mississippi and twelve cars fell into it on November 8, 2015, and eight classic cars were swallowed up by a massive sinkhole at the National Corvette Museum in Kentucky on February 2, 2014.

We are now seeing reports worldwide of winds blowing trains off their tracks, cars, truck and big rig trucks blown off the highways, planes crashing, and houses being torn apart by extremely strong winds.

No-Eyes envisioned extreme winters with blizzards and excessive snowfall, and summers with thunderstorms, tornadoes and large hail. Summer and winter would become mixed up in an hour's time— suddenly temperature drops. There will be a new light in the sky and it will be green all over, everywhere, she explained. The entire atmosphere will be tinged with a greenish hue. When the sky turns this color it is a warning of Phoenix Days, the birthing days of the great Phoenix. The Phoenix represented the dying of our planet and its rebirth, rising up from the mythical ashes to become a new world.

No-Eyes said Earth Watchers [Sky People] will no longer stop stuff from happening and mass deaths. Now they are letting humanity make its own unaware errors. She reprimanded humanity as being too lazy to learn lessons.

One of the more frightening visions was of nuclear plants, chemical warfare materials, and radioactive weapons leaking. No-Eyes said, "Earth Mother gonna dump burn stuff back up into peoples' face. That be only the start..."

Although I'm only listing three major environmental disasters, there are much more taking place worldwide. After Japan's mega-thrust 9.0 magnitude earthquake and tsunami on March 11, 2011, Fukushima Daiichi Nuclear Plant experienced three meltdowns and releases of radioactive materials beginning the next day. It is the largest nuclear disaster since the Chernobyl disaster of 1986 and the second disaster (after Chernobyl) to be given the Level 7 event classification of the International Nuclear Event Scale. Unconfirmed reports claim Fukushima plant continues dumping thousands of tons of radioactive water into the Pacific Ocean and has already killed thousands of fish from Japan to California and Alaska's coasts.

In the past few years, there have been deepwater oil drilling disasters like the one with BP Oil Company in the Gulf of Mexico off the Louisiana coast on April 20, 2011, which resulted in 4.9 million barrels of oil gushing into the Gulf, and in 2015 a toxic mine spill from the Gold King Mine at Silverton spilled millions of gallons of arsenic, lead and other toxins into the Animas River which runs through Durango, Colorado. The river, normally a deep green, turned bright orange from the spill's heavy metals. Farmers, animals, birds, and fish were impacted by what the Environmental Protection Agency (EPA) called an accident. A catalog of mine waste spills lists the historic spill at Silverton, Colorado at 127 million tons of material that polluted nearly 100 miles of the Animas River.

Maya Elder Predictions

In Dr. Ardy Sixkiller Clarke's book, *Sky People,* she writes about her journey through Belize and Guatemala to interview Maya elders and medicine people. The indigenous people she spoke to readily admitted that the Sky People have warned them of a time of great change. Dr. Clarke felt they disclosed this information because of her Native American heritage. They were told there will be wars and Earth shaking, that we are living in the fourth world, but a fifth world is coming soon, and now it's too late to stop it. They have been told that many sad things are about to happen to Earth. There will be signs in the heavens if people will take the time to look skyward, but the elders say people are too busy to look.

On Maya elder told her, "This is the fourth world, Señora. It has been destroyed before. Each time, people were careless with the Earth. There is a reason why we are here. We were placed on this planet to look after it. We have been allowed to evolve as a people [the Maya], but we have not been able to perform the task given to us. A day is coming when we must answer for our disregard of our mission. On that day, the Earth will be turned upside down. They [Sky People] warn us that we must prepare for the future."

Aboriginal leader Alinta aka Lorraine Mafi Williams (1940-2001)

For thousands of years Australian Aboriginals have lived in harmony with Mother Earth, but there was a time long before they arrived on Earth, they came from a distant place in the stars, according to the ancient legends. In Steven McFadden's book, Ancient Voices, Current Affairs: The Legend of the Rainbow Warrior, he cited the late Australian Aboriginal leader, visionary, activist and filmmaker, Alinta, and her wise words to the world.

"We the Australian Aboriginals have been on our traditional land, the Land of the Everlasting Spirit, for tens of thousands of years. Our culture is rivaled by no other, though we have been in seclusion for the last two hundred years. We are re-emerging from that seclusion now to show ourselves as no one has ever seen us.

"Our creation stories take us back into the Dreamtime, beginning when the earth was one landmass [Panagaea]. At that time the four races—red, yellow, black, and white, lived side by side. There, they lived as one people, creating a world of harmony, balance, and mystery.

"As Aboriginals, we have kept our culture intact for thousands of years into the present time. Now we are ready to share our wondrous culture with the other people in the world. It took the white people only fifty years to destroy a million years of our culture, but the core of it still remains strong. Our elders are telling us to go out and tell everyone so that no one can say they didn't hear."

Land of the Everlasting Spirit

Alinta continued, "Our land, Australia is called Arunta, the land of the Everlasting Spirit. Our old people tell us that we originally came from a planet that had seen its time and just blew up. See, our people were like refugees, and they went and lived in the stars in the Milky Way. The seven spirit brothers and seven spirit sisters came to Earth. They came when the Earth was one big landmass.

"They came to erect an energy grid. Because you see, the planet Earth is among the smallest of planets. And it is really not in the galactic system where all the other planets exist. We believe Earth is just a little bit outside the plane of the Milky Way galaxy in space. Because the Earth is so small, when the planets line up in a certain way, the pull of the galactic energy is so strong that it could just suck planet Earth into the spiral plane of the galactic system and toss it all around.

So, my people were given the knowledge to create this energy grid because the planet that they were previously on did not have such a protective structure, and it was destroyed. They realized that their new home, Earth, needed to have such an energy grid in a strong, healthy condition to withstand periodic energy pulsations from the galaxy.

Otherwise, it would quickly be drawn into the plane of the galaxy and experience devastating turbulence. But our ancestors had learned this lesson, and so they came to Earth to erect an energy grid, or an Earth truss, to help the Earth when it undergoes changes. (Alinta was referring to the ley lines that encircle Earth.)"

Alinta on The Sacred Rainbow Serpent

"In our old way, we call the energy grid Boamie, The Sacred Rainbow Serpent, whose colors reflect the beauty of the Earth and sky, the Rainbows. The multicolored coils of the Rainbow Serpent are reflected in the precious stones that are concealed in the Earth's crust. It is called the Rainbow Serpent because it has all the colors of the rainbow—gold and silver, and also diamonds, the rubies, the emeralds, and the uranium. You see, it is the foundation, the Earth's crust.

"Since my people erected the energy grid, the Earth just sort of sails through the periodic lineups without any difficulties. Both men and women are very knowledgeable in how the energy grid works for the whole system. We know what each mineral in the Earth is supposed to do, and what men's and women's responsibilities are to keep the grid strong and healthy."

The Balance is in Jeopardy by Alinta

We are very concerned about the energy grids of the Earth. They are there to help the Earth maintain its balance. Crystals and other minerals feed energy to the energy grid. They have been used for millions of years that way. For the health of the Earth, the crystals must be free to let the energy flow to the grid.

But now minerals, metals, and jewels have been removed from the Earth to such an extent that the Earth's balance is in jeopardy. Uranium, in particular, is important for this task. When it is all gone, the Earth will be totally out of balance.

Mining has an influence on the human race, too, and the human body. The human being is a link between the Heavens and the Earth. By keeping our bodies in balance and in harmony, we can keep the Earth healthy too, and that in turn supports our health. I use crystals for healing, but I do not believe huge crystals should be taken from the Earth to be sold to private collectors. It's more valuable to leave them in the Earth.

In Edgar Cayce readings, he gave us the ways in which gemstones enhance the vibrational energies of their wearers by interacting with the vibrational patterns naturally found in the human body. The stones draw in and give off positive energy. According to the Cayce readings, each stone has a unique spirit, vibration and "fire" that has the power to "bring that which fires the imagination of those who are very selfish or it may bring peace to the wearer." (3657-1) This reading goes on to explain that the vibration can be determined by how the stone was formed: "The diamond is selfish in its very nature, while you will find that the pearl is a natural consequence of irritation? And it will bring either peace or irritation to the wearer as will the diamond..."

I suggest planting a crystal in the Earth and doing a healing ceremony as Indigenous people have suggested. My mentor Ed McGaa "Eagle Man" taught that people should go out in nature and find their own special *wotai,* a Sioux word for a personal stone. Ed found his Wotai in a river bed and carried it with him all the time. A *wotai* stone is a special stone chosen by Great Spirit to send protection, guidance, and visions to a person...a bit like a guardian angel or spirit guide. Each person's *wotai* will be different, and it will call to you.

Alinta on At a Crucial Junction

"We have been told that within every one million years, there is a seven-thousand-year-long Earth shift. Then we begin to go into a new world like we are doing now. By our reckoning, we are actually at the end of a seven-thousand-year shift now and we are beginning to enter a new million-year-long epoch.

"Our people and our teachings are very similar to the teachings of the North American Indians. But we have different interpretations and we know our responsibility—taking care of the Earth through the energy grids. We perform our task by giving thanks to the Earth through the songs, dances, and ceremonies.

Right now there are two things—The Earth is undergoing its earthly changes, which is normal for this time in our development. But because there's been so much destruction to the energy grid, especially the gold, which is nearly exhausted already—and now they are after the uranium—there is a great danger to the stability of the Earth.

"Gold has driven men mad for thousands of years, leading them to lie, steal, cheat, murder, and make war...all this wickedness to get the gold. Humanity has become greedy and as a result, wicked. That has led to fighting, war, and disease. People have forgotten their responsibility to the Earth, for want of the gold. And now it's the uranium.

"As well as the Earth, humanity has to go through its changes. We've all got to rejuvenate and to create a new world on the same physical substance. And we are going through it. There's no safe place on Earth. We've just got to ride it out, but if we are in balance within ourselves and in balance with the Earth, then we are healthy.

"At the end of each change—every time we come into a new world—the Great Creator says: 'OK humanity, you must start your change now, too, and go into the new world—but you must do it in accordance with the Earth, as well as yourself, with heart."

Ed McGaa "Eagle Man" (1936-2017)

I met my friend and teacher, Ed McGaa, in Ketchum, Idaho in 1993, and one year later he returned to Idaho to conduct a sweat lodge ceremony and vision quest for thirty participants. It was an amazing event that brought in ancient spirits. Ed has performed hundreds of ceremonies worldwide with "The Rainbow Tribe," and never charged for any of his sweat lodge ceremonies. He is a member of the Oglala Lakota and American author. He received his bachelor's degree from St. John's University, earned a law degree from the University of South Dakota, and has studied under Chief Eagle Feather and Chief Fools Crow, Sioux holy men. He participated six times in the Sun Dance ceremony, and served as a fighter pilot in the Marine Corps in Vietnam, flying 110 combat missions, receiving 8 Air Medals and 2 Crosses of Gallantry. Not only is he a brave man, but a spiritual leader who speaks his truth.

Ed McGaa wrote this in his book, *Mother Earth Spirituality— Native American Paths to Healing Ourselves and Our World*, "You say ecology. We think the words Mother Earth have a deeper meaning. If we wish to survive, we must respect her. It is very late, but there is still time to revive and discover the old American Indian value of respect for Mother Earth. She is very beautiful, and already she is showing us signs that she may punish us for not respecting her. Also, we must remember she has been in this universe for the one who is the All-Powerful, the Great Spirit Above, or *Wakan Tanka*—God.

"Brothers and sisters, we must go back to some of the old ways if we are going to truly save our Mother Earth and bring back the natural beauty that every person seriously needs, especially in this day of vanishing species, vanishing rain forests, overpopulation, poisoned waters, acid rain, a thinning ozone layer, drought, rising temperatures and weapons of complete annihilation.

"Weapons of complete annihilation? Yes, that is how far the obsession with war has taken us. These weapons are not only hydra-headed; they are hydra-headed as well-meaning that they are the ultimate in hydrogen bomb destruction. We will have to divert our obsession with defense and wasteful, all-life ending weapons of war to reviving our environment. If such weapons are ever fired, we will wind up destroying ourselves. The Armageddon of war is something that we have all been very close to and exposed to daily.

"Our planet is under attack. It is not an imagined problem. This calamity is upon us now. We are in a real war with the polluting, violating the blue man of Black Elk's vision.

"In conclusion, our survival is dependent on the realization that Mother Earth is a truly holy being, that all things in this world are holy and must not be violated, and that we must share and be generous with one another. You may call this thought by whatever fancy words you wish—psychology, theology, sociology, or philosophy—but you must think of Mother Earth as a living being. Think of your fellow men and women as holy people who were put here by the Great Spirit. Think of being related to all things? With this philosophy in mind as we go on with our environmental ecology efforts, our search for spirituality, and our quest for peace, we will be far more successful when we truly understand the Indian' respect for Mother Earth. *Mitakuye Oyasin!* We are all related."

I felt that if Ed could give me a message from the spirit world he would. Shortly after his death on August 25, 2017, I was walking my dog at a nearby park when I noticed seven usual brown crows in a nearby tree, squawking. They weren't the usual black ravens of Idaho. I went home and searched the internet and finally found what kind of raven it was. What a shock! The Brown-necked raven is a larger bird than the carrion crow though not as large as the common raven. It has similar proportions to the common raven but the bill is not so large or deep and the wings tend to be a little more pointed in profile. Those were the raven at the park.

As I read more about them, again I was shocked. This species is not indigenous to the United States. They inhabit North Africa, down as far as Kenya, the Arabian Peninsula and up to the Greater Middle East and southern Iran. How in the world did they Brown-necked ravens appear in southwestern Idaho?

The next day I returned to the park and a few of them were still there. I captured the one below. Thank you for saying goodbye, Ed. I miss your wisdom and truth!

Brown-Necked Raven from Africa visiting Idaho.

And there appeared a great wonder in Heaven; a woman clothed with the sun and the moon under her feet, and upon her head a crown of 12 stars. Revelation 12:1 (1+ 12 = 13).

Chapter Ten
THE FATIMA PROPHECIES

Through the years I have written and discussed on talk shows perhaps one of the strangest events to have been witnessed by thousands near Fatima, Portugal in 1917. The events that took place over a span of six months and always at high noon and on the 13th day of the month was peculiar in itself, but the descriptions of what was witnessed by the children and those who had gathered can only be that of highly evolved beings. Even the sun falling from the sky on October 13, 1917, which was witnessed by thousands gathered in Fatima that day, perhaps was more than a miracle, but the act of technologically-advanced beings who wanted to prevent World War One.

For three small children high strangeness began one spring day in 1916 as Lucia dos Santos, nine, and her two cousins, Francisco, eight, and his sister, Jacinta, six, tended sheep at Chousa Velha, a field near the town of Fatima, Portugal. The children were startled by an approaching snow-white radiance from the east. It moved silently until the children could see it was the figure of a perfectly handsome young man, whose body seemed to be enveloped in a brilliant light.

The angel asked the children to come closer to him and said, "Do not fear. I am the Angel of Peace. Pray with me." Prostrating himself, he touched his forehead to the ground as the children copied his actions. Then he prayed three times, "My God, I believe, I adore, I hope, and I love you. I implore your pardon for those who do not believe, do not adore, do not hope and do not love You."

While the angel began the prayer for the third time, the two girls joined in. Francisco could not hear the angel, yet he was caught in their fervor. During the visions, Francisco could only see the angel. However, Lucia was the only child to see, hear and respond to the celestial being as well as the following year when a beautiful lady visited the children.

The angel rose from the ground and promised the children, "The hearts of Jesus and Mary are attentive to the voice of your supplications." He then vanished. The experience was so profound for the children remained prostrate for a long time, barely conscious of their surroundings while reciting the prayer the angel had given them.

The radiant being appeared one more to the children in midsummer and later in the fall of 1916. On the final visit, he came with a chalice and holding a host above it. Drops of blood fell from the host into the chalice as the angel descended to the ground and the chalice remained suspended in mid-air. He again prostrated himself and declared three times, "Most Holy Trinity, Father, Son, and Holy Ghost, I adore You profoundly and offer You the most precious Body, Blood, Soul, and Divinity of Jesus Christ, present in all the tabernacles of the world, in reparation for the outrages, sacrileges, and indifference by which He is offended. By the infinite merits of His Sacred Heart and those of the Immaculate Heart of Mary, I beg of You the conversion of poor sinners."

It appeared the angel or celestial being might have used the children's Catholic teachings and beliefs to calm their fears. The angelic-like being did not identify himself, but the children believed from his teachings he had to be Archangel Michael.

From the children's first encounter with an angelic being until their next visitation on May 13, 1917, with a beautiful angelic woman, they spent hours praying as the male angel had instructed them to do.

May 13, 1917

Sunday, May 13, 1917, Lucia, Francisco and Jacinta were tending their sheep as usual at the Cova da Iria, a large, basin-shaped pasture owned by Lucia's father. Knowing that their flock grazed peacefully, they decided to play among the rocks and construct a small wall. That's when a brilliant flash lit up the cloudless sky. Thinking a storm was approaching, they herded the sheep toward home. It wasn't long before a second flash lit up the sky, and that's when they saw the figure of a radiant young woman of incredible beauty standing on top of a small, sturdy holm oak tree. Like the angel, the lady had a brilliant aura around her. She wore a white garment with a mantle over her head with her hands pressed together as if in prayer. In her hands, she held a string of pure-white rosary beads with a sparkling white crucifix attached.

The lady spoke gently to the children to alleviate their fears, "Do not be afraid; I will not harm you."

Lucia, the eldest child, spoke first, "From where have you come?"

"I come from Heaven," the Lady replied.

"And what is it you want of me?" Lucia questioned.

I have come to ask you to come here on the 13th day of each month, at this same hour (exactly at solar noon), until October. Then I will tell you who I am and what I want."

Why was the Lady so secretive about her identity and why the 13th day of each month for six consecutive months through October 13 at solar noon? It appeared this angelic being had a time agenda. Even Lot and his family had to flee Sodom and Gomorrah on a set date and time before the wicked cities were obliterated. The Lady knew the children's whereabouts, and yet she requested their presence on the 13th day of the month and at solar noon.

Before the Lady departed she asked the children if they were willing to offer themselves to the service of God, accepting all suffering that might come to them and prayerfully surrendering it to God, living and praying for the conversion of mankind to spirituality. Lucia agreed to the Lady's request for herself and her two cousins.

The Lady continued, "Then you will have much to suffer, but the grace of God will be your comfort." As the Lady said this, she parted her hands and a great ray of light streamed from each hand directly upon the children. Lucia later said that she felt the presence of God at that moment. They were consumed in Heavenly bliss or a trance-like ecstasy. Before the Lady departed, she asked the child to say the bead each day to obtain peace for the world and end the war."

The Lady was referring to World War I. In April of 1917 the United States entered into World War I as Lenin and Trotsky were organizing the Bolshevik revolution that culminated in November of 1917. On the day the Lady appeared to the children, May 13, 1917, a group of horsemen was given orders by Lenin to ride into a Moscow church filled with children, where they destroyed statues and charged the children, killing many of them. Throughout the Lady's visitations, she continued to warn humanity to stop their selfishness and materialism or pay with the great chastisement.

June 13, 1917

Fatima's townspeople began to hear about the children's miraculous visions. On June 13, Lucia, Francisco, and Jacinta returned to the Cova da Iria with fifty people at the appointed hour—solar noon. At the designated hour a brilliant flash of light appeared and the children knelt before the light oak tree and became enraptured by what they could only see. When Lucia asked a question and paused, the crowd could only hear a faint buzzing sound coming from the top of the tree.

During the visitation, the Lady told the children she would return on the 13th of July and asked them to pray every day. Lucia asked the Lady if she would take her and her cousins back to heaven with her. The Lady replied that it wouldn't be long before Francisco and Jacinta joined her, but Lucia would live many years to fulfill her destiny.

The Lady's ominous prediction came true. Francisco died of Spanish influenza, complicated by several months of pneumonia in April of 1919. One year later, Jacinta joined her brother, dying from similar causes February of 1920. A year later in 1935, the children's bodies were exhumed and although Francisco's body had deteriorated, Jacinta's body was found to be incorrupt, despite quicklime had been thrown over their corpses due to the contagiousness of deadly influenza.

The great pandemic killed 50 to 130 million people worldwide between 1917 to 1920, more than the Bubonic Plague killed from 1347 to 1351. The greatest mortality was between the ages of 20 and 40, missing the very young and the very old, which makes it odd that Francisco died at age 11 and Jacinta died at age 10. In only two years, the influenza-infected a fifth of the world's population and half of the U.S. soldiers serving in Europe's battlefields fell to influenza, not the enemy.

Following the Lady's foreboding predictions that Francisco and his sister Jacinta would have early deaths; two magnificent rays of light poured from her outstretched hands and surrounded the children. The children later reported that a heart stood out from the Lady's body on the left side of her breast and was circled and pierced by large thorns that seemed 'real' and not a 3-D holographic image.

As the apparition departed, a loud explosion was heard, accompanied by a small smoke-like cloud that left the top of the oak tree. The smoke-like cloud then departed in the eastern sky, the same direction the Lady always appeared.

July 13, 1917
On the 13th of July, approximately five thousand people arrived at the Cova to see the next visitation by the Lady. Again, the Lady did not disappoint the crowd by providing them with more illusions.

Lucia told the Lady that she was fearful because many people, including her mother and her priest, believed she and her cousins had created a hoax. Lucia believed that if the Lady created a miracle, it would leave no doubt about their story and the Lady's visitations. The Lady replied, "Continue to come on the 13th of each month. In October I will tell you who I am and what I want of you. And I shall work a great miracle, visible to everyone, so that all may believe."

During this visitation, the children were heard to gasp in horror and become pale. They later explained that the Lady had shown them a dreadful vision and had given them an urgent message to be kept secret until much later date. When Lucia was asked by the Bishop of Leiria in 1943 to reveal the third secret given to her, she struggled with the idea and felt God had not clearly authorized her to act. She was under strict obedience in accordance with her Carmelite nun life and didn't want to disobey her superiors. By October of 1943, Lucia became extremely ill with the influenza and pleurisy and she believed that she was going to die. The Bishop of Leiria then ordered her to put the third secret in writing, which she did. The secret was then sealed in an envelope with a strict message that it should not be opened until either 1960, or at her death, whichever came first. The year 1960 came and went without any disclosure from the Catholic Church. Seven years later, in February 1967, a Vatican spokesperson revealed that Pope Paul VI had concluded that the time was not yet at hand to disclose the Lady's message.

On May 13, 2000, 83 years (8 +3 = 13) after the first apparition of the Lady to the children of Fatima, Cardinal Sodano announced that the Third Secret would be released. He implied that the secret was about the persecution of Christians in the 20th century that culminated in the failed assassination of Pope John Paul II on May 13, 1981. Most followers of the Fatima prophecies believed this latest revelation by the Vatican was untrue.

Oddly, Lucia died on February 13, 2005, at age 95. The date of her death fell on the 13th day of the month, which seemed beyond coincidence—perhaps further evidence of celestial intervention and a warning of a coming event related to 13.

Will the Church ever disclose the final message? With the Vatican's astronomers making strange remarks about extraterrestrial existence, is it possible their remarks are tied to the three Fatima Secrets? I believe they are related, and I believe newly elected Pope Francis knows what apocalyptic event or events were foretold to the children of Fatima, and that is why he has surrounded himself with the number 13.

After the Lady had given the secret message of July 13, 1917, she said, "In order to save souls, God wishes to establish in the world, devotion to my Immaculate Heart. If men do what I tell you, many souls will be saved and there will be peace. This war [World War I] is going to end soon, but if men do not stop offending God, not much time will elapse before another and more terrible war will begin in the reign of Pius XI.

"When you shall see the night illuminated by an unknown light, know that it is the great sign that God is given you that He is going to punish the world for its crimes by means of war, famine, and persecution of the Church and the Holy Father. To prevent it, I shall come to ask the consecration of Russia to my Immaculate Heart and communions of reparation on the first Saturday of each month. If my requests are heeded, Russia will be converted and there will be peace. Otherwise, Russia will spread her errors throughout the world, provoking wars and persecutions of the Church. The goodwill be martyred and the Holy Father will have much to suffer; certain nations will be annihilated. But in the end, my Immaculate Heart shall triumph...She [Russia] will be converted [eventually], and a certain period of peace given to the world."

It seems odd the Lady would threaten the world, but then say the no matter what happened with Russia, that country would eventually be converted, and a 'certain' period of peace given. In other words, peace would not last. Why was it so important for Russia to be converted when many countries haven't followed the tenets of Christianity?

Russia did invade parts of Ukraine. On July 17, 2014, Russian rebels believed they were targeting a Ukrainian military plane, and instead their fired missile hit Malaysia Flight 17, a Boeing 777, flying from Amsterdam to Kuala Lumpur. All 298 people aboard were killed.

Shortly after the July 1917 visitation, many skeptics began to talk. The Freethinkers (members of an anticlerical movement that had brought about suppression of the Catholic Church in that country) claiming, "the superstitious idiots [in this Church], are desperate to have something to support their unfounded religion, they are provoking mass hysteria and hallucination."

August 13, 1917

The District Administrator over Fatima was a prominent Freethinker. Angered by the crowds and commotion created since the children's absence from the Cova, he hoped the entire fiasco would end. He drove to Lucia's house on the morning of August 13 and ordered the children into his carriage under the pretext of driving them to the Cova. Instead, he took them to his house in a nearby town, where he detained them for several days.

During those few days, the children were interrogated constantly in the belief they'd change their story or that they'd reveal the secret message of July 13. When this harassment didn't work, the administrator threatened to jail them, and then he tried to bribe them with gold. Nothing worked. As a desperate last measure, he isolated each child and then told them they would be boiled in oil if they didn't tell the truth. All these frightening tactics failed.

Despite the children's absence on that day, a crowd of over eighteen thousand had gathered at the Cova at noon. When the news arrived the children had been kidnapped, many people became angered and disappointed and began to leave.

But on the appointed hour, solar noon, an explosive sound was heard and a flash of light was seen near the little oak tree. The sun dimmed, and around the tree, a small white cloud formed, and, after several minutes it rose into the air and dissolved. Next, the whole area turned into a kaleidoscope of colors, tinting the clouds, the landscape, and the people. When at last the miraculous display was over, the crowd was shaken but thrilled the Lady had kept another promise.

August 19, 1917

Four days after the children's release, the Lady appeared to the children at a hollow called Valinhos. The appearance was accompanied by another display of magnificent colors. Witnesses described a "magnificent aroma" which lingered on the tree branches where the Lady usually hovered.

The Lady was displeased with the way the children had been treated and said that because of the kidnapping and detention the promised miracle for October 13 would be less spectacular. She said the crowd would have seen Joseph and the child Jesus giving a blessing of peace, followed by the appearance of an adult Jesus blessing the people. With Jesus would have been appearing his mother as the Lady of Sorrows traditionally associated with Calvary. Then, she also would have appeared to all as the Lady of Mount Carmel.

September 13, 1917
At exactly solar noon on September 13, an estimated crowd of thirty thousand had gathered in the Cova to see the sun darken and the stars appear. Many in the crowd saw a great globe of light or orb approach silently from the eastern sky and descend to the oak treetop. At the same time what seemed to be white flowers or clusters of flower petals drifted down from the sky and dissolved before hitting the ground. Many people had photographed this remarkable vision.

The Lady told the children they must pray daily. It is interesting that in referring to the rosary, the Lady always used the Portuguese term, *o terco*, which means one-third or five decades, but the rosary she carried seemed to be of five decades. Again, she promised a final miracle on October 13 and then disappeared from the children's sight. People reported that the orb of light rose from the top of the little tree and moved toward the eastern horizon and vanished.

In the last ten years, large orbs or spheres have been sighted in the sky worldwide, including hovering over UK crop circles.

October 13, 1917
Heavy rain poured from the sky all morning as 70,000 to 80,000 people gathered at the Cova da Iria to witness the final miracle at the appointed hour, high noon. It was noted that many atheists, skeptics, and Freethinkers stood in the rain, ready to jeer should the promised miracle fail. Most of them believed the people were hypnotized by the children's adulation for the Lady and they too were experiencing mass hallucination.

The children soon arrived, but their parents feared the crowd would become violent if the miracle didn't happen. Lucia told her mother, "Don't be afraid, Mother. Nothing evil will happen to us." At exactly solar noon the lady appeared to the children as the crowd viewed a column of blue smoke that appeared and disappeared three times in the vicinity of the children. The children were oblivious to the phenomena and gazed at the beautiful Lady who hovered over the remains of the little oak tree, which by now had been stripped of its bark and branches for souvenirs.

Lucia stepped forward and asked, "Madam, who are you and what do you desire?" With tenderness, the Lady replied, "I am the Lady of the Rosary. People must cease offending my Divine Son, who they have already much offended. Therefore, let the rosary be recited daily. Sincerely ask pardon for sins. The war will end soon, and the soldiers will return to their homes. Let a chapel be built here."

Then the Lady spread her hands and magnificent rays of light beamed from them toward the sun, which seemed to have lowered in the sky. Lucia cried out, "Behold! The sun!"

At that instant, the rain stopped falling and the clouds pulled apart, revealing what one witness, Dr. Jose Maria Proenca de Almeida Garrett, described as "a disc with a sharp rim and clear edge, luminous and lucent, but not painful to the eyes. The comparison of the sun with a disc of smoky silver, which I have heard even at Fatima, does not seem to be apt. It had a clearer, more active and richer color, as changeable as the luster of a pearl. It was not round, as the moon is; it did not have the same character or the same light. It seemed to be a burnished wheel cut from the nacre of a shell." Note that the prophet Ezekiel of the Old Testament described something as extraordinary when he was visited by celestial beings or extraterrestrials.

In the Old Testament (1:4-1:24) Prophet Ezekiel said, "And I looked, and behold, a whirlwind came out of the north, a great cloud, and a fire enfolding itself, and brightness was about it, and out of the midst thereof as the color of amber, out of the fire. Also, out of the midst thereof came the likeness of four living creatures. And this was their appearance; they had the likeness of a man. And every one had four faces, and every one had four wings. And their feet were straight feet, and the sole of their feet was like the sole of a calf's foot, and they sparkled like the color of burnished brass...

"The appearance of the wheels and their work was like unto the color of a beryl: and they four had one likeness: and their appearance and their work was it were a middle of a wheel."

Dr. Garrett continued, "This is not the banal comparison of cheap poetry. Thus my eyes saw it. The phenomenon should not be confused with that of the sun shining through a slight fog...because the sun was not opaque, diffused, or veiled. In Fatima, it had light and color and its rim could be clearly seen!"

The crowd was mesmerized by what appeared to be the sun quivering in the sky. Then it appeared to spin on its axis like a terrible celestial pinwheel. It whirled faster and faster and from its rim fantastic streamers of light flashed across the sky and Earth, coloring the landscape and the crowd in a montage of colors—red, violet, blue, yellow, white.

Meanwhile, the children were focused on the Lady, unaware of the events happening in the sky and around them. They watch the Lady, dressed in a radiant white garment with a blue mantle bordered by a golden threat, joined by Joseph and the infant Jesus, both wearing red and blessing the world. The vision then changed to what Lucia could only see, the Lady of Sorrows, traditionally associated with Calvary, accompanied by an adult Jesus. The Lady then faded as if a holographic image and reappeared again, but this time bearing the scapular as the Lady of Carmel.

As the sun continued to awe and dazzle the crowd for four minutes longer, it suddenly stopped momentarily and then continued to spin and spew out a variety of colors. Twelve miles away school children sang a hymn of praise as the colors transformed their rustic village into a kaleidoscope of colors. Others present at the display were both amazed and fearful, asking God for his forgiveness.

For a second time, the 'sun' stopped spinning, and then it resumed with the multi-colored lights and spinning. Suddenly, the sun ripped away from its stationary place in the heavens and threatened to crash to Earth, causing intense heat to the terrorized crowd. Many in the crowd fell to their knees and prayed aloud for God to spare them and forgive them of their sins, convinced it was the end of the world.

Just when it appeared the sun was going to destroy the Earth, the fiery disc returned into the sky, in its normal position. When the shaken masses rose from their knees, they discovered that they were no longer soaked from the pouring rain earlier, and the ground was bone dry.

What is so extraordinary about his event is it was only witnessed within a 15-mile range, and not one astronomer at the time noted anything unusual with our sun that day. Some authors have theorized it was a giant UFO. Also, how could the sun be described as "smoky silver" with a rim and "not round like the moon?"

How was the Lady able to see into the future?

Lucia announced the coming period of peace, but there would be no peace as the Lady predicted. Twenty-two years later, World War II was underway in 1939, which lasted until 1945. The chastisement was well on its way as the war, including the Holocaust claimed approximately 75 million souls.

In 1927, Jesus supposedly spoke to Lucia from a tabernacle, instructing her to divulge part of the secret given to her in July of 1917, including what the Lady of Fatima had told her about five scourges that would befall humanity. The first sign given happened as the Lady predicted when she said, "When you shall see the night illuminated by an unknown light, know that it is a great sign that God is giving you that He is going to punish the world for its crimes by means of war..."

On the night of January 25, 1938, all of Europe and part of North American witnessed the most intense display of the aurora borealis (the northern lights). That night one of the largest solar flares in recorded times, probably an X-Class solar flare, was released from the sun and aimed at Earth. The sky glowed red, green and blue over the whole of Europe. The immense arches of crimson light with shifting areas of green and blue radiated from a brilliant Auroral Crown near the zenith instead of appearing as usual in parallel lines. The show lasted over London from 6.15 p.m. until 1 a.m. People called the fire brigade believing that the glow was the reflection of some giant fire. Although there are records of such electronic displays setting fire to telegraph wires as early as 1857, there has not been a storm of such magnitude in recent times. If such an event happened today it would wipe out modern radio and electronic communications worldwide and satellites for months and maybe years.

While World War II was believed to be the first scourge, the second was the rise of communism. Lucia had said that if the world ignored the Lady's request, every nation, would come under Communist domination. The third and fourth scourges it is said involved the Catholic Church and the faithful being persecuted and an unnamed pope that would suffer greatly—perhaps even martyrdom.

The fifth and final scourge was the most terrible prophecy of all where several nations would be annihilated. Is it possible that the fifth scourge will be in 2016, and be another World War or a natural cataclysmic Earth event from outer space?

Here is another event to ponder. On Monday, April 4, 2001, a sunspot called active region 9393 by scientists unleashed a major solar flare at 5:51 p.m. EDT. Radiation from the new flare was so intense it saturated the X-ray detectors on two spacecraft used by the U.S. government to determine the strength of the solar blasts. The blast was even larger than a 1989 solar flare that led to the collapse of a major power grid in Canada. Radiation from the new flare was so intense it saturated the X-ray detectors on two spacecraft used by the U.S. government to determine the strength of the solar blasts.

That night I tuned in to hear radio host Art Bell on Coast to Coast AM, broadcasting from Pahrump, Nevada. He couldn't contain himself as he described the blood-red Aurora Borealis lighting up the Northern Nevada sky. At the time, I lived in Tucson, Arizona. I rushed outside to witness a brilliant crimson-red aurora that covered the Northern Sky. I sensed that it was an ominous sign that something evil was going to befall humanity. I was right!

Six months later, 9-11 happened in New York City, where planes, and perhaps bombs, brought down the World Trade Buildings; killing 2,977 souls (this number totals 25 and 2+5 = 7, the number of Heaven and Angels).

Chapter Eleven
EXTRATERRESTRIAL WARNINGS

From 1992 to 1999 Barbara Marciniak wrote a series of channeled books given to her by the Pleiadians. In her book, *Family of Light,* the Pleiadians said, "As we share the dark part of the story with you, such as the covert and perverted sexual practices of your rulers, it is not for us to name names. You will discover for yourself that in every country around the globe, those in the highest of positions have been put there because they are qualified by their perversions to hold powers over others. This has been a secret for eons, but today everyone is coming out of the closet, so to speak.

"Do not become frightened when your leaders fall. It is all designed so you can know the worst of family secrets: that parents sexually abuse their children from generation to generation because they do not know love. Love must prevail. You must clean your biological line, the ethers and the astral plane because the new children wanting to be born will only be attracted by a frequency that guarantees they will be cherished. Without the cherishing of your children, you do not guarantee the continuity of humankind on Earth. This also requires that you respect and cherish the sexual act, for the quality of your couplings will determine the frequency in your energy field."

The Pleiadians continued, "The mind controllers and those who influence the weather and all aspects of your economy, religion, education, and medicine will be revealed because you are now ready to take charge and influence yourselves. Those responsible for your plight think they are so much better than you; however, their darkness creates endless difficulties for them.

"You must begin to heal these wounds. Your compassion and forgiveness must include an understanding of existence on a scale broader than any apparent singular 3-D events, a realization that these misuses of power are predominant throughout the pages of the Book of Earth. The healing must be deep. In this process, you will find your power and ideally, heal your wounded leaders, and wounded they are indeed. Some will self-heal; others will proclaim their shame and, once they have exposed their darkness, become great leaders. However, most will create their own destruction, and you will have to clear the astral planes of their polluted forms."

Interestingly, the Pleiadians talked about strange things in the sky. "Unusual sightings in the heavens will continue— streaks and balls of light, comets, mysterious fires in the skies, unusual lightning and bizarre phenomena. We remind you once again that without the dark you would not see this play of light. The cosmic frequencies involve many layers of plans. The Creator is in everything, so is anything natural? Is it not all connected? Frequency control of your mind will become a paramount issue of concern on your planet: how you are given visions through television, computers, music, movies, and through invisible microwave transmissions that influence your thought patterns and your patterns of living. Mind control will be seen as the ultimate battle with darkness.

The Pleiadians warned, "If human beings do not change—if they do not make the shift in values and realize that without Earth they could not be here—then Earth, in its love for its own initiation and its reaching for a higher frequency, will bring about a cleansing that will balance it once again. There is the potential for many people to leave the planet in an afternoon. Maybe then everyone else will begin to wake up to what is going on. There have been events all along stimulating you, encouraging you, and bring you to the realization that there must be global change. There are grass-roots movements that are going to grow phenomenally. What happens to Earth depends on how willing everyone is to change.

"What is your responsibility in this? How willing are you to change? The time has come not to just talk about it but to do it. As you commit to change in your own life, you automatically make the change available to the entire planet.

"Earth is striving for its integrity. The planet feels at this time deprived of its integrity, dishonored, and unloved. Earth loves you and gives you a place to operate; it is a living organism. Earth is about to reestablish its integrity and let you understand the importance of loving yourself by loving Earth. Love yourself and love Earth, because they are the same.

"All of you must learn to honor your bodies because without your bodies you would not be here, and without Earth, you would not be here. Your body and your planet are your two greatest gifts and the most valuable things you own. Ideally, you would express a sacredness and honoring and cherishing and love of Earth and your physical being. This would resonate in your home, your property, the land you are associated with, and the land of your body as well.

"Everything of Earth can be used if Earth is loved and honored in the process. It may be difficult to imagine a gang of oil workers, before they set the bit into the ground, holding hands and asking for guidance and permission to penetrate Earth. Yet, if this were done, things would be much more in harmony."

Messages from The Zetas

In 1993 a gray-haired woman named Nancy Lieder, with an eccentric personality came onto the internet scene with her predictions from a group of aliens known as the Zetas. Nancy has claimed that since childhood she's been in contact with these beings and had taken part in their hybrid program, actually meeting one of her hybrid children. In preparation for her communicator role for them, Nancy was given proprietary information on MJ12 and Planet X's arrival into our solar system in the 1990s which would cause a massive shift of the Earth's axis. When 2003 passed without a catastrophic event, she again claimed the Zetas told her the Earth would shift in 2012. Again, it didn't happen.

Although many of Nancy's Earth changes and extreme weather predictions have proven true in the last ten years or more, her dire predictions of Planet X (also known as Wormwood and Nibiru), a brown-dwarf or failed star, that arrived in our solar system in the 1990s, but hidden near the sun, hasn't proven accurate...yet. She still maintains that the accelerated Earth changes, extreme weather globally, sinkholes, anomalies in the sky, booms, shaking not related to earthquakes, larger than normal earthquakes and strange behavior in animals, are impending warnings of Planet X's destructive powers on the planet. She points out to the thousands of people have captured duel suns in our sky for the past few years and posted their videos on YouTube.

In the 1990s, Nancy wrote of "Manifest Clues" that would confirm her predictions of Planet X and its approach to Earth, which are happening today.

1. Loud booms from clapping air caused by plate movements.
2. Erratic weather explained away as global warming.
3. Increasing incidence of earthquakes.
4. Violent wave action swamping ocean-going ships.
5. Dramatic flashes of light caused by methane gas flares as trapped gas is released from pockets under moving plates (explained away as lightning).
6. Increasing magnetic diffusion (blamed on sunspot activity).

7. Interference with communications—Internet, radio, television, cell phones – in the months before the passage almost total interference.

Keep in mind that Nancy and the Zetas presented these clues in 1997, long before many of the manifestations began a few years ago. She also pointed out strange manifestations seen in the sky; the moon out of place caused by the Earth's wobble. She says this wobble is also creating severe weather everywhere.

In several photographs of the Sun sent back from the SOHO telescope, there appeared to be large objects of some kind; UFO motherships to some, but moons of Planet X to Lieder. Nancy also predicted as early as 1997 that the inbound Planet X had a tail of space debris tagging behind it and we'd see increased meteors, asteroids, and comets headed our way in the coming years.

There have been a great number of meteors sighted in the past two years, and asteroid fly-bys. Scientists warn us there could be another like the Chelyabinsk Russian meteor that exploded on February 15, 2013, with the force of at least 20 nuclear bombs, producing shock waves that blew out thousands of windows, damaged buildings and left more than 1,491 people injured. What else might be lurking out there?

According to Nancy, the reason for the chemtrail phenomenon that began in the mid-nineties by unmarked jets laying down off-white plumes in varying patterns of Xs, tick-tack-toe grids, cross-hatched and parallel lines across the sky was to cover-up Planet X. The Zetas claim that global governments fear public knowledge of coming Earth changes which might create a public panic.

So far not one governmental agency has admitted anything on this top-secret program. Can you imagine the trillions of dollars this clandestine operation must have cost so far, and that we, the tax-payers, are paying for it?

ET Contactees Betty Andreasson Luca and Bob Luca

Invisible, multi-dimensional beings are all around us and watch us every moment. They are the "Watchers" mentioned in the Bible, Daniel 4:13, the book of Enoch and even the Dead Sea Scrolls alluded to the Watchers of heaven. In the Dead Sea Scrolls the following passage from the Zadokite Document, related to the practical organization of the Essene community at Qumran.

For many, that be that have strayed thereby from olden times until now, and even strong heroes have stumbled thereby. Because they walked in the stubbornness of their hearts, the Watchers of heaven fell...So too their sons [hybrid offspring?] whose height was like the lofty cedars [giants]...fell. So too all flesh that was upon the dry land. They also perished.

The Betty Andreasson Luca and Bob Luca abduction encounters became known when Raymond Fowler investigated and wrote about their incredible abductions through the years by grey beings and tall human-like beings in his books, *The Andreasson Affair*, *The Watchers* and *The Watchers II*.

Betty Andreasson Luca's small grey alien abductors called themselves "The Watchers" and Caretakers of Earth's life-forms. They told her that they have been on Earth since our beginning on planet Earth. There was another type of entity that Betty encountered that appeared more human-like called the Elders. These white-robed, white-haired entities looked nearly identical and appeared to control the small grey aliens.

In 1967 Betty was told that "love is the greatest of all...because of greatest love, they cannot let man continue in the footsteps that he is going."

They also told Betty that "Mankind will become sterile. They will not be able to produce because of the pollutions of the lands and the waters and the air and the bacteria and the terrible things that are on the Earth...Man is destroying much of nature." They keep seed from man and woman so the human form will not be lost.

"We are the Gardeners of the Earth...We travel in the universe putting people and animals on many different worlds. You, Earthlings, have your legends about us, you refer to us as the Gods in the Sky, you talk of our flaming chariots. Now we are to give you information as the origin of life on Earth so that you can pass on the knowledge to one who shall come after and shall go into the world and write of these things, for it is time that the people knew the truth of their Gods before we initiate the second stage." (Betty was told by her abductors that she was chosen to give a message to the world.)

Betty was told that she had a photographic memory and that's why she was given this information—which she will never forget—and which she will much later pass on to another who will come her way.

Another point the Watchers conveyed to Betty was that they are Gardeners, and a gardener has to remove deadwood...he has to pluck unwanted weeds. They also said, "Man is so new upon Earth that no human has the right to even attempt to judge what we do...We must ensure that the works of Man do not pollute Space and endanger people of other worlds...Our purpose is to save your world. To save it from what threatens to be suicide. To save it from the utter pollution...New weapons will be developed. Man will enter space with the next hundred years. Thus it is that we are interested."

Similarly like Mary Summer Rain's teacher No-Eyes and her prediction of the "Phoenix Days," Betty Andreasson Luca encountered a giant eagle-like bird, perhaps a Phoenix, and heard a thundering voice she believed was God.

During Betty's husband Bob's regressive hypnosis, he said, "The future is not to be known by us, as it is something that can be given at times when it's deemed proper, but it is not our decision to determine when that time will be. It is the decision of the Elders, those who watch over, make the decisions and...help us if necessary.

An example would be...to give a personal warming that would enable them to avoid a bad situation. On occasions like that, people are given a glimpse into the future event...on the scale of an earthquake or a volcanic eruption. The person that is given this information may make it known, and often they are not believed. But people miss the point. Oftentimes, these people are given that information because, at that time, there may be thousands of people involved. The message may be to only one or two people— to listen, to believe—and for that reason, all through the course of their life cycle in the manner that they are supposed to.

Bob went on to say that we are watched all the time, "We are all constantly being monitored. Nothing that you do in your life escapes them. It's just like...a recorder. Your life, your existence on the Earth plane, is all recorded from the time you are born until the time you die; everything is there. How you react, what you do during your life. Even your innermost thoughts, feelings, and emotions. They're all recorded. It's all part process. This process determines how rapidly you will advance and what your next step or phase will be, what teachings you need to receive, what hardship you must undergo to deepen your understanding. It's all recorded."

The hypnotist asked Bob, "Are you saying that some level of life is fair?"

"Life is wonderfully fair. Those of us in this plane just don't understand it. When you see a small child that becomes ill and dies, people weep, they cry, they grieve. They grieve for themselves. The child does not need to be here any longer. The child has already advanced, much as you would skip a grand in school. It is not a bad thing. People that are sick or injured...their faith is being tested. The reactions are recorded. This determines whether or not they need more teaching. They need to advance spiritually. Can they go to the next step? Is there more they must learn? When the physical body leaves, you do not die, people need understanding. Life is stages, like a never-ending school."

Bob was asked under hypnosis why there is evil and he replied, "Evil on the earthly plane is the negative aspect. Evil on the larger plane is part of the overall plan that gives us all a chance to advance and rise about it. Everyone in the earthly plane has the ability to do evil. Those that don't—those that fight evil, those that learn and overcome evil, and those who have advanced—have gained tremendously in the next realm. Everything in nature...has a plus and a minus, a light and dark, a negative and positive, a good and bad. It must be, for without some content of evil, there can be no good. There can be no growth."

The hypnotist then asked, "We need evil for good!"

Bob replied, "We do not need evil for good. We need choice. The Creator gave us choice. We cannot use that choice unless we have two choices to make—evil or good. It is so simple."

The hypnotist was taken aback by Bob's answer. "I'm feeling that as we evolve as a civilization—won't there be more good, more kindness?"

"That would be due to those who are advancing. And, yes, eventually there will be. But, there will be some very distressing times before that happens."

Again the hypnotist asked, "What do you mean—distressing times?"

"As the population of this planet increases, there will be those that have. There will be those who are greedy. There will be those that have not and are starving or will starve. There will be much dissension. There will be more conflict. The world, this plane, is not perfect. There will be evil. There will come a time when evil will be wiped away. That time is not close at hand. Our growth will not cease. Rather, we will advance into further planes of existence."

Bob continued, "Because the people of this plane as a whole are not very advanced spiritually. Technology is advancing. Spirituality, unfortunately, is not keeping pace. Man is developing many things which are harmful to him, which he does not understand. Man needs spiritual growth badly."

When asked where animals fit in, Bob said, "Man will be very surprised to find where animals fit in. I told you: All that is done is recorded, and many foolish people think the harm they've done to animals will not count. It will! All that the Creator's made is not to be taken lightly. And the most lowly to the most magnificent, much is to be learned. Animals exist on more than one place for a reason."

Bob was asked to define the Creator, he said, "That is like asking a person to define to you the length and breadth and depth of space, or the universe. It is not within this mind to comprehend all that the Creator is."

Plejaren Contactee Billy Meier

Billy" Eduard Albert Meier was born February 3, 1937, and is a Swiss citizen who is the source of many controversial photographs of alleged UFOs, which he has presented to the world as proof of his contact with extraterrestrial beings. He has produced countless photographs and film footage of beam ships and even metal samples and recordings. Meier has reported continued contact with extraterrestrials he calls the Plejaren, and claims they look similar to humans. The Plejaren come from a world called Erra, and that is located in a dimension which is a fraction of a second shifted from our dimension, about 80 light-years beyond the Pleiades, an open star cluster.

Michael Horn, liaison to the English-speaking world on the Billy Meier contacts for over 30 years, and an authorized representative for the book on the Meier case, And *Yet They Fly*, by Guido Moosbrugger was a guest on my Rainbow Vision Network several times through the years. While watching Michael Horn's documentary, The Silent Revolution of Truth, about Meier, I was stunned by the clarity of UFO photographs and film footage taken through the years, which critics believe were models made by the one-armed man. How can you refute the photographs when photoshopping and special effects were not available during the 1950s and early 1960s? If Billy Meier did fake them, he was leaps ahead of Hollywood's special effects and Lucas' Industrial Light and Magic Studio.

I don't agree with everything Billy Meier claimed through the years, such as his claim that only Plejarens are visiting Earth at this time. However, he did say that other beings are observing and monitoring us. There's plenty of compelling evidence Meier was given higher knowledge especially when it comes to his predictions. Meier's photographs may not be believable by skeptics, but his detailed prophecies, many have come true already, can't be denied.

Billy Meier predicted AIDs, the 9-11 attack on the World Trade Center, global warming and the discovery of water on Mars long before these events happened. Meier claims that he was instructed to transcribe his conversations with the extraterrestrials, many published in the German language. These books are referred to as the Contact Notes (or Contact Reports). There are ten volumes published between 1978 and 1980 of the Contact Reports (titled Plejadisch-Plejarische Kontaktberichte). Some have been translated to English, edited and published in the out-of-print four-volume set, Message from the Pleiades, by Wendelle S. Stevens.

Meier's information from the Plejarens are detailed and deal with subjects ranging from spirituality and the afterlife to warnings of mainstream religions, human history, science and astronomy, ecology and the dire condition Earth would be in years into the future. That time has now arrived.

Meier was told this by the Plejarens long before it was evident, "Earth human, I see the great expanses of the Earth; the almost boundless oceans, the great continents, mighty mountains, the vast forests, bubbling springs, the flowing brooks, rivers and all the lakes, and I see how they will all, at the hand of man, be harmed and made sick, destroyed, and the majority will be annihilated." Below are a few of the 162 predictions given to Billy Meier on August 24, 1958, by the Plejarens:

Even next year on September 13th, 1959, using rocket propulsion, the Earth human, respectively the Soviet Union, will make a hard landing of an unmanned object on the moon; and on April 12th, 1961 an Earth human will climb high in the sky with a rocket to orbit around in the Earth's outer space, then on February 3rd, 1966 an aerospace object will make a soft landing on the moon, then in 1968, the outer fringes of Earth's space will be left, and later the first trip to the moon will be undertaken, whereby up until the year 1972, five (5) manned moon landings will take place through the U.S.A., while a sixth moon landing—supposedly the first—on August 20th, 1969 will rest only on world-wide staged deceit, a result of the political armament race with the Soviet Union.

Criminal leaders of commerce will be amicable towards million-dollar payments and million-dollar golden handshakes and engage in maladministration and thereby drive even quite traditional companies to ruin, as also the commoners in private bankruptcies will walk away when they can no longer control their finances because they are driven away from reliable money and are equipped with plastic money in the form of plastic cards with which they subsist in the circumstances of their indebtedness, with sundries paid for on credit, and get into horrendous debt, whereby also special companies come into existence for the administration of plastic cards, while the banks will be in on that, with plastic cards they will name credit cards, in order to make their customers dependent, whereby they quite particularly have their eye set on the youth who thereby pile up immense mountains of debt which drive them into need and misery.

The morals of very many people will completely sink, whereby many villages and every city will be a Sodom and Gomorrah as the prostitution of adults and children takes on completely boundless forms. Many young people will, in every form and manner, deteriorate to extremism in everyday life as well as in their professional life, whereby drug, medication, alcohol and narcotic addiction take the upper hand. In the coming time, many blood banks will be contaminated by viruses and will make the people sick. The human will be ever more unscrupulously addicted to greed for money and wealth, whereby he would secretly commit the murder of his parents, which would never be solved, in order to inherit from them.

The human will populate the Earth, the air and the seas more and more and take all the living space which is for the native wildlife and thereby exterminate countless species and varieties.

The drug problem will gain more and more ground, whereby internationally organized criminal gangs will maneuver even children into the vicious cycle of drug addiction. And through the fault of humans, chlorofluorocarbons sluice through the atmosphere, the Earth will burn, and melanoma and non-melanoma skin cancer will take hold and demand many deaths, and all that because, through human irrationality, the majority of the ozone shield, which protects against the rays of the sun, will be destroyed, whereby the atmosphere will be like a curtain full of holes and the strong and burning light of the sun will burn the skin, and the eyes of many people will be permanently blinded.

Towards the end of the Second Millennium researchers will clone animals and alter their genes any way they like, and in the Third Millennium researchers will have the audacity to create invitro humans who are intended to serve as human spare parts stores for organs.

Some of Meier's other prophecies include a 9.0 earthquake that will last for five minutes off the coast of Oregon (along the Cascadia Subduction Zone) and a huge earthquake in San Francisco that will topple the Transamerica pyramid building.

According to Michael Horn, witnesses such as retired Lt. Col. Wendelle C. Stevens watched Meier take "photos of the future," in 1978, which revealed the aftermath of the San Francisco earthquake. Interestingly, the cars in Meier's photographs were said to be of a more rounded design than in the seventies and were lacking rearview mirrors.

Although car manufacturers have prototypes of cars without mirrors on the sides and for rear-view parking, laws do not allow cameras on new cars yet. After 5 years of trying to convince lawmakers of cameras there are still mirrors on the sides and a rearview mirror. I suggest if you live in San Francisco that you watch for this car of the future and then prepare for the big one on the coast of San Francisco and Oregon.

Even with all the dire predictions by the Plejarens, there's hope for humanity as indicated in these prophecies: And in distant times it will be, when the Fourth Millennium after Jmmanuel's (Christian) time reckoning comes, that the Earth and its humanity will have its creational order again, and there will be true love and unity, true freedom and harmony, as well as true worldwide peace.

And in distant times it will be that the people will hurry through the universe from one end to the other in great and powerful spaceships, and they will have no more boundaries. And in distant times it will be that the forests, wetlands, meadows, and fields bloom again, as also the deserts, which will be enlivened and planted, and in which many kinds of trees, bushes, grasses, and flowers will reveal their glory, so the Earth will be a wonderful garden in which the human will respect and honor all that lives, creeps and flies.

Recently, Michael Horn stated that Billy Meier was warned by the Plejaren beings on the scope of the COVID-19 pandemic and it being proven prophetically accurate, which is bad news for us on Earth because we don't listen. Visit Michael's blog at www.theyflyblog.com

Mojave Incident

While on a business trip to California in 1990, author Ron Felber met with his longtime associate who told him about Elise and Tom Gifford (they asked Felber to use alias names and not their real names—Steve and Dawn Hess for the rewrite titled *Mojave Incident*), a couple who had endured a disturbing event while in the Mojave Desert some thirteen months earlier. Ron thoroughly investigated their UFO/alien encounter story, which included hypnotizing the couple one year later to uncover more of the story.

In 1994, Ron rewrote the original 1994 *Searchers* book, describing the weird alien beings encountered by the Hesses in a remote part of California's Mojave Desert. Not long after the publication of *Mojave Incident*, the Hesses started using their real identity for an interview Coast to Coast AM and a documentary for television.

The story is different from any alien abduction ever written about in ufology because of the three types of aliens encountered— hundreds of them coming down from a huge mother ship above the desert floor, how the beings scanned the ground as if extracting something from it, how they held Dawn and Steve hostage for hours and the message given to the couple uncovered through hypnosis.

Steve said this, "They [aliens] may have been here all the time existing spiritually, then becoming physical. They were from other planets, but are more spiritual now. A power and a force."

When asked why they are here, Steve replied, "To deliver a message that the world needs to be as one. That if there's a war or massive destruction, they will intervene."

Dawn provided more information during her hypnosis session. "They want to make contact with the population. Tom and I are specimens; imperfect like the human race. When we're ready to communicate with them face to face, then possibly the world will be, too."

When asked where they come from, Dawn replied, "There are five galaxies. Theirs is the next closest. In order for all five galaxies to work together one day, they have to start and they're staring with us, so we'll be united galaxies." Then she added, "I know where the universe ends. Our universe ends where theirs begins. Our universe ends when all its matter stops mattering to us and starts mattering to them"

Everyone was stunned by Dawn's strange words, trying to understand their meaning.

Dawn continued, "God created our world in his image, but no theirs."

"Are there many different kinds of Beings?"

"Yes. Different ones. Different hybrids."

"When do you think this communication will happen between the aliens and humans?"

"I don't know."

"In my lifetime?"

"How long will you live?" she retorted.

"In a normal man's lifetime?"

"Our children's," she answered at last.

Dawn was then asked if Earth's population is regularly watched and she answered, "By many different kinds of beings sent on missions from the One Supreme. There's one Supreme Being that controls all of them. He sends missions here. They're not here of their own accord."

She was asked if they are friendly and she answered, "They are neutral. They could care less." When asked what does the One Supreme want, she said, 'For all the galaxies to live harmoniously together."

Dawn claimed that she and her husband thought their daughter had alien DNA because she was born nine months after the frightening alien encounter. Even stranger is their daughter has the rare Rh 0 negative blood, which has strange properties. A few ufologists believe that those people who have this unusual blood have alien DNA.

Chapter Twelve
TIME TRAVELER JOHN TITOR

Proof of a time traveler's existence may have taken place in November 2000. A blogger on the internet calling himself John Titor blogged he was a time traveler from the year 2036. John spent the next four months answering every kind of question put to him, which included photographs of his time machine and its operation manual. People began asking about the physics of time travel, why he was here and what he thought of our society. Many dismissed the condescending and sometimes peevish answers by John, while others were angered or frightened by his tantalizing answers to many subjects and his predictions.

If John was a hoaxer, he certainly was a great actor and well-versed on many subjects. I, for one, believe the story might have validity, especially in light of American physicist Hugh Everett's (November 11, 1930-July 19, 1982) many-world interpretation of quantum physics and the experiments that prove there might be many unseen levels to our existence.

First, let's examine John Titor's predictions and thoughts of time travel.

John said he returned to the year 2000 to obtain an IBM computer built-in 1975, called the 5100, which did exist and was manufactured by IBM as he stated. The computer was one of the first portable computers ever mass-produced and disappeared in the early 'eighties. John also admitted he was related to one of the IBM engineers who worked on the 5100, and that's why he was picked for the time travel mission. John traveled back to 1975 to meet a relative and obtain the 5100 and had it altered for his time. The computer could translate computer languages unknown and unpublished before 2036. He added the reason for the visit was that the UNIX computer code in his timeline had a glitch, and some sort of UNIX system registry stops in the year 2038 (note: another Y2K bug is predicted for 2038) and that the 5100 could read and change the legacy code written by IBM before the release of that system and still create new code in APL and basic. According to John, IBM engineers were probably sworn to secrecy about the 5100 computer and its amazing capabilities. He further stated that the reason he was picked for the mission was that his grandfather was directly involved with the building and programming of the 5100 IBM computer.

Although this seems illogical to go through such trouble for a computer part, NASA and many others search for computer parts all the time. John was surprised he was selected for the time travel mission and stated he was not a computer expert, but he believed the computer had some intricate coding that we depend on now. John added that time travel is known and will be discovered soon in our time.

John made many predictions, often frightening for our timeline. John said in his timeline World War III would end in the year 2015, and WWIII started with an attack on Israel, which is what happened when Hamas rebels launched rockets at Israel. The state of the world is showing some eerie similarities to the pre–World War II global picture foretold by John. If timelines are malleable and can be changed, perhaps we still have time to change the future.

Not all predictions made by John Titor have come to pass. He said another civil war would take place in the United States. But he may have known about the attack on New York City's World Trade Towers on September 11, 2001, when he said New York City's skyline would change. He discussed mad cow disease, in which he said we've been lied to about CJD (Mad Cow) and how devastating it is. One blogger asked about the year 2012, and if the world would end as predicted by the Mayan calendar and John replied, "Yes, there are unusual events in 2012 but they do not cause the world to end. Unfortunately, I have decided not to discuss events that you or I can't do anything about. It is important that they are surprised. Perhaps you are familiar with the story of the Red Sea and the Egyptians."

Was John referring to the Japanese tsunami on March 11, 2011, one year before the 2012 Mayan calendar predictions?

John also predicted a nuclear strike by Russia by 2015 against the major cities in the United States, China, and Europe. He said, "The United States reacts with counter-attacks. Many U.S. cities are destroyed. The Capitol of the United States is moved to Omaha, Nebraska."

John was asked if some sort of new world government was in place by 2011. And John's response was, "On my worldline, in 2011, the United States is in the middle of a civil war that has dramatic effects on most of the Western governments."

Hopefully, this event happened in his parallel world or timeline and will never happen in ours.

John talked about his youth. "In the year 2012, I was 14 years old spending most of my time living, running and hiding in the woods and rivers of central Florida. The civil war was in its 7th year and the world war was three years away. The next time John was asked what started the civil war he answered the civil war will be started between the Democrats and Republicans. Since Obama was elected the Democrats and Republications in Congress have shown little or no bipartisanship. Many issues and bills remain in limbo. Either the events John predicted will never happen or were delayed for several more years on another timeline.

John referred to our current society and seemed to see our world as beyond help when he stated, "Have you considered that your society might be better off if half of you were dead? While you sit by and watch your Constitution being torn away from you, you willfully eat poisoned food, buy manufactured products no one needs and turn an uncaring eye away from millions of people suffering and dying all around you. Is this the 'Universal Law' you subscribe to?"

John had great disdain for our society when he said, "Perhaps I should let you all in on a little secret. No one likes you in the future. This time is looked at as being full of lazy, self-centered, civically ignorant sheep. Perhaps you should be less concerned about me and more concerned about that."

Ouch! Perhaps he was right about the majority of humans on the planet at this time being self-centered.

The future and past may be far more fluid and malleable than we think. In John's parallel universe, another Civil War occurred in the United States and World War III was a part of history, but in our current reality, it has not happened and hopefully, it will never happen. But he did say that the civil war sometime in our time that was instigated by the Democrats and the Republicans. And look at all the verbal abuse they are slinging at each other over the impeachment of Donald Trump. Could this be the beginning of the Civil War that John had read about in the history books?

John stated that timelines can be changed and nothing is set in stone. *En masse* human consciousness can alter events and timelines.

Chapter Thirteen
FATHER MALACHI MARTIN

The late Father Malachi Martin believed the Catholic Church has known about the existence of extraterrestrials for years. On Coast to Coast AM with Art Bell in 1996, Art asked Father Martin why the Vatican would "muscle their way into Mount Graham's observatory" with the University of Arizona. Father Martin replied, "...because at the highest level they know what is in deep space and what great influence it will have on our world in 5 or 10 years." Was Father Martin referring to Planet X?

Can we conclude the Catholic Church has been aware of the alien existence for centuries? The Catholic Church contends that astrology is against their doctrine, however, astronomy isn't, and maybe numerology isn't either. The Vatican, the Jesuits and the University of Arizona unveiled a new telescope centered on Apache sacred ground, on Mount Graham in southeastern Arizona in early 1990. Worse, the Vatican named the telescope "Lucifer," which stands for "Large Binocular Telescope Near-infrared Utility with Camera and Integral Field Unit for Extragalactic Research." The question is why did the Vatican go to such lengths to erect a giant telescope named "Lucifer" on sacred Native American land? What are they looking for in the heavens? Is it related to the third secret of Fatima and the Book of Revelation that describes the end times?

Mount Graham is one of the most sacred and holiest places for the Apache and it's believed to be a stargate or portal for deities and other-worldly entities to enter our world. Many of these stargate portals supposedly exist throughout the world allowing supernatural intelligent beings to move in-and-out of dimensions.

The Vatican Observatory Research Group or-VORG) operates the 1.8m Alice P. Lennon Telescope with its Thomas J. Bannan Astrophysics Facility, known together as the Vatican Advanced Technology Telescope or VATT, at the Mount Graham International Observatory (MGIO) in southeastern Arizona where sky conditions are among the best in the world and certainly the Continental United States. Mt. Graham is near Tucson, Arizona, in the Apache San Carlos reservation. At 3200 meters it is one of the highest peaks in Arizona. Above all, though, it is the single most sacred site of the Apache Nation.

Mount Graham or Dzil Nchaa Si An, known by the local natives as 'Big Seated Mountain' because of its distinctive profile, is an important religious reference point for the Apache: their ancestors are buried there; their medicine-men go there to collect therapeutic herbal plants, and the Apache shamans perform their sacred rites there.

The Apache and extraterrestrials seem to be linked in other ways. It is said that the Apache has a great dislike for the owl which goes back to their legends. The owl, the snake, and coyote are considered evil to them. Could there be a stargate on Mount Graham for extraterrestrials? Perhaps the Apache, like millions of so-called aliens abductees worldwide, recall seeing an owl. Owls, amongst other animals, often appear as a disguise to replace the images of the actual alien abductions and a medical examination that took place. And it is suspected that these screen memories were implanted within the abductees by the aliens to prevent mental trauma from the abduction.

The Apache tribal members website states they have tried to sue the University of Arizona, the Vatican and Jesuit Order to cease the building and desecration of their mountain, but lost their fight (what a surprise!).

Author and Researcher of ancient mythology and paranormal phenomena Tom Horn discussed his visit to the Arizona observatory on Coast to Coast AM talk radio show on March 25, 2013. He stated that Jesuit Brother Guy Consolmagno, astronomer to the Vatican, said the Vatican had nothing to do with the telescope's naming. German astronomers were responsible for the name L.U.C.I.F.E.R, which is an acronym for "Large Binocular Telescope Near-infrared Utility with Camera and Integral Field Unit for Extragalactic Research."

Many critics claim the naming of Lucifer telescope shows the Vatican's alliance to their true master—Lucifer or Satan, by using God and Jesus as shills to hide their deception.

While living in Tucson, Arizona in 2001, I visited Tucson's other Observatory—Kitt Peak National Observatory, 56 miles southwest of Tucson. I noted while on a tour that many areas were roped-off to visitors. I remember asking the tour guide if astronomers were searching from a large object reportedly coming into our solar system known as Planet X. He grimaced and didn't answer. His attitude was very disconcerting.

Could the Vatican be searching for in the heavens for the elusive Planet X? I would suspect that they have found it already.

Many conspiracy theorists speculate it's "wormwood" which appears several times in the Old Testament from the Hebrew term לענה *la'anah*. The only time the word is used is in the New Testament and in the book of Revelation: *The third angel blew his trumpet, and a great star fell from heaven, blazing like a torch, and it fell on a third of the rivers and on the springs of water. The name of the star is Wormwood. A third of the waters became wormwood, and many died from the water because it was made bitter.* (Revelation 8:10–11).

Could the U.S. government or the Vatican be planning a false event and could that event be Project Blue Beam? Project Blue Beam, often referred to as a myth, was an essay written and published by the radical Fundamentalist and Quebec separatist Serge Monast, dated 1994. He claimed that the governments of the world were going to create a grand illusion in the following order:

First, is a series of artificially created earthquakes at "certain precise locations on the planet," which will uncover archaeological evidence that will "be used to discredit all fundamental religious doctrines."

Second, is "a gigantic space show." This will involve "three-dimensional optical holograms and sounds, laser projection of multiple holographic images to different parts of the world, each receiving a different image according to predominating regional national religious faith. This new 'god's' voice will be speaking in all languages." These staged events will show the "new Christ" or Messiah and will be a false Second Coming.

Third will be the "Telepathic Electronic Two-Way." This involves "telepathic and electronically augmented two-way communication where ELF, VLF and LF waves will reach each person from within his or her own mind." These communications will fake a communication from God.

Fourth, according to Monast, would be "the universal supernatural manifestation with electronic means." He said it would take on three specific "orientations." One would simulate an alien invasion, which would then provoke nations with nuclear weapons to strike back.

Was this plan concocted by the Vatican and the Illuminati's One World Government? First, there is the false alien invasion scenario—presumably, this could be done with a fleet of black triangle craft, but could they blanket the world? Doubtful. But then, regarding the religious fakery, are "they" really going to blanket the world with 3-D holographic images of God, the Blessed Virgin Mary, Jesus, Krishna, Allah or UFOs? Is it feasible that they could use mind control to broadcast a message in all languages of the world? Again, doubtful. And could they convince us to abandon our previously held faiths? Well, maybe if it involved an alien invasion.

President Ronald Reagan hinted at such a scenario in his September 21, 1987 speech from the 42nd Session of the United Nations General Assembly:

"...In our obsession with antagonisms of the moment, we often forget how much unites all the members of humanity.

Perhaps we need some OUTSIDE, UNIVERSAL THREAT to make us recognize this common bond. I occasionally think how quickly our differences would vanish if we were facing an ALIEN THREAT from outside this world. And yet, I ask you, is not an ALIEN FORCE already among us? What could be more alien to the universal aspirations of our peoples than war and the threat of war?..."

In 2014, President Bill Clinton told late-night talk show host Jimmy Kimmel that when he was the leader of the free world, he tried unsuccessfully to investigate what the government was hiding regarding UFOs. When Kimmel asked if he would have told the public had he found evidence of real aliens, Clinton smiled and said "Yeah."

Then, in 2015, during a visit to Kimmel's talk show, President Barack Obama, in tongue-in-cheek fashion, said "the aliens won't let [disclosure] happen. You'd reveal all their secrets, and they exercise strict control over us. I can't reveal anything."

During Hillary Clinton's 2016 bid for the White House, she made several comments throughout the year about her intent—should she be elected president to make government UFO files available to the public. "If there is something there, unless it's a threat to national security, I think we ought to share it with the public," she told Kimmel.

When former President George W. Bush appeared on Jimmy Kimmel Live on March 6, 2017, to promote his book, *Portraits of Courage*, and Kimmel didn't waste any time trying to get Bush to admit that he may have looked for and seen alleged secret government files on UFOs. Kimmel began the "interrogation" by asking Bush "a question that's very important to me and very important to the country. When you were in office, did you go through the secret files—the UFO documents, because if I was president, that would be the first thing I did."

Even before Kimmel finished asking the question, Bush immediately replied, "Maybe." Then, he told Kimmel, "You know, it's funny. My daughters asked the very same question." When Kimmel asked if Bush would be allowed to tell his daughters what was in those files, the former commander-in-chief said "No." "Now that you're out of the office, you can do anything you want, right?" Kimmel pressed.

"True, yeah," Bush said, adding, "But I'm not telling you." Kimmel: "You're not telling me what? Are you not telling me that you looked at them?"

Bush: "I'm not telling you nuthin'!"

The brief UFO secret files portion of the conversation ended when Kimmel asked Bush if there were great secrets that the former president knows that he can't share with people. Bush confirmed it and indicated he would never divulge those secrets at any future point in his life.

In a June 2019 ABC News interview President Donald Trump responded to a question about the rise in reports of unidentified aircraft by US Navy pilots, "I think it's probably—I want them to think whatever they think. They do say, and I've seen, and I've read, and I've heard. And I did have one very brief meeting on it. But people are saying they're seeing UFOs. Do I believe it? Not particularly."

Asked if he has been told that extraterrestrial life was found, Trump said: "We're watching, and you'll be the first to know."

Maybe Trump should look into the sky more often while in the White House. A mysterious aircraft that's now being considered to be an unidentified flying object caused the lockdown of both the White House and Capitol Hill as security executives scrambled to identify if the aircraft is a possible threat on November 26, 2019.

According to Fox News, the UFO was discovered by Capitol securities Tuesday morning as it triggered an airspace alarm over the Capitol, prompting the secret service to launch emergency procedures just in case the "UFO" could cause a serious threat to the U.S.' main political seat.

The security around Capitol Hill also warned the people outside to stay out of the area as they continue to identify what the flying object could be and avoid any catastrophic events just in case. The situation escalated to "Air Con Orange," which is given only if a suspicious aircraft is detected to be uncomfortably close to the Capitol Hill and White House's secured perimeter. However, Air Con Orange should only be up for a few minutes before security personnel can determine if the situation should be escalated or downgraded. Those in Capitol Hill were advised to leave the premises but were allowed to go back in after 30 minutes.

Based on the report, the aircraft was simply something that got mixed signals prompting it to enter restricted airspace. As a response, the security forces of both Capitol Hill and the White House had to send jets to scramble whatever was hovering above them.

A military official said the alarm could have been caused by birds, a drone or some type of "weather anomaly." Since when can't the military tell a UFO from a flock of birds, a drone, or weather anomaly on radar? Interestingly, the ETs decided to buzz the White House during the impeachment hearings. Were they sending a message to Congress—stop the insanity?

This isn't the first time the White House has been buzzed by UFOs. It happened in 1952 and was known as the "Washington flap, the Washington National Airport Sightings, or the Invasion of Washington," where a series of unidentified flying object reports from July 12 to July 29, 1952, were seen over Washington, D.C. On July 19, 1952, seven UFOs were spotted on radar.

At 8:15 p.m. on Saturday, July 26, 1952, a pilot and stewardess on a National Airlines flight into Washington observed some strange lights above their plane. Within minutes, both radar centers at National Airport, and the radar at Andrews AFB, were tracking more unknown objects. USAF Master Sergeant Charles E. Cummings visually observed the objects at Andrews, he later said that "these lights did not have the characteristics of shooting stars. There was no trails . . . they traveled faster than any shooting star I have ever seen."

I can tell you this with absolute certainty after my own UFO experiences and an encounter with aliens, that they do exist. A number of species visit Earth with different agenda, and some of them live on (or in) our planet. Expect a huge number of sightings in 2020 and perhaps even a landing in public view. Mass sightings of orbs and other craft will make headlines worldwide.

More of Father Malachi Martin's Revelations
Father Malachi Martin, an Irish Catholic priest and controversial author, born July 23, 1921, and died July 27, 1999. He was originally ordained as a Jesuit priest and became Professor of Paleontology at the Vatican's Pontifical Biblical Institute, and from 1958 he served as a theological adviser to Cardinal Augustin Bea during the preparations for the Second Vatican Council. Through the years he became disillusioned by reforms in the Church and renounced his vows in 1964, moving to New York City. His 17 novels and non-fiction books were often critical of the Catholic Church. He believed the Church should have disclosed the third secret of Fatima, Portugal as the Virgin Mary had requested. Two of his books, The Scribal Character of The Dead Sea Scrolls, 1958, and Hostage to the Devil, 1976, dealt with Satanism, demonic possession, and exorcism.

Father Malachi Martin's Accusations
Father Malachi Martin said, "Anybody who is acquainted with the state of affairs in the Vatican in the last 35 years is well aware that the Prince of Darkness has had and still has his surrogates in the court of Saint Peter in Rome."

From 1958 until 1964, Jesuit priest Martin served in Rome where he was a close associate of the renowned Jesuit Cardinal Augustin Bea and the Pope. Released afterward from his vows of poverty and obedience at his own request (but as a priest), Father Martin moved to New York and became a best-selling writer of fiction and non-fiction. He often made references to satanic rites held in Rome in his 1990 non-fiction best-seller, The Keys of This Blood, in which he wrote: "Most frighteningly for Pope John Paul [II], he had come up against the irremovable presence of a malign strength in his own Vatican and in certain bishops' chanceries. It was what knowledgeable Churchmen called the 'superforce.'

Rumors, always difficult to verify, tied its installation to the beginning of Pope Paul VI's reign in 1963. Indeed Paul had alluded somberly to 'the smoke of Satan which has entered the Sanctuary'. . . an oblique reference to an enthronement ceremony by Satanists in the Vatican. Besides, the incidence of Satanic pedophilia—rites and practices— was already documented among certain bishops and priests as widely dispersed as Turin, in Italy, and South Carolina, in the United States. The cultic acts of Satanic pedophilia are considered by professionals to be the culmination of the Fallen Archangel's rites."

Father Martin said, "Satanism is all around us. We deny it at our peril. I could point out places only minutes from here [New York City] where black masses are being celebrated. I know of cases of human sacrifice—the sacrifice of babies. I know the people who are doing these things."

The Mysterious Death of Justice Antonin Scalia
From the moment I heard about Justice Antonin Scalia's death on February 13, 2016 (13 is an Illuminati number, at age 79 (7+9 = 16 and total 7 another Illuminati number) I suspected murder. (Learn more about the power of number 13 in my book Mystic Revelations of Thirteen).

The owner of the ranch claimed he found Scalia with a pillow over his face. That doesn't sound like a natural death. On Thursday, February 25, 2016, the Washington Post reported that U.S. Justice Antonin Scalia spent his last hours with members of a secretive society of elite hunters at a West Texas ranch. The exclusive fraternity for hunters is called the International Order of St. Hubertus, an Austrian society that dates back to the 1600s. This society was founded in Bohemia in 1695 by Count Franz Anton von Sporck, which is now in the modern-day Czech Republic.

Besides the ranch owner stating Scalia had a pillow "over his head," this detailed with the fact that a physician had declared him dead over the phone and the family didn't want an autopsy. This prompted speculation about foul play and the "obvious" role of the Obama administration in Scalia's "untimely" death.

On "Trunews," End Times, radio host Rick Wiles discussed "the possible occult connections" to the death of Justice Scalia Wiles explained that the "Luciferian" "devil-worshipers" who control the government are out for blood, noting that Lupercalia is observed between February 13 and 15. Scalia's body was discovered on the 13th. "There's always human sacrifice involved," he said.

There's a clandestine club called the Bohemian Club in San Francisco, which is associated with the all-male occult Bohemian Grove, also a secret club located in Sonoma county—Russian River area. The Bohemian Club has seen the likes of former President George H.W. Bush, a member, and reportedly Dick Cheney and Bill Clinton were participants. Strange rituals take place there. The Bohemian Grove is a 2,700-acre virgin redwood grove in Northern California, 75 miles north of San Francisco, where the rich, the powerful, and their entourage visit with each other during the last two weeks of July while camping out in cabins and tents and performing strange occult rituals.

It was in 1`995 that I discovered the shocking book Trance-Formation of America by Cathy O'Brien and Mark Phillips about children who have been abducted for mind-control experiments and other horrible occult rituals by the CIA. Cathy O'Brien was taken as a child and endured horrible physiological and sexual abuse. It was all part of the Central Intelligence Agency's MK-Ultra Project Monarch mind-control operation. The most shocking information was about the people involved—Dick Cheney, Bill and Hillary Clinton, and George H.W. Bush. The repeated sexual assault on children and even games where children were hunted like animals on a hunting ranch in California is too frightening to fathom. The book has been dismissed by some as pure fantasy yet it makes you wonder about Scalia's mysterious death and connection to an elite society linked to occult practices (i.e. Jeffrey Epstein's link to the famous). Cathy and Mark say the sexual and satanic rituals are so widespread it involves clergy, justices, law enforcement, and politicians.

Isn't it time we had our eyes wide open to the darkness that invades our world so we can transform the anger, hate, and abuse into love, light, and forgiveness? Much healing needs to take place on our planet if we are to survive and evolve.

Chapter Fourteen
A DYING WORLD

In 1971, singer/songwriter Marvin Gaye released, The Ecology album, which included the haunting song, Mercy, Mercy Me. Marvin was a visionary, who realized the disastrous road humanity was taking years ago with the environment.

Mercy, mercy me
Ah things ain't what they used to be, no no
Where did all the blue skies go?
Poison is the wind that blows from the north and south and east
Woo mercy, mercy me, mercy
Ah things ain't what they used to be, no no
Oil wasted on the ocean and upon our seas, fish full of mercury
Ah oh mercy, mercy me
Ah things ain't what they used to be, no no
Radiation underground and in the sky
Animals and birds who live nearby are dying
Oh mercy, mercy me
Ah things ain't what they used to be
What about this overcrowded land
How much more abuse from man can she stand?

Although Marvin's plea for us to awaken in 1971 was not heeded, there's still time to make changes and start the healing process for future generations. If we give up the fight, all is lost.

Have you ever watched Michael Jackson's 1997 Earth Song video? Michael was addressing us, humanity and society in general. Concerning the fact of what we have done to the Earth, all the forests are being destroyed at an unprecedented rate and the bond we once had with the animals is gone. Because of the ecological unbalance and environmental problems, Earth is dying. The main message by Michael Jackson is for "people to hear the voice of the planet" and he encouraged people to do something about it. At the end of the video, Earth is cleansed with violent winds and the animals come to life and flourish again, water, air becomes pure again, and the trees come back to life.

In a paper published in Science Magazine, January 2015, Johan Rockström argued that we've already messed up with regards to climate change, extinction of species, the addition of phosphorus and nitrogen to the world's ecosystems and deforestation. We are well within the boundaries of ocean acidification and the pollution of freshwater globally. "The planet has been our best friend by buffering our actions and showing its resilience," Rockström said. "But for the first time ever, we might shift the planet from friend to foe."

Since 2007 the concentration of greenhouse gases in the atmosphere has risen to around 400 parts per million (the 'safe' boundary being 350 parts per million), risking high global temperatures and rising sea levels, droughts and floods and other catastrophic climate problems, currently taking place. But Rockström doesn't see it as all doom and gloom. He is confident that we can step back within some of the boundaries, by slashing carbon emissions and boosting agricultural yields in Africa to soothe deforestation and biodiversity loss.

But there are those who feel that humans aren't doing enough to save the planet. Grandmother Bernadette Rebienot of Gabon, Africa, one of the Thirteen Ingenious Grandmother, said at the International Council held in Phoenicia, New York October of 2004, "Our planet is sick from the never-ending ravages of people, pollution, deforestation, abusive power, jealousy, and hatred. As the Earth increasingly suffers, we have become more and more disoriented and have lost our way."

Grandmother Flordemayo said, "The pollutions in a mother is transferred into the womb. The first breast milk an infant receives is tainted with the chemicals the mother has ingested through the years from food, detergents, creams, deodorants, shampoos, cosmetics, hair dyes, including the other pollutions now found in our environment."

Included in this list now are opioids and pharmaceutical drugs. New research reveals that our blood is full of caffeine and often Xanax, an anxiety and panic disorder medication. If you need a blood transfusion, most likely you will get both in the blood.

In 2018 the CDC determined that approximately 1 in 59 children are diagnosed with an autism spectrum disorder (ASD). In the year 2000, 1 out of 150 children had autism. That is a huge increase.

Is it any wonder children and adults sometime in their lifetime will have cancer from the poisons and toxins in our environment? The travesty of this is humans have a choice to stop the destructive path we are presently on. We can stop the harmful substances manufacturers load into our food, the GMOs, the fluoride in our water, and hormones in our meat and dairy products by refusing to buy any of these products. The future, just like the past, is ours to change.

Grandmother Shinobu Iura of the Amazon Rain Forest of Brazil had a remarkable three-month-long encounter with star beings, who told her they were from another planet, one of an incalculable distance away from Earth. The beings left a message to the people of Earth, an alert, to tell us not to lose ourselves in our material and technological ways, not to forget our spiritual consciousness, not to forget God the great spirit-creator of all things. "They told us to stop disrespecting His creation and to stop the destruction of our planet, which is resulting in the sickness of the Earth and her inhabitants. They told us that this destruction would continue and that only a change to spiritual consciousness would give hope for our salvation. They warned us that it is necessary to be attentive to products created by technology that can pollute and destroy our terrestrial atmosphere. They said it was necessary to enter into a state of alert. This was twenty-eight years ago [1978] when these questions were not yet so grave."

In 2019, thousands of wildfires were set intentionally in Brazil rainforests to clear the land for grazing cattle. It is estimated that 1,740 square miles of the Brazilian Amazon—about 1.8 times the size of Luxembourg was deforested between 2017 and 2019 and then burned. Scientists believe that most of these fires were started to clear vegetation for farms or pastures since they appear to spread outward from adjacent deforested land. I witnessed the same in Belize, Central America during my visits in 1992 and 1996. Forest land was being clear cut and burned to plant citrus trees. The Rainforests are the planet's lungs.

Rainforests absorb carbon dioxide, a greenhouse gas, and produce oxygen, upon which all animals and humans depend for survival. Rainforests also stabilize climate, house incredible amounts of plants and wildlife, and produce nourishing rainfall all around the planet. Without the rainforests of the world, our planet would be devoid of life.

Grandmother Shinobu Iura was also told by the Star Beings that she was destined, along with many other conscious people worried about the same issues, to take this message to all the inhabitants of Earth before the grand catastrophe that would bring much destruction and disgrace to all humanity, something already prophesied by peoples with sacred knowledge.

The Grandmothers all say the Ancient Ones have told them that it is their job as Earthkeepers to care for Mother Earth and the animals. They believe that the Creator or Great Spirit resides in Mother Earth, the animals, the rocks, the trees, the water, the stars, the sun, and the moon. By observing and respecting nature, we learn how to live in balance on our precious planet.

Both of my indigenous mentors during the 1990s, Corbin Harney, Spiritual Leader of the Western Shoshone Nation, (1920-2007), and Oglala Sioux Ceremonial Leader and author Ed McGaa "Eagle Man," (1936-2017), taught me and a great many others about honoring all life on Earth. That all life is connected and has a consciousness, even rocks.

As most of you know, crystals have energy, and so do all rocks—they have a frequency that exists in all life. What worried the elders most is how we have become disconnected from each other and our environment.

If you don't think our planet is dying, think again! A great debate rages on between scientists whether or not Earth is warming, but it is agreed something dire is happening, whether human-caused or natural.

Both the National Oceanic and Atmospheric Administration and NASA calculated that in 2014 the world had its hottest year in 135 years of record-keeping. Not only did sea stars (starfish) melt and die *en masse* along the Western Coast of the United States from Alaska to Southern California, but other sea creatures and Earth creatures are disappearing at an alarming rate.

Thousands of sea lions are starving to death off the coast of California, deep ocean oarfish, rarely seen, have appeared off the coast of California recently, and sardines have suddenly vanished off the West Coast of California. More than 100,000 young Cassin's auklet seabirds have been found dead since October 2014, from Long Beach, California, to Scott Islands off the northern tip of Vancouver Island, B. C., Canada, where 80% of the Cassin's Finch breed some 3.5 million birds. Yet no viruses, bacteria, toxins or other causes of death have been found. The speculation is starvation, but why?

January 22, 2015, dinoflagellates Noctiluca scintillans or glowing blue algae, appeared along the seashore of Hong Kong. This form of algae thrives on nitrogen and phosphorous rich water caused by farm runoffs containing fertilizer and pesticide chemicals. This single-cell life form eats plankton and it itself is eaten by other ocean life forms. But when it glows at night it's a warning that the water is toxic to other life forms. The algae can also glow red, known as "red tide." Few animals can survive dead zones of oxygen-poor water. And once a dead zone sets in, it's hard for the ocean to recover.

Animal Abuse
Animals all around the world continue to be treated without dignity as if they were unintelligent, unable to reason, to feel pain, and exhibit emotion. Each day there are horrible stories of cattle and dairy cows, horses, dogs, and cats that have been abused or killed from abuse. Even small animals are used in laboratories and experimented on for food products, medicines, and cosmetics. Feral animals are hunted for the fun of it, not as a food source. Whales and dolphins are captured in fishing nets or die by large ships in the shipping lanes worldwide. In Japan, dolphin pods are herded into Taiji cove and slaughtered during the dolphin hunting season from September to March. Fishermen say the cull is a traditional part of their livelihood in an area that has fished dolphins and whales for thousands of years.

Activists like Yoko Ono, John Lennon's widow, added her voice to the Japanese to stop this dolphin bloodbath. In the Academy award-winning documentary, The Cove, activist Ric O'Barry tried to stop the killing and had his life threatened. As of 2010, the Japanese refused to screen this documentary due to the controversy over the film and the film's subject.

Again, I must include what UFO abductee Bob Luca was told by the benevolent Elders under hypnosis from Raymond Fowler's book, The Watchers II. When asked by the hypnotist where animals fit in spiritually, Bob said, "Man will be surprised to find where animals fit in. I told you: All that is done is recorded, and many foolish people think the harm they've done to animals will not count. It will! All that the Creator's made is not to be taken lightly. And the most lowly to the most magnificent, much is to be learned."

I've always felt that animals should be treated as we want to be treated—with love, dignity, and respect. After all, animals have lived on this planet as long or even longer than humans. Animals are intelligent and have souls—perhaps not like humans. Every animal and every living thing, including insects, hold the vibration and balance on our planet. The whales and dolphins sing their song and hold the vibration of the oceans, the birds, insects, and frogs all tone to Earth Mother and they hold the balance. Without insects on our planet, we would not exist. Every living thing has an electromagnetic frequency and with that frequency, life depends on each other—a spiritual and necessary symbiotic relationship.

African elephants are poached for their ivory and sold in Asian markets. Once 1.3 million elephants roamed throughout Africa, and now there are only 500,000 remaining on game reserves. Even rhinos are killed for their horns, and gorillas for their hands because certain countries believe these animals will bring them magical and curative powers.

Superstitious beliefs still dominate much of the world today.

Ancient peoples have considered Mother Earth a living breathing entity, but modern humans have forgotten that our planet allows us the gift of life. We have arrived in the twenty-first century destroying our natural resources at a phenomenal rate without any thought of the consequences, except those few who are trying desperately to stop the destruction of Mother Earth.

On Monday, November 25, 2019, President Donald Trump signed a bill, The PACT ACT (Preventing Animals Cruelty and Torture) that makes animal cruelty a federal felony, saying the measure would help us be "more responsible and humane stewards of our planet. This is only a small step to preventing animal abuse. In the future, let's intend that countries all over the world adopt rights for animals.

Plastic and Our Oceans Our oceans face a massive threat from something humans use every day: plastics. An estimated 17.6 billion pounds of plastic leaks into the marine environment from an equivalent of dumping a garbage truck full of plastic into the oceans every minute! As plastics continue to flood into our oceans, the list of marine species affected by plastic debris expands. Tens of thousands of individual marine organisms have been observed suffering from entanglement or ingestion of plastics permeating the marine environment—from zooplankton and fish to sea turtles, marine mammals, and seabirds. Plastics never disappear. Instead, they break down into smaller and smaller pieces, which act as magnets for harmful pollutants. When eaten by fish, some of those chemical-laden microplastics can work their way up the food chain and into the fish we eat. Yes, we are drinking and eating plastic daily. Is there any wonder that humans are dying of cancer at rates never seen before?

It's a vicious cycle that won't go away any time soon. A meager 9 percent of all plastic waste generated has been recycled. Recycling alone is not enough to solve the plastics crisis.

A recent study found that sea stars or starfish have been ingesting plastic for at least 40 years. Researchers were surprised to find that sea star specimens collected between 1976 and 2015 had similar amounts of microplastic in their stomachs, which means ocean plastic pollution started impacting sea life much earlier than previously thought.

Harming Earth Mother

Sir Isaac Newton (1642-1726), an English physicist and mathematician, believed that for every action, there is an equal and opposite reaction—in other words, Newton understood the universal law of Karma. Karma is what Asian religions believe is the result of an action, good or bad, that will influence a person's future with either happiness or suffering. However, humans have a bad habit of ignoring the ramifications of their actions.

For example, it was April of 2010 deepwater oil drilling was taking place in the Gulf of Mexico off the coast of Louisiana when BP's Deepwater Horizon oil rig exploded. It was the largest accidental marine oil spill in the history of the petroleum industry. Following the explosion and sinking of the Deepwater Horizon oil rig, which claimed 11 lives, the sea-floor oil gusher flowed through September 19, 2010. It is estimated that 4.9 million barrels (210 million US gallons) were released into the Gulf of Mexico.

The oil spill was disastrous enough killing hundreds of birds and marine life, but BP began spraying Corexit oil dispersant, a toxic chemical used to dissolve oil spills on the ocean surface. The U.S. government allowed the company to apply chemical "dispersants" to the blossoming oil slick to prevent toxic gunk from reaching the fragile bays, beaches, and mangroves of the coast, where so much marine life originates. But several recent studies show that BP and the feds made a huge mistake that has harmed everything from microscopic organisms to bottlenose dolphins.

The problem with the Corexit dispersants was it emulsified into tiny beads, causing them to sink toward the ocean floor. Wave action and wind turbulence degraded the oil further, and evaporation concentrated the toxins in the oil-Corexit mixture, including dangerous compounds called polycyclic aromatic hydrocarbons (PAHs), known to cause cancer and developmental disorders.

When BP began spraying the Gulf, it proved to be toxic to marine life, but when combined with crude oil, the mixture became several times more toxic than oil or dispersant alone. Beaches, wetlands, and estuaries became coated in thick oil. The fishing industry came to a halt as people lost their businesses. Those who lived close to the ocean or worked at sea became ill from the toxic oil spill and dispersants. As of 2013 tarballs could still be found on the Mississippi coast, and a 40,000-pound tar mat was discovered near East Grand Terre, Louisiana which prompted closed waters to commercial fishing.

Much of what happened to the Gulf from this disaster has never been fully disclosed to the public and its far-reaching environmental consequences to the Gulf of Mexico. It may take hundreds, maybe thousands of years, before the Gulf is restored to its prior state before the spill. There are reports that the oil still flows into the Gulf of Mexico and was never fully contained.

Everywhere around the world, huge amounts of oil and gas are being removed from Mother Earth—her lifeblood. If we don't find alternative solutions to our energy sources, that won't harm our planet, I fear we'll find as the Australian Aboriginals have, the Earth's grid will wobble completely out of balance and the poles will shift.

It appears this may be happening to our planet already as earthquakes increase in places that aren't known to experience earthquakes; strange booms continue to be heard worldwide along with shaking not related to earthquakes, according to the USGS (US geological survey) earthquake website. Mother Earth is warning us that we can't continue to disrespect her without disastrous consequences.

The great 9.0 magnitude earthquake of Japan happened on Friday, March 11, 2011, at 2:46 pm off the Pacific coast of Tōhoku. It is what scientists call an undersea megathrust earthquake. This earthquake occurred where the Pacific Plate subducted under the plate beneath northern Honshu. The break caused the seafloor to rise by several meters. The earthquake triggered powerful tsunami waves that reached heights of up to 133 feet in Miyako. The earthquake was so powerful it moved Honshu, the main island of Japan, 2.4 meters (8' feet) and shifted the Earth on its axis by estimates of between 4 inches and 10 inches. It also generated sound waves detected by the low-orbiting GOCE satellite.

The tsunami destroyed over a million buildings and killed as many as 16,000 (some estimates claim over 19,000 people died that day). The tsunami also caused history's worst nuclear accident, level 7 meltdowns at three reactors at the Fukushima Daiichi Nuclear Power Plant complex, and subsequently warranted the evacuation of hundreds of thousands of residents in a 12-mile radius of the plant. Many electrical generators were taken down, and at least three nuclear reactors suffered explosions due to hydrogen gas that had built up within their outer containment buildings after cooling system failure resulting from the loss of electrical power.

In 2013, Yushi Yoneyama, an official with the Minister of Economy, Trade, and Industry, which regulates Tokyo Electric power Co. (TEMPCO), was asked about the radioactive water going into the ocean from Fukushima Plant and he replied, "We think that the volume of water is about 300 tons a day." It is estimated the cleanup from Fukushima will take more than 40 years at a cost of US $11 billion.

We still don't know the total damage the radiation leak had on the ecosystem, but since the 2011 disaster, there have been mysterious die-offs in the Pacific and species like sardines vanishing deepwater oarfish never seen in shallow water, and the inexplicable death of thousands of sea stars along the West Coast from Alaska to California. These sightings may or may not have anything to do with the radiation released into the air and ocean from the Fukushima nuclear plant, but I find it highly suspicious. Birds are the ideal sentinels for studying the potential impacts of radiation on humans because they share many basic biological processes and are easy to observe.

For more than a decade scientists have analyzed avian species in another irradiated area, the 77,000 square miles contaminated by the 1986 explosion at the Chernobyl Nuclear Power Plant in Ukraine. Among their findings there: reduced numbers and longevity of birds; diminished fertility in male birds; smaller brains in some birds; and mutations in swallows and other species that indicate significant genetic damage. Barn swallows and wood warblers, among other species, are locally extinct.

The shameful part is we haven't learned our lesson about the catastrophic consequences of nuclear radiation after Pennsylvania's Three Mile Island accident in 1979, Chernobyl in 1986 and Fukushima in 2011. Even worse, some of the nuclear plants have been built on known seismic regions. According to BBC reporter Greg Palast, reporter engineers knew Fukushima might be unsafe, but covered it up. Based on the first-hand interview by a senior engineer for the corporation which built the Fukushima nuclear plants, and a review of engineers' field diaries, it was revealed that the engineers who built the Fukushima nuclear plants knew their design would fail in an earthquake. Their report stated: the plant was riddled with problems that, no way on earth, could withstand an earthquake. The team of engineers sent in to inspect it found that most of these components could "completely and utterly fail" during an earthquake.

In 2004, Leuren Moret warned the Japan Times of the exact type of nuclear catastrophe that Japan experienced and said: "Of all the places in the entire world where no one in their right mind would build scores of nuclear power plants, Japan would be pretty near the top of the list."

Japan sits on top of four tectonic plates, at the edge of the subduction zone, and is in one of the most tectonically active regions of the world. "I think the situation right now is very scary," said Katsuhiko Ishibashi, a seismologist, and professor at Kobe University. "It's like a kamikaze terrorist wrapped in bombs just waiting to explode."

Here's the kicker—for Earth's inhabitants—radiation stays dangerous forever, or as long as humans are likely to exist, but the most dangerous parts will have decayed to only a small proportion of their original activity after a few thousand years. I'm afraid that if we don't hurry and find alternative sources of energy that won't harm our planet and the environment, we are headed in for extinction.

There is solar energy, wind energy, and water energy available and yet not enough is being done. From the startling photographs sent back to Earth by NASA, I know that Mars once had an advanced civilization that misused their technology and science and destroyed themselves. When we view Mars from Earth, let us keep in mind that we can destroy ourselves if we aren't careful. No world is safe from their own folly.

Ocean Acidification

You probably haven't heard about this because our mainstream news isn't reporting on it—it's call ocean acidification which is increasing at an unprecedented rate. As humanity continues to fill the atmosphere with harmful gases, our planet is becoming less hospitable to life. The vast oceans absorb much of the carbon dioxide we have produced from the Industrial Revolution.

Due to Earth absorbing 25 percent of humanity's CO2, has spared the atmosphere severe consequences, according to some scientists. But in light of the extreme weather worldwide in the past few years, that may no longer be true. However, the news media can't hide the climate weirding of hurricane superstorms, fierce tornado cells, disastrous snowstorms, and record-setting global high temperatures.

The rising carbon dioxide in our oceans burns up and deforms the smallest, most plentiful food at the bottom of the deep blue food chain. One such victim is the sea butterfly. In just a few short decades, the death and deformation of this fragile and translucent species could endanger larger species that rely on the sea butterfly for food. This "butterfly effect," could potentially threaten fisheries that feed more than 1 billion humans worldwide.

Computer modeler Isaac Kaplan at the National Oceanic and Atmospheric Administration off in Seattle said that his early work predicts significant declines in sharks, skates and rays, some types of flounder and sole and Pacific whiting, the most frequently caught commercial fish off the coasts of Washington, Oregon, and California. The increase in carbon dioxide might have caused the huge die-off off sea stars from California to Alaska in recent years. Once a species immune system is weakened, it's vulnerable to disease.

Acidification can even rewire the brains of fish. Studies have found rising CO2 levels cause clown fish to gain athleticism, but have their sense of smell redirected. This transforms them into "dumb jocks," scientists claim, swimming faster and more vigorously straight into the mouths of their predators. These Frankenstein fish were found to be five times more likely to die in the natural world. Could this be a metaphor for humanity, as our recklessness and abuse of Earth propels us toward an equally dangerous fate?

Craig Welch from the Seattle Times and others have reported, carbon dioxide is changing the ocean's chemistry faster than at any time in human history, in ways that have potentially devastating consequences for both ocean life and for humans who depend on the world's fisheries as vital sources of protein and livelihood.

Fracking

Fracking, also known as hydraulic fracturing, is the process of extracting natural gas from shale rock layers deep within the Earth. Fracking makes it possible to produce natural gas extraction in shale that was once unreachable with conventional technologies. Fracking involves drilling and injecting fluid into the ground at a high pressure to fracture shale rocks to release natural gas inside. It takes 1-8 million gallons of water to complete each fracturing job. The water brought in is mixed with sand and chemicals to create fracking fluid. This is hard to believe but approximately 40,000 gallons of chemicals are used per fracturing.

Up to 600 chemicals are used in fracking fluid, including known highly toxic and carcinogenic materials such as uranium, mercury, ethylene glycol, methanol, hydrochloric acid, and formaldehyde.

Around 10,000 feet the fracking fluid is then pressure injected into the ground through a drilled pipeline. The mixture reaches the end of the well where the high pressure causes the nearby shale rock to crack, creating fissures where natural gas flows into the well. During this process, methane gas and toxic chemicals leach out from the system and contaminate nearby groundwater. Methane concentrations are seventeen times higher in drinking-water wells near fracturing sites than in normal wells.

This contaminated well water is used for drinking water for nearby cities and towns. There have been over 1,000 documented cases of water contamination next to areas of gas drilling as well as cases of sensory, respiratory, and neurological damage due to ingested contaminated water. In Bradford County, Pennsylvania methane gas, a highly flammable gas has seeped into groundwater from fracking. Residents there can light their water with a match from the methane gas mixed with their drinking water. Many people have moved now that methane gas pockets have formed under and around their homes.

There are those who could argue that we need this oil and gas, and at the moment that is true, but at what price? Fracking is also blamed on the swarm earthquakes taking place in the United States. Evidence continues to mount that fracking for oil and gas has caused hundreds of swarm earthquakes in southwestern Oregon, Nevada, Texas, Oklahoma, Ohio, and Kansas recently. These earthquakes might be linked to oil and gas fracking, but there could be something far greater happening. While the quakes are far more often tied to disposal of drilling waste, scientists also increasingly have started pointing to the fracking process itself. Oklahoma Geological Survey seismologist Austin Holland stated to his colleagues that this has been happening more than they previously recognized. Currently, there are 500,000 active gas wells in the United States.

I believe, like indigenous people, that more than fracking is to blame for the swarm earthquakes—like deep core Earth movement, and probably for Earth's warming.

Pesticides and Herbicides

Scientists are baffled by the collapse of bee colonies worldwide. Scientists have been trying to discover why millions of beehives have collapsed and died during the past six years. Dozens of different types of chemicals may be combining to wreak havoc on the pollen that the bees collect for their hives.

Do we ask too much of animals and insects while forcing them to work for us? Are they rebelling? Animals are very concerned with the quality of life—much more so than humans. When the quality of life is in question, the animals automatically migrate toward a more sustaining reality. They remove themselves into other domains of existence, for they are programmed to survive.

As I have written, animals are intelligent and flexible and have many more adventures than humans do. Animals don't need to build shopping malls, graveyards, watch television, text on cell phones, watch movies, and distract themselves with these forms of entertainment. Do you think animals get bored? Do you think animals ever wonder what to do? They have many, many adventures that you are not quite capable of understanding, though you will one day, and at night when they dream, they enter other realities.

Insects are represented in greater numbers than any other class of animals on your planet, and they take up less space. They keep a balance, for without the insects our planet could not exist. Insects are multidimensional and act as unseen guardians for many worlds. As you demonstrate your acknowledgment of intelligence in all forms of life, you begin to qualify as an ambassador or diplomatic representative of these various species. Life will become very strange indeed.

In the coming years, the awakened ones will bring a magnificent new upliftment, a new way of being, and a new prayer to Earth Mother. Understand that there is great intelligence in all life forms, and the experience of all life is waiting for us in the Library of Earth. Open your emotional selves and employ the vital force of love as the key to your spiritual evolution.

Half of the one million animal and plant species on Earth facing extinction are insects, and their disappearance could be catastrophic for humankind, scientists have said in a "warning to humanity." "The current insect extinction crisis is deeply worrying," said Pedro Cardoso, a biologist at the Finnish Museum of Natural History and lead author of a review study published Monday, February 10, 2020.

The disappearance of bugs that fly, crawl, burrow, jump and walk on water is part of a gathering mass extinction event, only the sixth in the last half-billion years. The last one was 66 million years ago when an errant space rock wiped out land-based dinosaurs and most other life forms.

This time humans are to blame. "Human activity is responsible for almost all insect population declines and extinctions," Cardoso told AFP. The decline of butterflies, beetles, ants, bees, wasps, flies, crickets and dragonflies has consequences far beyond their own demise. "With insect extinction, we lose much more than species," Cardoso said.

"Many insect species are vital providers of services that are irreplaceable," including pollination, nutrient cycling and pest control.

Dying Water

Around our planet, even in remote islands, our precious water is being polluted by pesticides and fertilizers that flow into the rivers and into the oceans. The toxins create toxic blue-green algae, poisoning Earth's waters. Pesticides and fertilizers that run into rivers and then into the ocean are causing coral reef around the world to die, a process known as coral bleaching. The corals that form the structure of the great reef ecosystems of tropical seas depend upon a symbiotic relationship with algae-like unicellular protozoa that are photosynthetic within their tissues.

There is a fragile balance for the coral reefs of the world. The following can contribute to coral bleaching: herbicides, bacterial infections, cyanide fishing, silt runoff, mineral dust from African dust storms caused by drought and even sunscreen, non-biodegradable, washing off tourists swimming, snorkeling or diving.

Factories in the United States, China and throughout the world have toxic spills, and some of these toxins are intentionally dumped into rivers and lakes. In the documentary, River of Waste, the movie examines the potential hazards caused by factory farms in the United States, particularly by waste disposal. It shows how large-scale corporate farms use growth hormones that threaten human health and the future of our planet.

Some scientists have gone so far as to call the condemned current factory farm practices as "mini Chernobyl's." In the U.S. and elsewhere, the meat and poultry industry is dominated by dangerous uses of arsenic, antibiotics, growth hormones and by the dumping of massive amounts of sewage in fragile waterways and environments. The film documents the vast catastrophic impact on the environment and public health as well as focuses on the individual lives damaged and destroyed.

My friend and mentor, Western Shoshone spiritual leader Corbin Harney (1920-2007) had a vision of water becoming extremely polluted. Water spoke to him and said, "I'm going to look like water, but pretty soon nobody's going to use me. In some places, the water's already got chemicals in it, so much that they can't use it. And people are just continuing to put poison in that water.

"When I went to the coast, the ocean water there looked sad to me. The water is saying I need help. Water talks like we do. It breathes air like we do. It's hard to believe, but it does. Everything drinks water, and everything's got a life to it."

Corbin wanted us to know that everything will suffer as our waters die. He believed that the Redskin People had a chance to survive because they are connected to what's out there. It is their prayers, he believed, that would help the water to continue to flow cleaner and purer.

Corbin was not a fatalist—he believed that if we unified in a common cause for the upliftment of Mother Earth, we could heal our waters and the entire planet, but it would take hard work and prayers to turn things around.

The Ancient Ones told humanity that it is our job to care for Mother Earth's creatures and all the kingdoms of nature, according to the indigenous Thirteen Grandmothers. In the creation myths handed down from generation to generation, it is said that in the beginning, wisdom and knowledge were gained from the animals, because the Creator did not speak to humans. The Ancient Ones observed all the kingdoms of nature—the stars, Grandfather Sun, Grandmother Moon. Everything on Earth has a purpose and consciousness and was needed to balance the planet, they believed. For every disease, there is a plant spirit to cure it.

Grandmother Agnes Baker Pilgrim, world-renowned spiritual leader and Keeper of the Sacred Salmon Ceremony for her people, reminds us, "If we don't take care of our animal kingdom, we ourselves are dying faster than we think."

Grandmother Agnes Baker Pilgrim says, "We forget that everything comes from Mother Earth, even the clothes on our backs. We are in denial about what we are doing. We must see ourselves in the whole context. We all breathe the same air. Let's make it clean and healthy."

The Grandmothers tell us that the Ancient Ones, their ancestors, revered the Earth and used ritual and gratitude to sustain Earth's balance. It is important to reclaim that reverence and holiness. It is time to go back to appreciation and respect for Earth Mother and all we have or there will be nothing left to appreciate. Every living thing on planet Earth has a reason to be here—it's the perfect order of the Universe. That is our spiritual lesson.

Now, something is threatening the West Coast of the Pacific Ocean. Tens of millions of voracious purple sea urchins that have already chomped their way through towering underwater kelp forests in California are spreading north to Oregon, sending the delicate marine ecosystem off the shore into such disarray that other critical species are starving to death.

A recent count found 350 million purple sea urchins on one Oregon reef alone—more than a 10,000% increase since 2014. And in Northern California, 90% of the giant bull kelp forests have been devoured by the urchins, perhaps never to return.

Hundreds of the spiny creatures have spread to coastal Oregon, where kelp forests were once so thick it was impossible to navigate some areas by boat.

The underwater annihilation is killing off important fisheries for red abalone and red sea urchins and creating such havoc that scientists in California are partnering with a private business to collect the over-abundant purple urchins and "ranch" them in a controlled environment for ultimate sale to a global seafood market. The explosion of purple sea urchins is the latest symptom of a Pacific Northwest marine ecosystem that's out of whack. Kelp has been struggling because of warmer-than-usual waters in the Pacific Ocean. And, in 2013, a mysterious disease began wiping out tens of millions of starfish, including a species called the sunflower sea star that is the only real predator of the ultra-hardy purple urchin. Around the same time, the purple urchins had two excellent breeding years— and with no predators, those gametes grew up and are now eating everything in sight.

The devastation is also economic: Until now, red abalone and red sea urchins, a larger and meatier species of urchin, supported a thriving commercial fishery in both states. But 96% of red abalone has disappeared from California's northern coast as the number of purple sea urchins increase six-fold, according to a study released this week by the University of California, Davis.

There is a bright side to this ecological disaster. Conservationists, commercial urchin harvesters, scientists and private interests are coming together with an unusual plan: Pay underemployed red sea urchin divers to collect the shriveled, but living, purple sea urchins and transfer them to carefully tended urchin "ranches" to be fattened up for sale to seafood markets around the world.

The warnings continue from scientists, environmentalists, Native Americans, Indigenous people worldwide and the Star Beings, and yet humans remain complacent about the threat to our planet's balance and health. What will it take to awaken us from our coma, and take drastic action for global healing? A small ripple in a pond can grow into a huge wave with everyone doing their part to change what could be a disaster. There are evolved beings that want to raise our consciousness, heal our collective karmas, and solve the many problems encounters or caused by our evolutionary course or lack thereof. We are always allowed to shift our consciousness to higher levels of spiritual growth.

You see, every soul is offered the chance to evolve, learn, heal, and grow. Right now if we continue on this dire course, a planetary disaster will take place and there will be no recourse. This is a crucial turning point in this timeline that could compromise or even abort the soul evolution in this world we share with many sentient beings, some that remain invisible to humans.

Unless your collective consciousness returns to a peaceful spiritual civilization of the Soul, you and the millions of souls on Earth might become one more on a long list of extinct species that have destroyed themselves or their planet. Mars is a reminder of one civilization that did just that! This happens more often than I can tell you.

But there will be superior beings who will help a planet evolve by seeded it again. That's how life continues in the cosmos.

Medicine Grizzly Bear's vision from 1990-1993

"On several different occasions, I was given a new vision while praying and meditating in our sacred sweat lodge ceremonies. I have had the same vision three different times, in three different parts of the country. I did not seek these visions, they came on their own accord, and sometimes vague in symbolism and content. I received the vision for a fourth and final time while during a sweat lodge ceremony at Mt. Shasta, this time the vision was very vivid. I can't tell you all of it, but I will tell you what it meant: I saw the Earth tilt twice, first to the west toward the Pacific Ocean, then it wobbled, and major disasters beyond the human imagination occurred; this activity was followed by fierce winds raging across the Earth. Shortly afterward, the Earth then tilted towards the east, toward the Atlantic Ocean, with people, animals, cars, buildings, factories, cities and everything in nature started sliding into the ocean. It was disastrous beyond imagination, with large chunks of the continent being swallowed by the ocean. Several times, both on the west coast, then on the East Coast, the ocean backed up, rose into the air, and like a giant hand, rushed toward the continent and grabbed masses of land. Then once again, fierce winds raged across the earth destroying everything upon the surface that wasn't hidden underground, or blocked by a natural mountain range. The Earth wobbled, and then finally settled. In the vision I desperately looked for a newspaper, something to give me a date; I saw 2012 on the headlines.

"Our Native Elders teach us that the Universe and Nature operates according to a definite system of laws. The laws are both spiritual and physical. To start from the Western frame of reference, for example, the Law of Physics states: For every action, there is a reaction. This reaction can be positive or negative. Our Native Elders have also taught us that another principle to live by the Law of Reciprocity: "don't take anything without giving something in return, be it plant or herb for healing, animals while hunting, fish for subsistence and ceremony; or food, water, and resources needed for subsistence or ceremony; or when praying and requesting help.

"Otherwise, the Circle is broken; the resources become depleted. Everything in Nature has its own spirit, in addition to being connected to the Great Spirit; therefore, our Native Elders have counseled us to always show Respect. This is another ancient Law; in other words, provide payment, offer a gift or donation, have a give-away, in exchange for the privilege of receiving something we need. In the traditional Native way, we always show respect by offering tobacco and/or food to the Creator, Nature, the Spirits, and our ancestors before taking the life force and spirit of any living thing; and we practice conservation and cleanliness as part of this philosophy. This philosophy is based upon the symbolic power, meaning, and purpose of the Circle: Life is sacred and holy, always approach it with respect, because what goes around comes around, be it positive or negative.

"We just can't keep taking without giving something back to the circle, otherwise, we destroy ourselves. In conclusion, it appears that humankind has forgotten the fact that this Mother Earth and the entire Universe is a Great Circle. They have forgotten or decided to ignore the ancient laws of Nature and the Universe, or what some cultures and religions even call the Great Creator's Laws. They have become too greedy, too selfish, and too far removed from Nature. As a result, humankind has created its own problem. We have created our own sickness. So the answer to the question, "why?" should be self-evident. Nature goes through cycles; the "Great Purification" as some Native spiritual leaders and prophets call it, is just another part of the universal cycle. Some will survive in the cycle, and others will not. Whether it is a form of punishment from a wrathful God, or from aggravated spirits and forces of Nature, or if it comes about simply as a negative physical and spiritual reaction according to natural law... is all a matter of one's perception, beliefs, and concept of reality.

What can people do to prepare for the potential purification? The Native Elders offer the following advice. "First of all, we as human beings must begin to individually and collectively take responsibility for our negative thoughts and actions against this Earth. We must begin to clean up the mess we have made and try to restore those things that have become polluted, damaged, or depleted. We must learn to assume responsibility for our actions, and try to put political pressure on industries, the governments, communities, and individuals to help find ways to clean up the pollution and destruction now being made by so-called civilization and technological advancement. We should begin to purify our mind, body, and soul by use of the ancient rituals and ceremonies that, since time immemorial, have been done with the Earth, and according to sacred laws and natural cycles. It is now time to give back to the Earth to do healing ceremonies for the Earth and to pray for and help each other. And the Elders further advice, perhaps we should begin to prepare for survival, by helping each other prepare for the Great Purification; let the rich help the poor, let the wise help the ignorant, let those who have plenty share with the poor. And this approach must be done with a good heart and in a spiritual way.

"As for the Native American people, our Elders advise: We are the original caretakers of this land. Bring back your sacred dances, rituals, and ceremonies. Perform the religious activities with cleanliness and according to traditional custom and law: No alcohol, no drugs, abstain from sex, and do not record or photograph these activities, and do not sell the religion for profit; otherwise, it will not be spiritual. The sacred dances and ceremonies are the tools and knowledge that was originally given to us, in the Beginning, to help keep the world in balance.

"As for the non-Indians, the advice of the Elders is: "IN ORDER TO CARRY OUT OUR SACRED DUTIES AND RESPONSIBILITIES AS CARETAKERS OF THIS LAND, WE NEED PROTECTION, PRESERVATION, AND PROPER USE OF OUR SACRED SITES, POWER CENTERS, TRADITIONAL RELIGION, AND CULTURE. IT IS FROM SUCH HOLY PLACES WHERE WE GET THE KNOWLEDGE, POWER, AND RESOURCES NEEDED TO HELP HEAL THIS EARTH AND EACH OTHER.

"The sacred sites and holy places, (in many different parts of the world, for many different races and cultures of humankind were put upon this Earth by the Great Creator, for a purpose and reason, such as for keeping the Earth in balance; and as a means for dealing with certain potential natural disasters and diseases in a spiritual way. Thus, another way concerned people can help prepare for the alleged Great Purification and potential predictions is to help the Native American people with their aboriginal and legal rights: Make your governments sanction and honor the American Indian Religious Freedom Act (PL9S-341), make your government, large corporations, exploiters, and tourists leave the sacred sites alone, and help support the traditional Native healers and ceremonial leaders so they can have the respect and resources they need to help the people and this country during the forthcoming Earth Changes and difficult times. Nobody knows this Earth better than they do; and without their unique knowledge, power, and abilities it will be difficult for anyone to survive into the future. History has already proven that fact in many cultures."

Chapter Fifteen
PRESIDENT DONALD J. TRUMP

At solar noon Eastern Time on January 20, 1017, Donald J. Trump, a business tycoon, and television personality, took the oath of Presidency as the 45th President of the United States. He will be the oldest president to ever hold the office of U.S. President at age 70 (Ronald Reagan was 69).

I felt January of 2016 that Donald Trump would most likely be the Republican candidate for President. By April of 2016, I predicted Donald Trump would be elected the 45th President of the United States on November 8, 2016, after experiencing a powerful vision of him taking the oath of Presidency on a cold, but a clear day on January 20, 2017, wearing a dark or black wool coat and Melania, his wife, wearing a light-colored coat.

My next confirmation was calculated by Trump's numerology. I used the title—PRESIDENT TRUMP, which totals 72 and 7+2=9. And because he would become our 45th President (4 +5 = 9), I sensed this was another sign that he would win the election.

Our 45th President of the United States Donald Trump was born on June 14, 1946, at 10:54 a.m. (some say at 9:51 am, but I'll go with the 10:54 am) in Queens, New York. He was born on a lunar eclipse which is the most dramatic spectacles in the heavens. An eclipse is one of the most powerful horoscopes any person can have.

Trump was born under an angular full moon eclipse with the Sun in tight triple conjunction with Uranus and the Node at the top of the chart—an empowering, rare and fateful alignment. At birth, the eclipse will last for your entire life—this affects the career orientation of Donald Trump.

First, let's consider that his Gemini sun eclipses his Sagittarius moon. The moon is our emotions. When emotions are hidden from the solar light, they can intensify "until they are forced to emerge through some kind of confrontation." Having Uranus conjunct the Sun encourages radical and sometimes childish behavior, and opposite the Moon makes personal relationships difficult. Uranian people tend to dislike following the lead of others and prefer to create their own way.

Trump has plenty of Leo in his chart—Leo Rising, Mars in Leo and Pluto in Leo. Leo can be driven to do admirable works, but his Moon in Sagittarius allows him to say whatever comes to mind. He just can't help himself. What's worse is that Trump's Leo tendencies are exacerbated by Mars, which is also in Leo. Oddly, there are no planets in Earth elements in Trump's birth chart which might explain why he doesn't see Earth's environmental needs. It also explains why he's all "fire and air"—energy, enthusiasm, verbose and full of ideas.

His Leo rising reflects his need to shine in the spotlight and be admired. At its best, Leo is driven to do admirable and important works that will gain him public recognition, but there's always a negative side. Statements by Trump such as, "I'm very rich" and "no one builds better than me" are examples of Leo gone wrong— the desperate need for attention taken to its extreme.

This tendency for self-aggrandizement is increased by the presence of Mars (planet of aggression) which is also in Leo, intensifying that need for attention, right on the ascendant where it becomes the projection of the personality. It's Mars which we see when Trump makes off-colored remarks and pushes his way through business dealings and at the presidential debates.

Trump also has a lot of Cancer in his chart. His Venus is in Cancer; his Saturn is in Cancer and his Mercury. His Achilles heel is in his relationships. With three planets in the emotional and family-oriented sign of Cancer, he has lots of sensitivity for those he loves. Cancer loves his home and family. His Mercury (mind) in Cancer reflects his emotionality when speaking and reacting to the words of others. Cancer is very intuitive and caring, although he may not show the tender side because of all the Leo in his chart. His Venus in Cancer reveals his desire to nurture and care for those he loves, which we can see in his relationship with his children, most of whom work with him in one way or another. Marriage has been tricky for Trump which isn't surprising with Saturn (tests and challenges) conjunct Venus (relationships) and Chiron (wounding and healing) in Venus-ruled Libra. I'm not sure that Melania will stay married to him forever—she's too sensitive, especially with his extramarital affairs in the past.

Although Donald Trump was given positive astrological placements in his birth chart and positive numbers in his birth date, he was given free-will to do what he wants in life—like all of us. We each have many roads to choose from. The problem is Trump doesn't want to listen to others! He's always gotten his own way since childhood and nothing will change that. He is extremely stubborn.

Donald Trump's Astrology

Trump's progressed Midheaven, revealed the evolution of his career path, moved from sensitive Cancer into Leo in March of 2016. This would have encouraged him to seek a greater role in the public eye, and right on schedule when he announced his candidacy for President in June of 2016.

Capella is his Star and grants him an energetic nature, inquisitiveness, and a love of learning. It imparts honor and prominent positions of trust. It also shows that Trump would acquire wealth and success in his life, and shows a pronounced tendency to be verbose and too talkative (that's an understatement!). Capella advises him to learn to listen to others to avoid misunder-understandings.

Donald Trump's Astrology

Sun is in 22 Degrees Gemini. Rising Sign is 29 Degrees Leo
Moon is in 21 Degrees Sagittarius. Mercury is 08 Degrees Cancer.
Venus is in 25 Degrees Cancer. Mars is 26 Degrees Leo.
Jupiter is in 17 Degrees Libra. Saturn is 23 Degrees Cancer.
Uranus is in 17 Degrees Gemini. Neptune is 05 Degrees Libra.
Pluto is 10 Degrees Leo.
N. Node is 20 Degrees Gemini.

Donald Trump's Numerology

Please note that I do not use the conventional way of calculating a birth number. I find this is much more accurate in my readings.

Example of Trump's birthdate: June 14, 1946

1946 + 14 + 6 1966 and this number totals 22, reduced to single-digit 4.

Donald Trump's birthdate 6-14-46 totals the master number 22, which means the Master Builder, dreams made manifest, ancient wisdom, realization, force of nature, the future, evolution, technology, Universal Love, God, retribution, redemption, love, war, leader, the Universe, personal power, charisma, service, the Divine imagination, idealist, expansive, visionary, government, Universal transformation, philanthropy, common sense, practicality. This is the 'God' energy brought to the material plane and put into form, and this vibration holds with it a great deal of responsibility. Because of its great power, the number 22 may result in outstanding ascendancy or disastrous downfall. The 22 can turn the most ambitious of dreams into reality and is potentially the most successful of all numbers.

Number 22 is the teacher and has chosen to reincarnate at this period in time. Destiny or Life Path 22s is the master builder. Whatever a 22 person thinks about is almost sure to manifest so they need to choose their thoughts carefully. If they are willing to work for what they desire they can achieve enormous prestige, success, and fame. And that's what Donald Trump has done.

Twenty-two number people are the most capable of the Life Path numbers and are endowed with many powers. They have a unique talent for manifesting ideas into the realm of reality. Sometimes they display what looks like insensitivity, but actually, they are very focused upon their goals. This is part of a spiritual directive to be detached from objects and the outcome of events. Many of them work for material gain, with the idea that their wealth should be spread among the masses.

Major attempts will be made to find a balance between the need to be self-sufficient and the need to honor debts of social commitment. Trump's innate restlessness and constant lack of satisfaction will inspire him to make huge and sometimes hasty changes during his term as President, especially in the world of finance and politics. Again, the year 2020 will be a roller coaster ride for him. The Democrats won't stop with their accusations and trying to have him removed as President.

Prophet Kim Clement on Donald Trump

In 2007, a modern prophet named Kim Clement predicted Donald Trump would win the election, and Hillary Clinton would lose. Kim Clement died in November of 2016 at the age of sixty. Clement, long before anyone was taking Trump seriously as a presidential candidate, not only predicted his successful bid for the White House, he also says he is God's choice and will become known as a "prayerful president."

So far this is true. President-elect Donald Trump set a record with the number of prayers during his inaugural ceremony.

"Trump shall become a trumpet, says the Lord," the South African Clement bellowed in a recording reportedly made April 4, 2007, in Redding, California. Clement went on to say, or sing, accompanied by his ever-present keyboard: "It shall come to pass that the man I place in the highest office shall go in whispering my name. But God said, when he enters into office, he will be shouting out by the power of the spirit. For I shall fill him with my spirit when he goes into office and there will be a praying man in the highest seat in your land."

2020 Prophecies and Predictions

He said something similar, according to the recording, on Feb. 10, 2007: "There will be a praying president, not a religious one, for I will fool the people, says the Lord. I will fool the people, yes I will, God says, the one that is chosen shall go in and they shall say, 'He has hot blood.' For the spirit of God says, yes, he may have hot blood, but he will bring the walls of protection on this country in a greater way and the economy of this country shall change rapidly, says the Lord of hosts."

"Listen to the word of the Lord, God says, I will put at your helm for two terms a president that will pray, but he will not be a praying president when he starts," Clement continued. "I will put him in office and then I will baptize him with the Holy Spirit and my power, says the Lord of hosts."

Dated April 4, 2007, a "prophecy" from Clement cites an "invasion" of news media and states: "For God said, I am not going to yesterday to bring the past back into existence, but I am moving into the future and bringing it into existence. For this nation shall once again pioneer the greatest move of the Spirit that has ever happened, says the Lord. And you are alive; you are alive in the midst of it!"

His specific citations of Trump follow: "The Spirit of God said, this is a moment of resurrection. For the Spirit of God says, honor Me with your praise and acceptance of this that I say to you. This that shall take place shall be the most unusual thing, a transfiguration, a going into the marketplace if you wish, into the news media. Where Time Magazine will have no choice but to say what I want them to say. Newsweek, what I want to say. 'The View,' what I want to say. Trump shall become a trumpet, says the Lord! I will raise up the Trump to become a trumpet and Bill Gates to open up the gate of a financial realm for the Church, says the Spirit of the Living God!"

Trump is referenced one more time in the Clement archive of prophecies, from June 27, 2015. He said God said, "Not at his time," referring to a crash to cripple America. You have been besieged for seven years, America. You have been surrounded by your internal enemies. Haters of America have stood up and then they have said there are those in the church that are anti-Israel. I say to you that there are many but there are many more that are in the church that is anti-America and anti what I am going to do in this nation. I will give you a president that shall bring some ease to your debt challenges and I will take the wealth of the wicked and for a season transfer it into the hands of the righteous and those who have given and poured out their blessing into My land and to My people, says the Lord."

In 2019, the Stock Market revealed it was "Highest Stock Market EVER recorded, best economic numbers in years, and unemployment was the lowest in 17 years

Clement said this, "Then we went to the Trump Tower because naughty Donald Trump is going to be put into a difficult position in a few weeks. But that's OK, we pray for him, too."

His message seemed to refer to the lewd conversation about women that Donald Trump had with Billy Bush in 2005 on a bus before his interview on Access Hollywood. Although Trump's words were lewd and disrespectful of women, the voters forgave him while Hollywood berated him. Those who made the loudest protest were the biggest hypocrites—many had sordid pasts.

Jesus reminded us in John 8:7 when a woman was caught in adultery, he bent down and began to write on the ground with his finger. "When they [the people] continued to question Him, He straightened up and said to them, "Whoever is without sin among you, let him be the first to cast a stone at her."

Sinners can become Saints. Some examples are well known. St. Paul was responsible for the murder of many early Christians before his dramatic conversion experience on the road to Damascus. And St. Augustine of Hippo led a life of arrogant pride and sexual immorality before offering his mind, heart and soul to God, thanks in part to the Letters of St. Paul and the prayers of his mother, St. Monica. Of course, Donald Trump has never harmed anyone physically, but his sin is his bombastic rhetoric and ego.

Kim Clement had a television show on the Christian network TBN until he became ill in 2015. He died of complications related to pneumonia shortly after Trump's victory on November 8, 2016. Born in 1956 in South Africa, Clement became addicted to heroin at the age of 17. His biography says he was overdosing on the drug in a bathroom bar when he was robbed and stabbed. He stumbled out into the street, fell in a ditch and felt he was dying when he cried out the name of Jesus.

He said, "I remembered then what an Anglican minister had said to me when I was 9 years old," he recalled in his testimony. "He said, 'Jesus walks the streets still today. One day you will need him, just call on him and he will touch you.'"

While in the ditch, he recalled, a hand reached out and lifted him up, a hand belonging to a Christian man who carried Clement to his car and drove him to a hospital. Clement then became a follower of Jesus and worked as music director, youth pastor and drug rehab counselor.

Clement also predicted that Donald Trump would serve two terms in office as the 45th President of the United States.

At this time, timelines are changing quickly and events can be changed. As I wrote earlier, the Democrats will vote to impeach Trump before Christmas for his Ukraine transgression to learn more about Presidential candidate Joe Biden, who has much to hide, and for threatening to withhold aid to Ukraine if they didn't help investigate Biden and his son Hunter, an attorney, who oddly, quit his job for Ukraine's largest natural gas company shortly after the investigation began with Trump. More will be revealed in 2020 about the Biden's relationship with Ukraine. There is more to the story!

Donald Trump's numerology number for **2020 is 6**. Six is the number of duty, responsibility, and justice.

Uri Geller's Prediction for Trump

World-famous psychokinetic spoon-bender and paranormalist Uri Geller tweeted the world in September 2016 that Donald Trump would win the election because — he has 11 letters in his name.

Geller's simple reasoning is that "11 is a very powerful mystical number." He wrote this about the following president all had 11 letters in their names.

- Barack Obama: 11 letters
- George W. Bush: 11 letters
- Jimmy Carter: 11 letters
- John Kennedy: 11 letters
- Bill Clinton: 11 letters
- Donald Trump: 11 letters

Joe Biden's birth name is Joseph Biden which also contains 11 letters, but this is an eight-year for him and eight will be a karmic year for him. Number 8 in numerology is the law of 'cause and effect' and he will receive exactly what he deserves depending on how he has lived his life. Joe Biden has shown a very peculiar habit of touching women and young girls without their permission. This has already come back to haunt him. There is something he and his son Hunter Biden are hiding that will also be uncovered in 2020 before the Presidential election and their involvement in Ukraine.

Geller noted that other historical figures with names having 11 letters include Anthony Blair, Nostradamus, Pope Francis, Colin Powell and, yes, Jesus Christ.

Trump impeached by Congress but not Senate on Wednesday, December 18, 2019, by the mostly Democratic Congress who voted and approved to impeach President Donald Trump. The future of the House's impeachment case against President Trump hung in doubt on Thursday, December 19, 2019, when House Speaker Nancy Pelosi, Democrat from California, said she will withhold the articles from the Senate if they do not get assurances of a fair trial.

I was stunned to learn that a great many people in the United States believed Trump was gone from office and Pence was our current President. Did anyone study government in school?

With Congress and the Senate coming to an impasse, nothing will happen until they reconvene in January 2020 after the holidays. I have never seen such bad behavior in adults, who behave worse than children. It has become an utter fiasco! House Democrats kept switching the offenses they claimed merited kicking Trump out of the Oval Office, ditching the bipartisan spirit they once considered essential. They tried to kick him out Russia, but Mueller's report did not find any collusion. Angered, they continued to dig until they found something else.

Even if the House of Representatives decides to pass the articles to the Senate, which is not a given at this time if they continue to hold out, and I believe they will, the damage from the game playing and wavering has been done.

Polls say the majority of voters what Trump removed from office, but like 2016, I didn't trust the polls that Hillary was leading in the Presidential race. If you read the poll articles usually 1,500 people are questioned. How can that be a majority of voters? The census taken in 2018 puts 327.8 million people residing in the United States, and 235,248,000 people were eligible to vote.

The Democrats will find that their fiasco of impeachment will have backfired on them in the 2020 polls. People are tired of the feuding in our government and will re-elect Trump in 2020.

UPDATE: As I predicted, President Trump was acquitted on February 5, 2020 by the Senate. After five months of hearings, investigations and revelations about President Trump's dealings with Ukraine, a divided United States Senate acquitted him on Wednesday of charges that he abused his power and obstructed Congress to aid his own re-election, bringing an acrimonious impeachment trial to its expected end.

Chapter Sixteen
BETSEY'S PREDICTIONS

My heart is heavy by the negative events that continue to escalate in our world—the disrespect of all life and our disconnect with each other and nature. In all the years I've lived on Mother Earth, I never could have imagined that our world would be so out of balance.

But there is hope. Most prophecies by the prophets and indigenous elders tell us that events can be altered and Earth changes can be lessened if we unite in prayer and if we take action against Black Elk's blue man (the Family of Dark) who is set on destroying our beautiful and unique planet through greed.

The truth is that there are multiple levels of activity going on behind what appears to be a play of incredible magnitude. Who is writing the lines—humanity! Together we are writing the lines and until we can figure out a point to the script, there is none. There is a focused group that has decided they would like to put forth their point in the script. There is just one problem with this, what they plan for us is not in harmony with the Creator. In fact, the plan this group has in mind has a great surprise—they intend to destroy the audience, the actors, the state and the theatre. Creator of All and benevolent beings are hoping that we, the audience, will come up with some other solution. If a new storyline is introduced with new characters then there will be a new ending, and the script will change into a love story rather than a tragedy.

This I know—we are about to witness incredible events never seen before, greater than we can imagine. Many parallel worlds exist with our own, worlds that sometimes merge into our reality. There are just too many stories of people jumping into past and future timelines. Many cataclysmic events prophesied in the last century by visionaries may or may not happen as timelines are altered by human intervention and by unseen celestial beings. We have free will and we have the power to change probable events and timelines headed our way when it comes or lessen the outcome.

We can no longer deny the frequency of Earth changes with super earthquakes 7.0 to 9.1 in the past ten years, volcanoes rumbling to life, sinkholes forming throughout the world, extreme weather and temperatures breaking records, hurricanes and tornadoes more powerful than we have ever recorded, birds dropping dead in the sky, millions of dead fish washing up on shores, and now we have space debris in the form of asteroids, fireballs, and meteors coming into Earth's atmosphere. Even comets nearing Earth in the past few years have increased. The planet's creatures are aware something is happening, for they are linked to our energy grid and hold the balance of our planet.

On February 19, 2013, a 'superpod' of thousands of dolphins spanning seven miles were spotted and filmed by tourists off the coast of southern California. Marine biologists call it an incredibly rare sight as thousands, or possibly even tens of thousands, of dolphins, swarmed together off the coast of San Diego, California. Also, whales have shown up off the Southern California coast in great numbers lately. Why? Are they sensing something happening deep within the Earth or did they sense the incoming meteor that hit Russia on Feb. 15, 2013, at 9:20 AM local Russian time, which was 7:20 pm Pacific time, the day thousands of dolphins gathered off the coast of California.

Mother Earth and animals are here to warn us, if we trust the, ad pay attention to what they are communicating. Animals and sea creature are connected to Mother Earth in ways we can't even imagine. It's is so important my teachers have said that we reconnect with Mother Earth and all life on this planet. But not only connect but show reverence! Mother Earth is a sentient being, and she's struggling to survive like all sentient beings do when faced with death, and she will do what is necessary to awaken us so that she can survive the horrible poisons we are putting into her daily.

We must realize that our planet has always had a violent past— volcanic eruptions, tectonic Earth movement, and massive glaciers that covered continents. The question is whether or not it can happen again? If my recurring dreams of violent Earth changes as a child were more than screen memories of the past, but true precognitive visions of our times now, then we are just beginning to see events unfolding.

It's evitable that Earth will experience mega changes in the near future and perhaps even a solar event if my premonitions are right. So what can we do? Trust your intuition, trust your heart and listen to Mother Earth and her warnings. Also, prepare for any disaster. Take time to visualize another outcome, meditate, intend, pray, and ask your Angels and Mother Earth to guide you to safe areas.

When humans honor life as the number one priority in their lives, there will be fewer Earth changes for our planet. But sadly, our monkey minds are more concerned now with electronic devices, how much food we can consume, the cars we drive, and what clothes we wear. If we, as a species, don't lift our values to Mother Earth, the sentient being that gives us life, then she will reach for her own higher frequency and bring about a cleansing that will bring about balance again. What happens in the next few years depends on us and how willing we are to change, to make a commitment to honor all living creatures and Earth, to find ways to heal Earth and love her. It's time to honor all life!

People have said our Mother Earth can heal herself and that was true in the distant past, but never in the history of our planet has over 7.8 billion people been using up all her natural resources at such an alarming rate. Not only are we using up natural resources, but polluting everything. How can poor Mother Earth compete with human abuse? She can't! More than one hundred years ago we didn't have all the technology we have now to cause such destruction in such a short time.

As the abductee Betty Andreasson Luca was told by the ETs— we are destroying ourselves with poisons and we will become sterile, and that's why they are created a new being from our DNA.

We make have a fraction of time to save our planet but time is quickly running out. We can make a difference if we unite. How one person can make a difference? Well, when two or more are gathered miracles do happen. His Holiness the Dalai Lama said it best, "If you think you're too small to make a difference, try sleeping with a mosquito."

Do not dwell on the events coming our way, but instead focus on a positive new world coming. When we come together in love and one heart-healing Earth, we create a "Prime Event" where we shift timelines. Communicate with Earth, listen to her, observe her and talk to her, and uncover ancient wisdom also known as the Living Library. There are many secrets held by Mother Earth, the Living Library, waiting for us to unravel if we take the time to acknowledge them.

Edgar Cayce, (1877-1945) known as the "Sleeping Prophet," gave thousands of trance readings on Atlantis, ancient Egypt, Earth changes and diagnosed illnesses for people, sometimes miles away. He said that a great many souls on Earth now once lived in ancient Atlantis and we have returned to learn lessons about the destructive powers of technology. If we don't learn those lessons this time we could be headed to disaster again.

So we must awaken and makes changes. There's no time to waste and sit back and be "spiritual couch potatoes." Each of us has to take up the responsibility for what is happening in our world and change our views about ourselves and our world and the reality we live in.

Remember our world is frequencies and in this timeline, frequencies are being lowered by the Family of Dark through toxic food, electrical devices, alcohol, drugs, television shows and movies on violence, sex, and the dark occult. Cellular frequency is affecting human sleep, our thinking and blocking our psychic ability. It's also harming animals, birds, sea creatures and all life.

We have been programmed as a species to believe we are powerless by the news, television and educational system. We are led to believe that we create reality some of the time, when in fact, we create reality all the time! When you dream—dream big, create a new world and new timeline. Believe nothing is impossible!

Also, remember that much of what is going on in our skies are 3-D holographic images—duping us. It is important to know what is real and what isn't. Holographic technology has been around for years and has advanced in ways you can't imagine.

Be mindful of this and what the Church or any other world organization or leaders announce about extraterrestrials and UFOs. What is behind their agenda? Are there more plans for our total control? Unless we awaken and change the path we are headed down, there are dire responsibilities to be faced. Granted we have been lulled into a zombie-like existence, but that's each and everyone's personal choice. Think of the events on our planet as a play and nothing more. We are like actors on a huge stage (Earth), and so how will you change the ending of the play—will the hero Luke Skywalker win or the antagonist Darth Vader take over? In order to change the play, you must rewrite the lines and unite with like-minded actors. No matter how evil things seem, keep in mind the Creator of All will not allow the dark forces to carry out their twisted plan. However, there are lessons to be learned by all souls presently on this planet. You choose to be here now and make a difference.

In 2020, a great number of souls will be born. They will of a higher frequency. These souls must be nurtured by loving and caring parents who can teach them about spiritual laws and most of all they need love. These children will be smarter, more intuitive with will have supernatural abilities. I'd like to think that the parents of these new souls will be prepared to help them understand their powers and gifts so that they can make major changes in our world. Sadly, schools are archaic in what they teach. Perhaps it will take a great cleansing for us to have an epiphany about how life should be lived and honored on our precious planet.

Most of us are so charged by electronics we find ourselves restless, fidgeting and twitching in our bodies, unable to integrate the energy. We need to detoxify our bodies to rise to the new frequencies.

To escape all the intense electronic energies happening on our planet at this time, connect to nature as much as possible by visiting the mountains, rivers, lakes, or ocean, any place that has negative-charged ions (positive-charged ions cause irritability and anxiety). Take time to quiet your thoughts and visualize a new world of integrity and beauty. It is up to each and everyone one of us to create a new world of peace and harmony, but it will take a great number of us coming as one mind to create this new world and timeline.

If our planet shifts, as many prophets have foreseen, it is of great importance to lift up our bodies to the new frequency. Remember our bodies mirror what is happening to our beloved planet—everything is a mirror and we are connected to this living planet. So it is important at this time that we honor our bodies with nutritious foods that raise our vibration level to help the planet in her need to heal. The normal vibratory rate of a human body has been determined to be between 62 and 68 MHz. The brain functions optimally between 72 and 90 MHz. When we are ill and catch a cold our body drops to 58 MHZ, 57 MHz the flu; 42 MHz cancer and at 25 MHz death begins. The good news is that as we awaken from our deep slumber and critical mass takes place this will uplift the planetary consciousness.

A shift is needed to cleanse the planet's surface and the astral planes that carry lower vibrations and dark entities. These dark entities have been here for eons and it's time to heal them along with our physical planet. People now are experiencing strange things with their bodies—lack of sleep, headaches (sometimes related to Earthquake and core movement), nausea and dizziness. These symptoms will escalate as our planet continues her struggle to survive and reach a higher vibrational frequency. We are also trying to escape radio waves sent through our planet by military and phone companies competing for our cellular business. Already these waves are affecting birds and other species. And I have no doubt it's affecting humans in a long list of negative ways.

5G cellular technology represents a massive upscale of network technology. It will provide data transfer rates many times faster than a blink of an eye, high bandwidth and greater opportunities for connectivity and reliability. Some 5G pundits contend that the new network generates radiofrequency radiation that can damage DNA and lead to cancer; cause oxidative damage that can cause premature aging; disrupt cell metabolism; and potentially lead to other diseases through the generation of stress proteins

It is important to remember is to have empathy for those who are frightened or skeptical about events taking place now. Those of you who are courageous, become ambassadors of light and show the fearful ones the way. As we move further into these times and begin to human-up there will be a heightened sense of love and compassion for all life and our planet. The old karmic patterns will be broken. Doors once veiled to us will suddenly open.

It's an exciting time to be alive, for us to learn and experience what our Mother Earth represents to us, even if it means many lives vanishing in the blink of an eye. Those souls will return with the remembrance of these lessons which will be forever embedded in their higher consciousness. A new world can then continue with the new Children of Light and their vision of a New Earth.

5g technology spread the Coronavirus worldwide

Dr. Thomas Cowan, M.D. hypothesizes that Coronavirus may be history repeating itself like the Spanish Flu of 1917-1918 and caused by 5G. It makes sense how our technology can disrupt the frequencies of our bodies! Just think what we've done to whales and dolphins with SONAR. I have written how we are **electrical beings** and everything in our world has a frequency. Now, 5G and thousands of satellites orbiting our planet are zapping us of our fragile frequencies. Thanks for nothing, Elon Musk, and your 100,000 PLUS satellites! The normal vibratory rate of a human body has been determined to be between 62 and 68 MHz (**megahertz**). The brain functions at 72 and 90 MHz. Death begins at 25 MHz.

Many of us are beginning to realize that we agreed before we came into our physical bodies that we'd come together at a certain time to bring light and love onto this planet and usher in a Golden Age. Others have forgotten and some have a feeling they are missing something in their lives, like an inkling of a long-lost dream, that there is a reason for us to be on here now. In either case, on one level or another, we are experiencing monumental changes in our consciousness and our physical bodies. Those knowing souls and the "New Children" born in the past 20 years will continue to raise the vibrational rate of Earth. This is what is being remembered at this time, and it will bring the Golden age into manifestation.

Earthkeepers come from the future as well, and they can help us access who we'll become as humans thousands of years from now. The Laika people of the Amazon know that the future has an infinite number of possibilities since everything yet to come is potential. That's why Earthkeepers like the Hopi, Maya, Inca, and many other indigenous tribes gather regularly to pray peace on the planet.

So which future will we create—a dying planet filled with hopelessness, despair, and hate, or a planet filled with love, balance, peace, and hope? The choice is ours. When we discover that we're dreaming of the world into existence, we will realize that we also create the nightmares of our reality. So let's get started dreaming heaven on Earth!

Weather

Again, Earth's weather will be unpredictable. Extreme cold—record-breaking rain and snowfall from the Northwest to the East Coast. Even the Southwest and the South will have colder than usual temperatures and lots of rain early 2020. The Middle East and much of Europe will experience strong winds, heavy snow, and blizzards. Summer will be extremely hot for the Northern Hemisphere and Southern Hemisphere. Straight-line winds will cause havoc for planes and homes and tornadoes will be stronger and last longer than in previous years. Scientists worry how tornadoes are getting more powerful each year and some have become huge, as much as a Class 4 with a mile-wide path of destruction. Even barometric pressure is unprecedented in today's tornadoes. With continued warming of the Pacific Ocean, there will be hurricanes hitting Mexico and Southern California.

Springtime will bring flash floods across Texas, the Southern United States, and New England again. Again, drought conditions will cause horrific wildfires, mostly caused by arsonists, which will destroy homes, lives, and nature. Watch for fire in Northern and Southern California, the Northwest and parts of Australia again. Nothing will be normal about our weather in 2020. Records will continue to be broken.

Surprise Comet

A surprise comet will come out of nowhere and bring awe and wonder to humanity in 2020. They may say this is a comet, but it won't be or is not the usual type of comet. At first, I thought that my vision was about Betelgeuse, the bright red star in Orion's shoulder. Betelgeuse was growing bright each day and then it wasn't bright anymore. Its luminosity has "fallen off a cliff"—a sign that the star could be on the verge of going supernova, scientists speculated. "I predicted that Betelgeuse will go supernova and be a brilliant light in the night sky in 2020, but low and behold Comet Atlas appeared as I was shown in my vision in 2019. Our ancestors believed that signs in the sky were omens of coming events.

Comet Atlas

A surprise comet did appear in the night sky. Emerald-green Comet Atlas is racing toward the inner solar system, and it could become the brightest comet seen in the night sky in over two decades, according to the astronomers. The comet was discovered by an observatory designed to protect Earth from asteroids and I predicted it will be visible during the day in May or June. The comet, also known as C/2019 Y4, was discovered by astronomers at the Asteroid Terrestrial-impact Last Alert System (ATLAS) in Hawaii in December 2019. In December it was a dim object, but the comet became 4,000 times brighter in only a month. This increase is far greater than astronomers had predicted, but it could potentially signal the comet may soon be much brighter. This is the comet had foreseen in late 2019 in a vision, although at the time I felt it was Betelgeuse, the bright red star (not a comet) in Orion's shoulder). Sometimes I shouldn't doubt my predictions!

Karl Battams of the Naval Research Lab said, "Some predictions for its peak brightness now border on the absurd." Comets are dirty snowballs. As the comet approaches the Sun, the heat will drive off some of the ice which makes up the nucleus (main body) of the object. If the comet holds its shape as it continues to heat, then Comet Atlas could grow as bright as the planet Venus (the brightest object in the night sky other than the Moon). The comet, currently near the orbit of Mars, is closely following the path taken by one of the great comets in history — the Great Comet of 1844.

For skywatchers in the northern hemisphere, this would be a sight-unseen since the dual shows of Comets Hyakutake in 1996 and Hale-Bopp the following year. When Hyakutake was at its peak, the tail of the comet stretched halfway across the sky.

As I predicted in 2019, a comet will bring awe and wonder to humanity. Watch for another city in the United States to have a major UFO city like the one in Phoenix, Arizona on March 13, 1997 when people were looking at the night sky for Hale-Bopp.

Moon Surprise

Scientists have been baffled how the moon rings as it is hollow. It is! Between 1972 and 1977, seismometers installed on the Moon by the Apollo missions recorded moonquakes. The Moon was described as "ringing like a bell" during some of those quakes, specifically the shallow ones. This phrase was brought to popular attention in March 1970, in an article in Popular Science. It's a satellite and was constructed by aliens. NASA will make surprise announcements in 2020 about the moon's odd anomalies.

Power Grid Outages

Take into account the age of the power grid and add a huge natural disaster or a terrorist attack, and millions of people could go without power for days or even weeks. Newscaster Ted Koppel once said he is prepared for any outage with freeze-dried food and water. Are you prepared? I feel this event is in our future and I'm not sure of the timeline yet. Southwest Colorado is not connected to the entire grid and would not be affected by a massive power outage. Other areas are not connected to the aging power grid, which might be good to consider if you plan to move.

Japan

The late Edgar Cayce (died in1945), known as the "Sleeping Prophet" said that, "the greater part of Japan would go into the sea." Although Cayce had some amazing hits, not all of his predictions were accurate—not yet anyway. However, Japan's 9.0 megathrust earthquake and disastrous tsunami struck on March 11, 2011, surprised scientists. Could it happen again? I have sensed for a long time that a huge earthquake, perhaps as much as 9.5 or larger could strike the South Pacific. I do not see Japan going into the ocean, but I foresee large earthquakes causing people to leave Japan from rising water to many coastal areas.

Iran

Iran will be in the news in early 2020 and it may involve hostages taken and some killed. They will threaten the United States and President Trump will respond with words. I don't see any missile retaliation yet, but if they do, it could be disastrous for both sides. Something will cause the Iranian people to pour into the streets and protest in anger about their government.

Alien 3-D Holographic Inserts

Holographic technology has been used for ages by aliens and more recently by our world governments. It's all about frequency. Aliens have used holographic technology to create wars, and enter images of our religious icons to control use. Again, it's all about frequency. How will you determine what is real and what isn't? Intuition and how it feels. Holographic inserts vibrate at a higher level than reality. We are already seeing holographic inserts in our skies.

Holographic inserts have been used on Earth for eons to manipulate and control consciousness and to change Earth's library of information to one of disinformation and lies. Those who use holographic inserts on our planet are not always here to bring light and upliftment to humanity. Many, but not all UFO sightings are holographic inserts and not real. There have been holographic inserts of one individual, designed in many fashions and cultures, projected simultaneously. That is why some of Earth's religious beliefs are parallel from one corner of the world to another when there was no physical contact, according to the Pleiadians.

We have been controlled like sheep by those who think they own us—from the government to the World Management Team to those in space or those dark beings that live beneath Earth's surface. We have been deprived of knowledge by frequency control. Events may or may not be real in the future. Earth is on a dimensional collision course, and many dimensions or probabilities will intersect one another at this time. Some of these realities will be shocking, depending on the level of shock each person needs to kick their consciousness into another paradigm. It doesn't mean destruction necessarily, but it could be a method to alter the way you view reality. You are about to take an unimaginable ride.

Governments are already working on this technology, and Japan is already working on a holographic image that can be touched. How will you determine what is real and what isn't in our skies and our news? Intuition and the way it feels. We are already seeing holographic inserts appearing in the sky—with increased UFO and orb sightings in the sky.

Yellowstone the Super Volcano

Lately, Yellowstone National Park has recorded hundreds of small earthquakes. Does that mean an eruption soon? Although scientists continue to warn that Yellowstone National Park, one enormous volcanic caldera, will erupt someday, but don't worry, it won't happen at least for over 100 years or more. In the distant past, Yellowstone has had at least three such eruptions: The three eruptions, 2.1 million years ago, 1.2 million years ago and 640,000 years ago, were about 6,000, 700 and 2,500 times larger than the May 18, 1980 eruption of Mt. St. Helens in Washington State. We've heard many predictions that Yellowstone is overdue—that it has a major eruption every 600,000 years on average, and since the last eruption was 631,000 years ago. You can see where this is going. It's way overdue, according to scientists. But for now, it is only a venting spot for deep Earth magma, and again, I don't foresee a mega Yellowstone eruption in the next 100 years or more.

3-D Printer Technology

This technology is still in its infancy but will make leaps in the next few year in the medical field with human parts. The term "3D printing" covers a variety of processes in which material is joined or solidified under computer control to create a three-dimensional object. The medical applications are infinite and are already being used in the operating rooms. Currently, students and other innovators are using 3-Printers to create ventilators for the Pandemic.

Flu and the Super Flu Pandemic of 2020

Late 2019, I predicted the usual flu season would be deadly for children and already this has proven true for 2020. In I wrote this on my website predictions page: *It has been 100 years since the Spanish Flu (also known as the 1918 flu pandemic) spread across the globe, infecting 500 million people and causing the deaths of 50 million people worldwide–which was three to five percent of the world's population at the time. I do foresee another flu pandemic later this year and into 2020.*

I feel the Coronavirus that is spreading worldwide and started in China will take thousands and probably millions of lives before it is contained or a vaccine is available. It was bio-engineered and accidentally released. People on social media continue to point fingers, but does it matter who created it? It's here and we must deal with it the best we can.

Did human thought *en mass* create our current world situation? In part, we did! Thought is energy and with 7.8 billion human souls on the planet, we are creating many of the negative events taking place worldwide now. Our fear is a magnet! The Marian apparition that visited the three children of Fatima, Portugal from May 13, 1917, to October 13, 1917, warned of coming events and told the children they must all pray to stop the horrific future wars. The future is still forming and not set in stone--it is constantly changing and our thoughts can alter major events. Most people believe that we are powerless in our world, but we are powerful spiritual beings and can change events if we come together in thought, intention, and prayer!

The Four Horsemen in the *Book of Revelation* symbolize the evils to come at the end of the world and they are riding in 2020. The figure representing conquest rides a white horse; war, a red horse; famine, a black horse; and plague, a pale horse. They are often called the Four Horsemen of the Apocalypse.

It appears China lied about the actual body count from the coronavirus. Some have claimed it could be millions already as bodies are quickly cremated. Each day the news reports how people in China are being quarantined in hospitals and their homes. There will be wars, plagues, and famine in 2020. Already Africa is being invaded by massive swarms of hungry locust devouring crops in Kenya, Ethiopia, Uganda, Tanzania and Somalia that will create future famine. United Nations officials blame the climate crisis for the unprecedented locust breeding that could create widespread famine. The deadly disease has now claimed the lives of more than 1,300 people in China and is threatening to become a global pandemic, while the conflict in Iran and the African locust invasion in the Middle East could cause unimaginable famine.

New York City, New Orleans and several cities in the United States will become ground zero for the Coronavirus as health workers try frantically to save those in critical condition. India has a small percentage of cases now but the virus will spread quickly to millions of people in that country and millions will leave this world very quickly. No one can save them!

We will say goodbye to celebrities and the famous before the end of the year.

Worst case scenario—couples will divorce, suicides and murder will increase with those who cannot handle the pain and fear. Those who are unemployed and hopeless may turn to rioting in the streets. When people are put in a corner and nowhere to turn, people often lose their minds and their tempers.

Pandora's Box has been opened literally, and the virus will continue to spread death worldwide. It is important to pray for both the living and those who have passed. The newly arrived souls are confused and will want to stay Earthbound, but they need your love and prayers to help them adjust. I wish that I could tell you that we can put the virus back in the box, but it's too late now. We can slow it if we come together in mass thought and prayer to change events, but humans believe they are powerless and victims.

How Long will COVID-19 last?

I have received a huge number of emails asking how long will the virus last. Well, that's up to us and how soon we awaken to the agenda planned for us and the planet. Since the age of seven, I was shown huge earth changes coming, but nothing about a virus until last year when I was shown a pandemic like the Spanish Flu of 1917-1918 would hit this year and kill many of us of every age. We are creating it with our electromagnetic thoughts. I know that's hard for us physical beings to comprehend. How soon will it take for us to awaken from this nightmare and become empowered spiritual beings instead of victims as we have been for eons? You have lived and died perhaps thousands of lifetimes. You are an eternal being. I foresee at least two years before the virus begins disappears. Some countries and parts of the United States will recover more quickly and be able to get back to some form of normalcy.

I ask that you to stop your fear and panic because fear will only make matters worse. Already Mother Earth is feeling our fear and panic and earthquakes again are growing stronger. She's trying to shake us awake! Be kind now, be compassionate to others because everything that we do right now is being recorded (the Akashic records). Our souls are being tested. Will you be greedy, angry, and unkind to others or will be step up and be a hero. Of course, I'm not saying to put yourself in harm's way. Just help others who are in fear, who need food, who need your comforting words or any other way you can comfort your fellow human. This drama has played out since we were created—the Family of Dark against those of the Light fighting each other for domination. For the souls who leave now, they will return to learn the lesson of love and empowerment in future lifetimes. Best we learn now! Remember your soul never dies--it will live on forever. Keep your vibrational rate up with music like Mozart, Bach, chanting, drumming, healthy foods and stay away from recreational drugs and heavy alcohol drinking that will lower your vibrational rate. Get in nature more and if you can sit beside moving water, i.e. a river or the ocean, which provides negative ions—the good ones!

The CDC is advising people not to take antibiotics with the Coronavirus. But you might try the herb Umcka found in South Africa and sold in most grocery stores. Its common names include African geranium and South African geranium. The root extract of Pelargonium sidoides is used as cold and flu medicine under various brand names including Umckaloabo, Kaloba, Renikan, Umcka, and Zucol. It works on the common flu and colds, and it might help with the Coronavirus.

A young Indian Astrologer Foresees the end of the virus

On August 22, 2019, on his YouTube channel Conscience, 14-year-old Abighya Anand, predicted that the world will enter into a tough phase starting November 2019 to April 2020. This 6 month period will see the spread of global disease and a rise in global tensions. On May 29th as the earth orbits away from this tough period, it will mark the decline of the global disease as the spread of it will be more manageable.

Let's pray that his vision comes true, but at this time I don't see it declining in May. I see the virus slowing ebbing in 2021.

Worst-Case Scenario for the Coronavirus

There will be an economic catastrophe. Globally, millions of people, children, young people, adults and the elderly will die of every nationality. Massive graves will be used and other countries will cremate bodies. Family members won't be able to say goodbye to loved ones before they die.

People will lose their jobs, their homes, and even those who once had money will find their finances dwindling. There will be looting and murder in the streets and homes. Suicides will increase and some will take their entire family with them, believing there is no hope for the future. and people will turn to religion and God again, begging for help. Marriage will fail as never seen before. The world's government won't be able to help. Military and health workers will walk off their jobs to save themselves. There will be world riots and horrible violence. Five to seven million will lose jobs in the next few months.

This is the worst-case scenario. If such a scenario happens most of us will move on to the Other Side, and there we will reside with the angels and our spirit guides for a few thousand years until the Earth has restored itself to a pristine planet and we can reincarnate again into physical bodies. Hopefully, when we return, we will have learned our lesson about honoring our home, Earth, and all living creatures. Nothing will be taken for granted. We will have learned how to use technology that will not harm the environment.

Best-Case Scenario for the Pandemic

People all over the world are coming together in prayer, intentions, and meditations on certain days. And together we can create a new world. Our thoughts will change timelines and events by moving the train onto another track where the Coronavirus disappears and never returns. *When two or more of you are gathered together in my Name, there am I also.* A new consciousness change must take place within each of us. Groups will come together to stretch their conscious awareness, to invoke the aid of the highest sources of knowledge to assist them in changing an apocalyptic event.

Here's a great analogy for our current situation.

If you watched the 1984 fantasy movie, **The Never Ending Story**, you know the hero, Atreyu, sets out to save the fantasy world of Fantasia slowly being devoured by a malevolent force called "The Nothing". Fantasia's ruler, the Childlike Empress, had fallen ill, and the young warrior Atreyu task was to discover the cure, believing that once the Empress is well, *The Nothing* will no longer be a threat. Atreyu is given a medallion named the Auryn that can guide and protect him in the quest. As he reaches the Swamps of Sadness with his beautiful white horse Artax, the horse is so depressed and sad, it begins to sink in the swamp, while Atreyu yells at it to stop its sadness so they can go on. The horse sinks into the swamp and Atreyu is left to go on to stop *The Nothing* from devouring Fantasia. As the despair envelopes us, we sink deeper into the swamp of sadness. Could it be that if we lift our thoughts and our hearts, the horrible Coronavirus (The Nothing) will vanish?

We are powerful, spiritual beings capable of miracles!

China Military Might and North Korea Missile Launches

With the COVID-19 pandemic mostly contained in China and now wreaking havoc on the United States, security analysts are closely watching Beijing's military moves in the South China Sea. In recent days, China has conducted military drills and deployed large-scale military assets to the maritime area while at the same time officially celebrating strides made in exploiting disputed energy resources in the fossil fuel-rich sea. Also, we should watch North Korea and its continued missile tests. Remember, China and No. Korea are close allies.

Planet X

As a child of seven, I had recurring dreams of disastrous Earth changes and I intuitively sense those changes are still coming. The Four Horsemen of the Apocalypse is riding—and we will see plagues, famine, earthquakes, volcanoes erupting and violent weather.

People all over the world are seeing what looks like another sun in the sky near our sun. Videos of sightings near our sun will continue to be posted on YouTube. Planet X, also known as Nibiru is passing through our solar system at this time and its magnetic pull on Earth is creating greater Earth changes. It won't be the end of the world, but there will huge changes on our planet as it wobbles even more. NASA has known about Planet X since 1984 and even admitted to its existence then.

Will the leaders of the world tell us that Planet X will disrupt our planet? No, because they don't want further panic. Perhaps the Coronavirus was intentionally released on the world, it was to create Martial Law without saying the word. Prepare for the worst, but don't panic. I often tell people to be like General George S. Patton who recalled past lives as an ancient warrior while in Europe during World War II. He believed, as I believe, that we all have a mission in life, so he didn't fear death.

UFOs, Orbs and Strange Sky Sightings

2019 was an amazing year for Unidentified Flying Objects. Once thought to be fictional works used to sell tabloids, 2019 was inundated with news of UFOs, aliens and strange phenomenon—including reports (complete with video) from verifiably sane sources. In May, the Pentagon admitted it investigated UFOs soon after Navy pilots claimed to not only have seen but recorded UFOs during training exercises in 2004 and 2015. In November, another report in Popular Mechanics confirmed that after the 2004 incident, two "unknown individuals" took the data tapes away and wiped the memory from the Navy hard drive. But while astronomers say humans finding aliens may take a long time—2019 was a particularly active year for UFOs visiting Earth, especially huge orbs dancing in the night sky. Alien beings are watching what happens with the pandemic COVID-19 and how we handle it. Why don't they assist us? Although abductees claim aliens have been told that a galactic law won't allow them to interfere with our world. But that can't be true, because alien beings have stopped missiles from firing on many occasions in the United States. That's interference!

According to the National UFO Reporting Center, on Sept. 21, 2019, in Gallipolis, Ohio, "a husband (former law enforcement) and wife (scientist), while sitting outside their recreational vehicle at a public campsite, witnessed a very bright light approach their campsite from the south in an erratic manner, appearing to slow or stop on several occasions as it drew near. It got within 50 yards, they estimate, of their campsite, at which time, out of a sense of alarm, the husband reached for his .45 caliber sidearm, but he felt unable to use his arm, or lift the firearm. The object, estimated by the witnesses to have been approximately 20 feet in diameter, hovered nearby for approximately 8 seconds, and then suddenly accelerated toward the west, and disappeared very quickly to the west."

According to reporting centers like MUFON (Mutual UFO Network), aliens prefer colder climes as "UFO hotspots include Washington State (the home of the National UFO Reporting Center), Montana and Vermont. Alaska and Maine are also popular states for alien encounters."

The states with the least alien activity are Texas, Louisiana, Georgia, Mississippi, and Alabama—despite former President Jimmy Carter logging an official report with the International UFO Bureau in 1969, claiming he had seen a self-illuminated, multi-colored UFO before giving a speech at the Lions Club in Leary, Georgia. Some of the orb UFO sightings have shown some strange acrobatic maneuvers and can split into several orbs. I sense these are monitoring devices, like our drones.

I predict in 2020 UFO activity will be the largest ever with mass sightings over major cities. Washington, D.C. and the White House could well have another visitation in 2020.

Recently, a NASA official says an ET invasion will take place before 2025. Strange remark for a NASA official. The highest-ranked official of the National Aeronautics and Space Administration (NASA), Charles Bolden, was put on sick leave for 6 months after he publicly declared that an extraterrestrial invasion would take place before 2025. A veteran of four space flights aboard the shuttles Columbia, Discovery and Atlantis, M. Bolden has logged over 680 hours in space and is the administrator of NASA since 2009. He shocked many people during a conference in Houston on Saturday, by declaring that "it's only a question of months, maybe years, before technologically advanced aliens invade our planet". "There are many scary things out there, and some of them have probably already taken notice of our existence," Mr. Bolden said. "We have estimated that there are at least 30,000 other civilizations in the Universe. We've been active in outer space for decades, so we've certainly already attracted the attention of at least one of them. We could be invaded at any moment!"

I am told by my spirit guides that a huge event is coming in 2020 involving aliens. Get ready!

Global Warming – true or false?

Authorities in the state of South Australia have issued a code red alert as the country continues to break temperature records with the mercury rising above 40 degrees Celsius. That's just an appetizer as the country's meteorological bureau has warned that the temperature may rise to 50.7 degrees. According to a study published in the journal Nature, climate change researchers found a link between extreme temperatures and Rossby waves, giant meanders that warp air currents in a observed in the atmosphere as well as in the world's oceans.

Weather and temperatures will be extreme, either extremely cold in the winter and record-breaking summer heat. Ice in the Arctic will continue to melt and many coastal in the Northern Hemisphere will find the towns inundated by rising waters in the coming years.

Chemtrails

As a child, I looked to the skies for UFOs and loved to watch fluffy white clouds in the sky. Occasionally, jets were passing over, leaving a contrail (water vapor) that disappeared almost instantly. I began noticing something different in our skies by the late 1990s when unmarked jets began laying down trails of clouds that would fan out on a beautiful clear day. By mid-afternoon, the sky would be covered in these grey-white clouds, now called "chemtrails." What are they? Conspiracy theorists believe the unmarked jets that create the chemtrails are geoengineering our weather or they are controlling us through lithium, barium, and aluminum.

Lithium is a calming drug and aluminum is known to cause dementia and Alzheimer's Disease. There are also theories that the chemtrails are used to cover Planet X near our sun. Think about this: chemtrails fall into our water, our food, the environment daily, and those who are doing this can't be immune to their spraying. They too will experience the negative effects of chemtrails. It will affect their children and future generations. Our separation and lack of concern for Mother Earth are creating huge changes taking place now—global warming, oceans warming, increased diseases, and dying animals worldwide.

What angers me is YouTube has removed the conspiracy theories and replaced them with videos explaining how chemtrails are normal contrails. Further generations will never know the truth or even seek it because they were told by their leaders and governments that conspiracy theories are ludicrous. Young people viewing the videos today have no idea what our skies once looked like before chemtrails. Our sky was always a beautiful azure blue with ordinary clouds, not like the wispy grey chemtrail trails laid down by strange jets. Now it's almost impossible to find conspiracy theories videos of any kind on social media.

If you put chemtrails, JFK's assassination, Roswell crash or 9/11 conspiracy theories into a search engine you will find a plethora of articles discrediting these conspiracy theories. How did the Coronavirus or COVID-19 sweep the world in a few short weeks? Sure, people travel worldwide, but not in obscure, remote places. There's a new theory that the virus spread from our 5g electromagnetic technology.

Dr. Thomas Cowan, M.D. hypothesizes that Coronavirus may be history repeating itself like the Spanish Flu of 1917-1918 and caused by 5G. It makes sense how our technology can disrupt the frequencies of our bodies! Just think what we've done to whales and dolphins with SONAR. But what if the chemtrails that have covered our skies contained viruses bioengineered to break down our immunity? I believe chemtrails have also contributed to world droughts and caused wildfires that raged in the Amazon Rainforest of South America, the entire U.S. West Coast, Northwest, and last year, the deadly Australian fires that killed 34 humans and a half billion indigenous animals.

A recent article states that viruses circulate Earth's atmosphere and fall from it, according to new research from scientists in Canada, Spain and the U.S. The study marks the first time scientists have quantified the viruses being swept up from the Earth's surface into the free troposphere, beyond Earth's weather systems but below the stratosphere where jet airplanes fly. The viruses can be carried thousands of kilometers there before being deposited back onto the Earth's surface.

"Every day, more than 800 million viruses are deposited per square meter above the planetary boundary layer—that's 25 viruses for each person in Canada," said the University of British Columbia virologist Curtis Suttle, one of the senior authors of a paper in the International Society for Microbial Ecology Journal that outlines the findings. "Roughly 20 years ago we began finding genetically similar viruses occurring in very different environments around the globe," says Suttle. "This preponderance of long-residence viruses traveling the atmosphere likely explains why—it's quite conceivable to have a virus swept up into the atmosphere on one continent and deposited on another."

Is it conceivable that unmarked planes spraying chemtrails on the Earth's population helped spread COVID-19 worldwide or was the Jetstream responsible?

Some of you are probably wondering how our government could conduct such horrific programs on us. Easy! They have been conducting experiments on unsuspecting civilians for years. The government/military detonated nuclear weapons underground beneath the Southwest desert. Many people in surrounding towns developed horrible cancers from the radiation. In 1950, the U.S. Navy sprayed a cloud of bacteria from ships over San Francisco to find out how susceptible an American City would be to a biological attack. Many people became ill with pneumonia-like symptoms. Remember the Gulf War's Desert Storm Operation where soldiers complained of a mysterious ailment, but the government denied every their illness existed. Between 1929 and 1974, it is estimated 65,000 people were victims of forced sterilization in at least 30 states, and nearly 7,600 people were sterilized under the orders from North Carolina's Eugenics Board. There more, like the mind control experiments, MK Ultra and Project Monarch conducted on adults and children.

What is happening today with the Coronavirus is no accident. Was it a bioengineered accident? According to a military expert weeks ago, it was bioengineered. Was it on purpose to cull the herd of Earth's 7.8 billion population? At this point, it doesn't matter who did it or why it was done, the virus happened.

We must awaken to how we've been controlled for eons. We can stop them through our positive thoughts and visualization if we come together on social media. Visualize the virus evaporating into the sky and turning into snowflakes or some other benign element.

Trump's Space Force

May the Force be with you (Star Wars)! On December 20, 2019, President Trump officially signed into law the US Space Force (not associated with NASA), the sixth military branch and first devoted to organizing, training, and equipping personnel to use and defend military space assets. With the 2020 National Defense Authorization Act that Trump signed last Friday, US Air Force Space Command becomes Space Force but remains within the Air Force, much like the Marine Corps is a part of the Navy Department. Why would Donald Trump want to create a Space Force? Does he expect an outside force to attack our planet? But there's more to it than that. Trump is aware of the alien presence like all Presidents before him, and he feels that some of them are not friendly.

Through the years NASA has captured what appears to be UFOs around the Space Shuttle missions. Although NASA always finds some rational explanation to explain away what appears to be spaceships under intelligent control and other videos that standout as real UFO footage. The STS-48 Space Shuttle Discovery orbiter mission was launched on September 12, 1991, from the Kennedy Space Center in Florida, with the Upper Atmosphere Research Satellite as its primary payload.

While in orbit at 20:30-20:45 GMT on September 15, 1991, cameras captured multiple bright UFOs that appeared to be flying under intelligent control. Although NASA suggested the UFOS were actually ice crystals, several other researchers rejected the claim. Kasher, Professor Emeritus of Physics at the University of Nebraska suggested they could be UFOs or more precisely extraterrestrial spacecraft.

Aliens have been warring against each other on and above our planet for eons.

Avatars and Humans

Remember the 2009 movie *Avatar* where a human consciousness could inhabit another biological being? This is our future. Already scientists are discussing ways to upload our brains to the Cloud. Remember that Science Fiction is just a vision of the future.

Mysterious Booms The mysterious booms and strange noises heard worldwide in the past few years suddenly stopped in late 2019 but will resume again in 2020. I believe the booms are warnings of deep core Earth movement. Usually, a large earthquake happens within two weeks after the booms are reported Mother Earth always has a way of warning us before a major event—that's if we listen to her and heed her warnings, i.e. animals and sea life behaving in odd ways, earthquake lights before a huge earthquake, unusual weather. The booms will increase as our planet continues to experience stretching and pulling deep within the Earth as it wobbles in space.

Another theory on the mysterious booms—Earth was being pulled into a parallel world or alternate reality. As of March 2020, there have been few reports. During the past few years, people reported hearing trumpet sounds—was it Angel Gabriel blowing his horn to announce the coming Coronavirus plague?

Sinkholes
Sinkholes will again be in the news worldwide and no explanation for them by scientists. Sinkholes are created by our warming Earth as and methane gas rises to the surface and causes explosions. Due to Earth's movement along the U.S. East Coast, there will be more homes exploding from natural gas lines. Many of the gas lines are aging. The problem is two-fold.

Magnetic North Pole is Shifting but Why?
and a slew of civilian applications, is continuing its push toward Siberia. "The WMM2020 forecasts that the northern magnetic pole will continue drifting toward Russia, although at a slowly decreasing speed –down to about 40 km per year compared to the average speed of 55 km over the past twenty years," the US agency said in a press statement.

Elon Musk Plans to Launch 42,000 Space X Satellites

Earlier this year, US National Oceanic and Atmospheric Administration and the British Geological Survey (BGS) were forced to update the World Magnetic Model a year ahead of schedule due to the speed with which the magnetic north pole is shifting out of the Canadian Arctic and toward Russia's Siberia. The BGS and the US National Centers for Environmental Information have released a new update to the World Magnetic Model this week, confirming that the magnetic north pole, whose coordinates are crucial for the navigation systems used by governments, militaries Starlink is the project launched by Elon Musk's space exploration company SpaceX which aims to put up to 42,000 satellites in orbit with the aim of bringing high-speed internet to even the most remote corners of the globe. Though only 120 of the satellites are up and running, they're already wreaking havoc with astronomical research. The brightness of the satellites means that when they cross a piece of the sky being watched by a telescope, they leave bright streaks that obscure stars and other celestial objects. Last week astronomer Clarae Martínez-Vázquez of the Cerro Tololo Inter-American Observatory (CTIO) in Chile tweeted that 19 Starlink satellites crossed the sky and disrupted the work of the observatory because they were so bright they affected its exposure. "Rather depressing... This is not cool," she added.

Not only are we polluting Earth, but we also are polluting outer space. It is estimated that there are about 200,000 pieces of space junk floating around in space between 1 and 10 cm (0.4 and 4 inches) across and that there could be millions of pieces smaller than 1 cm. Satellites will stay in orbit, probably forever!

Elon Musk's Space Starship Rockets Keep Exploding

Space Starship was set to begin test flights by the end of 2019, but SpaceX 's rocket suffered a huge setback following another disastrous test. The monster spacecraft partially exploded during a ground test in Boca Chica, Texas. The failed test saw the top of the rocket blown off, sending plumes of gas into the air. Thankfully, the rocket was unmanned during the test, and no-one was hurt. UFO hunters accused SpaceX of cutting their live feed from a rocket in space after a UFO appeared.

The next explosion happened on Jan. 19, 2018. I believe that a recent NASA launch failure and the explosion of the Falcon 9 was a message to us from aliens to stop exploring space. Is this the real reason for Trump's Space Military Force? And now another loss for Space X with a huge explosion. Do ETs want us confined to Earth because they don't want a violent species to infest space?

Until we humans become a more peaceful species, Star Beings will not allow us to be part of the Galactic Team. We must first learn to get along with each other, or we will be confined to Earth forever. They will let us explore the Universe in unmanned spaceships, but it will be a much longer time before humans live on the moon and Mars.

Russia and Putin
Saber-rattling and a possible attack between Russia and the United States in Syria. It appears to be an accident, but Russians will be angered and blame the U.S. for the attack. There could be some kind of retaliation for this so-called accident. WWIII could begin by some strange event or accident involving either Russia, China or North Korea. Our prayers are needed now. Someday in the far future, Russia will become an inspiration to the world as the prophet Edgar Cayce predicted.

More Troops to the Mideast
Trump will send more troops to Iraq and Afghanistan. I see a massive explosion in Syria like a bomb dropped on a major city.

Bestselling Books
Bestselling books both fiction and nonfiction will be memoirs, true near-death experiences, true historical stories, books on faith and religion, and books by and on politicians. True stories about heroes will become bestsellers. Books on famous people who survived the Coronavirus will be best sellers as well.

Medical Advances

There will be great advances in certain kinds of cancer this year and other diseases. I've seen a vision of the blind seeing with something planted in their heads. I don't think the blind will see with their eyes, but with their minds. We will see more amazing advances in bionics. Although scientists are working with levitation, they soon will be able to lift large objects in the air— they appear to float. Eventually, a Star Wars-type of lightsaber weapon will be developed that can stun, paralyze or kill. Eventually, a vaccine will be made to stop the Coronavirus but it will take until early 2021.

Isis — Isis will continue their attacks and killing worldwide. The attacks and carnage will continue and destruction of antiquities and life in cities throughout the world as if nothing can stop them, but they will be eventually stopped in the years to come. But for the next five years, I see visions of blood flowing in the streets of the world, planes being shot down from the sky, and bombs exploding in cities. Innocent people will be slaughtered. These terrorists are well versed in occult practices and numerology and it's is no coincidence that the 11th district of Paris was hit on the 11th month and the 13th day. They are just puppets being controlled by those who remain hidden as well as their far-reaching agendas for Earth. Terrorist cells will continue their attack on cities in European cities. Canada, be alert for suspicious people at airports and churches. I can't tell you when or where, but I urge you to trust your intuition/gut feeling if you get a feeling not to go to a movie, concert, sporting event or any large event.

Isis will continue its attacks worldwide. The attacks and carnage will continue and destruction of antiquities and life in cities throughout the world as if nothing can stop them, but they will be eventually stopped in the years to come. But for the next five years, I see visions of blood flowing in the streets of the world, planes being shot down from the sky, and bombs exploding in cities. Innocent people will be slaughtered. These terrorists are well versed in occult practices and numerology and it's is no coincidence that the 11th district of Paris was hit on the 11th month and the 13th day. They are just puppets being controlled by those who remain hidden as well as their far-reaching agendas for Earth. Terrorist cells will continue their attack on cities in European cities. Canada, be alert for suspicious people at airports and churches. I can't tell you when or where, but I urge you to trust your intuition/gut feeling if you get a feeling not to go to a movie, concert, sporting event or any large event.

Since publishing this book on January 1, 2020, the Coronavirus pandemic has hit every country in the world. Theorists are now fighting an invisible enemy that cares little about color, religion or race. Isis and other terrorists will fight for their lives.

Dec. 21, 2019 – Lucid Dream of Tsunami

The Cascadia Subduction Zone, that starts off the coast of Northern California and continues up to Vancouver, British Columbia, will someday let loose and cause the greatest natural disaster along the coasts of Oregon, Washington and parts of Vancouver. It is a sleeping giant, this giant has been quiet far too long. The last megathrust earthquake to hit off the coasts of Oregon, Washington, and Vancouver, occurred on January 26, 1700, with an estimated moment magnitude of 8.7–9.2. The megathrust earthquake involved the Juan de Fuca Plate from mid-Vancouver Island, south along the Pacific Northwest coast as far as northern California. The generated Tsunami also moved inland along the coast of Washington for miles.

Early this morning I had a lucid dream of a huge tsunami while I was swimming in a coastal cove. The water was dark like the West Coast Pacific Ocean. Does that mean a powerful earthquake is going to hit along the US West Coast? I pray this prediction will not come true. Usually, when I have vivid dreams, they come true. The last time I had such a dream was one week before the 7.1 earthquake that shook the Mojave Desert of California on July 5, 2019.

Famous People Leaving Us in 2020

Already the Coronavirus is taking the lives of celebrities and famous people from us. It will get worse as months pass. Supreme Court Justine Ruth Ginsberg's life essence is very low at this time. She will probably leave us in 2020 as well as Prince Philip, Queen Elizabeth's husband, who turns 99-years-old on June 10, 2020. Pope Francis will probably leave us due to the Coronavirus. However, I foresee many souls born in 2020, the new advanced children, who were here in prior lifetimes, returning to help the planet. They will be blessed with amazing psychic talents—telekinesis, telepathy, seeing and communicating with spirits, and recall of past lives. They will behave exceptional gifts in math, music, art, and will show these talents early in life. Also, a famous and much beloved 1960s singer/songwriter will leave us suddenly. Keep those who pass over in your prayers—our prayers for those living and those who will die in 2020. Prayers do matter!

Pope Francis

In my book, *Mystic Revelations of Thirteen,* I wrote that Pope Francis is linked to occultism and uses numerology. He believes the number 13 gives him power and protection. But it's no secret the Vatican Church has a long history of occult practices. Francis was elected Pope on March 13, 2013 (3+13+2013 = 13), he was 76 years old at the time (7+6=13), and he selected the name from the Francis of Assisi, the 13th-century friar, and saint, known for his humility toward nature, animals and the poor. Francis was ordained to the priesthood on December 13, 1969. His episcopal motto was

Miserando atque eligendo taken from Bede's homily on Mathew 9:9:13 which means because he saw through the eyes of mercy and chose him. Number 13 is associated with the Illuminati. I can't say Francis is involved with the Illuminati but there are several mysteries about him and his connection to the number 13.

Recently, Pope Francis made a statement that he would not live long. Will he be the last Pope as many prophets have predicted? I do not see Pope Francis living long, perhaps passing from the Coronavirus, and his death will bring about a great holy war. He will either resign or pass on in 2020.

There will be more sexual abuse forthcoming from children who have been abused by both priests and nuns.

Earthquakes and Volcanic Eruptions

As Planet X aka Nibiru passes through our solar system, its passage will bring huge earthquakes and volcanic eruptions worldwide. A mega-earthquake is building (9.0 +) and will hit probably around the Pacific Rim of Fire. Northern or Southern California (not in a big city)—perhaps the Mojave desert again. A 5.7 earthquake shook residents in Salt Lake City, Utah on March 18, 2020, and over 600 aftershocks have followed. Then on March 31, 2020, a 6.5 magnitude earthquake hit Central Idaho, near Stanley and the Challis area. Although the earthquake caused some landslides, no one was injured. The 5.7 earthquake near Salt Lake City may have triggered the earthquake in Idaho. Again, I foresee continued powerful earthquakes in the Northwest and possibly another large one in Salt Lake City.

Our Sun Although seismologists won't admit this, there is a connection between solar eclipses and powerful earthquakes. Everything is connected in our world and the universe. Scientists say the gravitational pull of the Sun and the Moon produces the tides, so it makes sense gravity could affect plate tectonics and potentially trigger earthquakes. In a solar eclipse, the Earth, Sun, and Moon are aligned, so you'd expect the effect to be greatest. Is there a correlation between eclipses and earthquakes? The short answer is yes, but it's not really the eclipse that increases the probability, but the lunar phase. Solar flares and geomagnetic storms hitting earth can also trigger large earthquakes. Everything is connected.

The sun will awaken in mid-2020, and produce some X-Class flares and CMEs Earth-directed. We will also see increased strong earthquakes in vulnerable areas like the South Pacific and much of the Pacific Ring of Fire along with increased volcanic eruption—some major volcanic eruptions in Iceland and Italy. Italy's Mount Etna could erupt and cause major loss of life in late 2020.

Vanishing Retail Stores and Theaters

One day malls will become extinct and so will movie theaters. People would rather order online through the internet or stay homes and watch movies. Hollywood and movies will be forever changed due to the Coronavirus. Many retail chain stores will close and small businesses will fail due to the time they were forced to be closed from the COVID-19 lockdown across the United States.

Sick and Misguided Children

Sadly, I see children killing children because they are programmed through television and video games that life is not precious. These children could have been inspiring leaders, but they have been mind-controlled by the Media, Television and violent movies and video games. They have become emotionless zombies who no longer respect life. People at large gatherings will be targets for those who want to commit mass murder. Whenever you attend any large event, always, ask your guardian angel for divine protection.

More NASA Revelations

Watch for NASA to announce astonishing discoveries about the origins of our solar system, our Sun, Mars, the Moon and about black holes. They are going to make some outrageous claims and maybe hint about ancient alien structures on Mars and the Moon. Are they preparing us for the big disclosure?

Other Side Communications

Benjamin Franklin claimed that he was working on a device that would record messages from the dead. In 2016 watch for news about an invention that will prove we can communicate with the Other Side and dead people. But will the right kind of spirit answer? Maybe not!

Oscar Night

Tom Hanks might accept the 92nd Academy Award on January 13, 2020, for Best Actor in his portrayal of Fred Rogers in the movie, *A Beautiful Day in the Neighborhood,* which could also receive Best Picture category or the movie *1917.* I see Joe Pesci receiving Supporting Actor award for his portrayal of a mobster in *The Irishman,* but not much more for this movie. **UPDATE:** South Korea's *Parasite* movie ran away with many Oscars including the best foreign-language picture and best picture. Joaquin Phoenix was awarded best actor for his role in Joker, Brad Pitt for best supporting actor, Laura Dern, best-supporting actress, and Renee Zellweger, for best actress in the movie *Judy.* Although I had foreseen Renee winning the best actress, I had forgotten to include her in my predictions.

Many indie companies like Showtime, HBO and Netflix are all producing their own movies, but the Academy refuses to acknowledge them in the awards.

The British Royals

The scandal for Prince Andrew, Duke of York, will continue as more young women, victims of Jeffrey Epstein, come forth about their sexual involvement with him. Eventually, Prince Harry and his wife Meghan Markle will make the United States or Canada their new home sometime in 2020. Another baby for Prince Harry and Meghan in 2020—this time a baby girl. Severe health problems for Prince Phillip, the Queen's husband, who turns 99-years-old on June 10, 2020. His life force is very low. It could also be a bad health year for Queen Elizabeth, who will turn 94 on April 21, 2020. I have seen that when couples married for a long time and one spouse dies, the other follows shortly after.

Recently, Prince Charles was infected with Coronavirus and is now out of self-isolation, but others in his family may not fare as well as from the virus.

Princess Diana

It has been 23 years in 2020 since the deaths of Princess Diana and Dodie Fayed on August 31, 1997 (a number that totals 11, an Illuminati number). New information will surface and show that Princess Diana and Dodi Fayed were murdered in Paris. It was a ritualistic murder—a sacrifice.

9-11 Conspiracies and Facts

As more time goes by and the younger generation becomes of age, the events of 9-11 will be a distant memory of planes going into the two tallest buildings in New York City on September 11, 2001, killing nearly 3,000 people. History can be manipulated and changed to what historians want us to believe. It's happened in the far past. Lately, any conspiracy theories video that once abounded on YouTube is hard to find. These videos have been replaced by debunkers.

The Trade Towers were constructed in the 1970s and were built to withstand a plane crashing into them with the strongest steel and reinforcement, yet on 9-11-2001, the two-building fell within minutes of being hit by commercial planes and pancaked down as if explosives were set inside them. It appeared to be a demolition explosion. Experts have given pro and con theories on their destruction, and no one seems to agree whether explosive could have been used, but firefighters and police and other first responders heard and witnessed what appeared to be explosions in the buildings.

But here is the strangest part of this prime event. Proponents of the World Trade building demolition theories allege that the number 7 building —a 47-story skyscraper that stood across Vesey Street north of the main part of the World Trade Center site, was intentionally destroyed with explosives. Unlike the Twin Towers, which appeared to be giant 11s reaching into the sky, number 7 World Trade Center was not hit by a plane, although it was damaged by fires that burned for seven hours until it collapsed.

Unlike the Twin Towers, 7 World Trade Center was not hit by a plane, although it was hit by debris from the Twin Towers and was damaged by fires which burned for seven hours, until it collapsed completely at about 5:20 p.m. on the evening of September 11. It was a new building and opened in May of 2006. Several videos of the collapse event exist in the public domain, thus enabling comparative analysis from different angles of perspective. It's interesting that the 9/11 Commission Report and the Federal body charged with investigating the event, required seven years to conduct its investigation and issue a report. Conspiracy theorists maintain that building 7 was demolished because it may have served as an operational center for the demolition of the Twin Towers, while others suggest that government insiders may have wanted to destroy key files held in the building about corporate fraud. The WTC buildings housed dozens of federal, state and local government agencies. What was so important to destroy and kill 3,000 people in the process?

My symbolic dream in the fall of 2000 indicated that implosion was planned for the World Trade buildings one year before the event. My dream was of a giant apple tree full of leaves and apples, and suddenly the leaves and apples began to fall to the ground and within a few minutes, the entire tree was sucked into the ground and vanished. Of course, I didn't understand the symbolism that the tree was the "Big Apple" aka New York City until the event happened.

The Year 2038
The Y2K that was supposed to cause computers worldwide to shut down in 2000, never happened. Another Y2K computer disaster is looming for 2038. It is claimed that Y2038 is so bad it could be worse than Y2K. Just like Y2K, if left unchecked, Y2038 could cause major issues for any computer systems. But just like Y2K, it could be nothing.

Round Houses in The Future

In the future, homes will be round, mirroring nature. It is beyond me and Indigenous people why modern humans built square houses. I first learned about roundhouses from my father who planned to build a roundhouse near the lake resort we owned in the Snake River Canyon of Idaho. It never was built, but the idea stuck with me all these years. Then I read about Richard Buckminster Fuller (1895-1983) and his geodesic dome houses. One of his early models was first constructed in 1945 at Bennington College in Vermont, where he lectured often. However, the U.S. government recognized the importance of his work and employed his firm Geodesics, Inc. in Raleigh, North Carolina to make small domes for the Marines. With a few years, there were thousands of such domes around the world. Sadly, the idea of roundhouses has been lost.

Native Americans realized that birds build round nests and that everything in nature seemed to be round. The oldest forms of indigenous shelter were often round in shape. (think the Southwest USA Hogan, Mongolian Yurt, North American Teepee and the Greek Tenemos, among others.) Why did our ancestors choose to build circular structures? Because the ovid shape—eggs, Earth, stars, moon, sun, tree trunks, and stones—is what they saw reflected in the surrounding natural environment. And, as usual, Mother Nature knows best. Wind and tsunami waves move naturally around a round building rather than getting caught at (and potentially ripping off) corners. A rounded roof avoids 'air-planing'- a situation where a strong wind lifts the roof structure up and off of the building. There are dozens of interconnected points in round homes. These are sites where builders can connect parts of the building.

In the past, the connecting materials were rope, vine, and hides. Modern materials are engineered components like a center radial steel ring, steel brackets, seismic and hurricane ties, bolts and steel cables. These connect the structural pieces and give the building a unique combination of flexibility and strength- qualities that cause them to be significantly safer in severe weather conditions like earthquakes, extreme winds, and heavy snowfall.

Donald Trump's Destiny

The Democrats have tried to have Trump removed since 2016 when he was elected with the Russian fiasco. The Special Counsel investigation, headed by Robert Mueller, was an investigation of Russian interference in the 2016 United States elections and suspicious links between Trump associates and Russian officials, conducted by special prosecutor Robert Mueller from May 2017 to March 2019. Nothing was proven after months of investigation to link Trump to the Russians. Now the frustrated Democrats have found what they consider new evidence against Trump for withholding aid to Ukraine from information on Joe Biden's son Hunter Biden, who was conveniently given a great job in Ukraine at a natural gas company. Although Hunter Biden, 49, denies any wrongdoing, his father has continued to be very defensive about his role in Ukraine.

I predict that damaging information will be uncovered about Hunter and Joe Biden's role in Ukraine. Donald Trump was born on June 14, 1946, in Jamaica, New York, which totals 22 and reduces to the single digit of 4. The number 22 is considered one of the most powerful numbers, able to turn all dreams and desires into reality. On November 8, 2016, Donald J. Trump was elected our 45th President as I had envisioned seven months before when I had a powerful vision of him taking the Oath of Office wearing his long black coat and a very chilly January 20, 2017 day in Washington, D.C., with his wife Melania beside him in a light-colored coat. I was right! And I feel that the vision of Trump's shocking win was part of a divine plan.

2020 is a 22 Master Number Year. 2020 is a year of angels. 2020 will be a year for the battle for America's soul—or a test to see if we still have one. Donald Trump's number is 22, his soul urge. Logical thinking and systematic work belong to number 4, but on the negative side number 4 could appear weak, tenacious, stubborn, too set in ways, and impractical. But because 2020 is a 22 year, and Donald Trump is a 22, I foresee protection around him and unusual luck.

In 2016, I accurately predicted Mike Pence, a Gemini, born on June 7, 1959, would be Trump's Vice President days before he was selected. I find it beyond coincidence that Mike Pence is a Gemini, like Trump, and seven is a part of their birthdate. Mike Pence as born June 7 and Trump on June 14 (7 + 7 = 14). They have a destiny together.

At this time, he will be acquitted by the Senate no matter what the Congress throws at him and will go on to win the 2020 election for another 4 years. But the controversy and anger with the Democrats will not end there. They will try again to have him removed before 2024 but it won't work. As I predicted in this book in the original publication Donald Trump was acquitted by the Senate on February 5, 2020.

As of December 14, 2019, Trump seldom gets kudos for his achievements because the news media is so focused on all the negative things they can dig up. Trump has always made it known he's not a fan of the press. The United States has the lowest unemployment record ever and the Stock Market has made its biggest gains. Many of you are probably making big gains on your 401Ks holdings. Would anyone want to rock the boat or have it sink when things are going well?

Added to the list of Trump's accomplishments December of 2019:

An agreement on a new U.S.-Mexico-Canada trade deal.

A new budget including more than $1.3 billion for a border wall and blocks a government shutdown.

House approval of the U.S. Space Force, a brand-new branch of the military.

Government family leave that will be a model for a proposal for the public

Tentative agreement on trade with China and resuming in 2020.

Approval of Trump's 50th Federal Appeals Judge.

Confirmation of a new Food and Drug Administration chief.

The signing of a pro-Israel anti-Semitism executive order.

Trump biographer Doug Wead wrote this of the President's actions in the shadow of impeachment. "Perhaps, for now, what he accomplished this week (Dec. 9 to Dec. 13, 2019) will be overshadowed by the impeachment, but by next summer, the impeachment may be seen as mean-spirited and partisan, and the string of victories will add to his incredible list of victories going into reelection season," he said.

Wead, who spent months inside the White House interviewing the president and top aides, said that he hadn't been surprised by Trump's aggressive fight on impeachment and his campaign to rack up wins.

"During impeachment, any other president would retreat into the bunker and be consumed with defense. Endlessly gaming various scenarios. Instead, Trump, the businessman, is looking for a way to use it to his advantage," he said.

"He is the master magician, waving one hand to distract, while with the other hand, he makes the trick work. In this case, the Democrats provided this unwanted distraction, but he clearly seized on the moment," Wead added.

Before you write to me about how terrible Trump is and that I clearly must be getting faulty information from my spirit guides, I will say this again as I have indicated on my website—Trump is human, and therefore not infallible. I do not think he is perfect or without faults. Who is? In this timeline, he is the best for the job.

Again, I predicted he will be cleared of any wrongdoing by the Senate and will go on to win the 2020 Presidential election, that's if there is an election in November. At this time I do not see a normal election as the Coronavirus rages on into 2021. Trump so far has not handled the Coronavirus pandemic well and has not been truthful with the American citizens. Some people can't handle disaster well, and he certainly has shown he can't. Events are changing very quickly and timelines changing. Trump may stay in office for another year with the U.S. presidential election moved to November 2021.

Joe Biden

Currently, Joe Biden is falling in ratings as self-described democratic socialist Bernie Sanders and 38-year-old Pete Buttigieg move ahead of him in the Iowa Caucuses. Joe Biden was born on November 20, 1942, and will be 78 years old in 2020. His Sun sign is Scorpio, his Rising sign is Sagittarius and his moon is in Taurus. Scorpios are notorious for secrets and their Scorpion sting—their anger. He was recently accused of sexual misconduct and this could hurt his chances of winning in the next election.

Biden's birthdate totals 20 and reduces to the number 2. As a number two, he is intuitive, poised, tactful, but on the negative side, he can be over-emotional, self-centered, moody, touchy, and easily upset as he has demonstrated recently when asked by a citizen about his son Hunter's involvement in Ukraine.

As the Vice President to President Obama, many felt he was not a strong Vice President and often made continual blunders and misquotes. He continues to make misquotes and strange remarks on social media now that he is confined to home isolation. While in Iowa this past August, Biden said, "Poor kids are just as bright and just as talented as white kids." And then he tried to correct himself by saying, "wealthy kids, black kids, Asian kids."

Its true politicians say some pretty stupid things under the stress of campaigning, but Joe is infamous for it.

Again, I mention that Joe Biden has been seen as inappropriate touching of women and young girls and has acquired the nickname of "Creepy Joe." It might be harmless, but there appears more to it, especially after reporters have asked him about it and he makes light of it. Several children have recoiled at his touch and whispering in their ears.

If Bernie somehow becomes the Democratic nominee, he will never be president. Joe Biden and his son Hunter Biden will be investigated for more on of their involvement in Ukraine. They aren't as innocent as they claim. Already Hunter Biden is being investigated for 156 million dollar counterfeiting scheme.

Hillary Clinton

As of December 6, 2019, Hillary has not officially jumped into the Presidential race, but there are hints and rumors that she will run again. I foresee her running again, but she will not get far.

Remember when Hillary was running against Donald Trump and all the health issues she was having—making strange comments, having coughing spells, and falling? Again, I see that she has health issues that will be compounded when she enters the race against Trump. It's Déjà vu!

Here's why Hillary lost and will lose again. Hillary was born Oct. 26, 1947, in Chicago, Illinois. Her sun sign is Scorpio. Scorpio is also in her Rising sign, in the planet Mercury, and in the planet Venus. Scorpio is the scorpion, known for its painful sting. Hillary can be short-tempered, and she doesn't forgive easily. She makes hasty decisions. Hillary has Uranus in Gemini, Jupiter in Sagittarius, Mars in Leo, and her moon is in Pisces (this is the sign of the fish going in two different directions)—indecisive. Hillary's star is Princeps which gives her prominence in education, science, and government affairs. She has a competitive nature. The truth is Hillary and Bill Clinton are part of an elite cabal group and they are involved in dark occult practices. Their involvement in the dark side of life will eventually be their undoing and eventually, the truth will be revealed.

In the book *Trance Formation of America* about the documented autobiography by MK-Ultra Project child victim Cathy O'Brien and her handler Mark Phillips. It's about the horrible things that were done to Cathy O'Brien through mind control by the CIA. The book describes Hillary, George H.W. Bush, and Dick Cheney's involvement with Cathy and other victims of sexual abuse. Many of you have read about all the people associated with the Clintons through the years that died under mysterious circumstances. And recently former President Bill Clinton was named as a friend to American financier and convicted sex trafficker of young women Jeffrey Epstein. Bill visited Epstein's sex playground on his Island retreat in the Virgin Islands. Do you think it's any accident that Jeffrey Epstein died in jail under mysterious circumstances? He was murdered by those scared that their names would become public and their heinous involvement revealed.

They should be scared because more of their story will unfold in 2020! These people are powerful and they are extremely dangerous. It will become known that dark occult rituals went on at that Island retreat.

The latest news story is that former New York Governor Mike Bloomberg, an Aquarius born on February 14, 1942, is considering Hillary as his vice president running mate. I doubt she will join him now. Even if she joins him, I don't foresee them winning the 2020 Presidential election.

Another mystery is why Hillary hasn't been thoroughly investigated for her breach of secure emails? During her tenure as United States Secretary of State, Hillary drew controversy by using a private email server for official and even classified communications rather than using official State Department email accounts maintained on secure federal servers. The FBI examination of Clinton's server found over 100 emails containing classified information, including 65 emails deemed "Secret" and 22 deemed "Top Secret." An additional 2,093 emails not marked classified were retroactively classified by the State Department. This could have been grounds for a formal hearing on her treasonous act. The emails secret or top secret information could have easily been hacked by another country, yet nothing was done to Hillary. The question is WHY?

Bernie Sanders

Bernie was born on September 8, 1941, a Virgo, and will be 79-years-old in 2020. Bernie is a decent man but he will never be President of the United States. He experienced a heart attack in October of 2019, and I sense he could have another one in early 2020. Unfortunately, Bernie was born on the 8th day, which is a karmic number and hard to live by. Those born on the 8th day of the month usually have a difficult time achieving their goals and dreams.

Tom Steyer for President in 2024

You may not have heard of him yet, but you will. He is a candidate in the 2020 Democratic Party Presidential primaries. His television ads are on his concern about the climate crisis that no other candidate is currently discussing, not even Trump. His star is rising and his name will be known by everyone in the next few years. Thomas Steyer was born on June 27, 1957, born under the astrological sign of Cancer, a water element. He is a billionaire, an American hedge fund manager, philanthropist, environmentalist, liberal activist, and fundraiser. Steyer gained a more national profile in 2017 when he launched a campaign to impeach President Donald Trump.

His astrology shows that he has a sound mind and creative ideas. He is witty, sociable and has a friendly personality that people are attracted to. He has a talent in writing that will bring him honor and success. He will make a great impression upon those he comes into contact with the public and in politics. His name numerology totals 5 which is very lucky and successful. He will be liked by all (I know that's hard to believe). Although 2024 is too far in the future, I feel he could easily become U.S. President in 2024. Steyer's Life Path number is 1, the total of his birthdate. A person with a Life Path of 1 is hardworking and a natural-born leader, with a pioneering spirit. These people have a strong desire to be number one, which means a person with this number can manifest their destiny easily. Due to their determination and self-motivation, they won't let anything stand in their way of accomplishing any goal. A number 1 person has the desire to accomplish great things in their lifetime. He is a pioneer, an innovator, and capable of great success and achievement. When he expresses his passion from the heart, he will achieve amazing things in the world. Examples of number 1 famous people—President George Washington, Martin Luther King, Author Ernest Hemingway, CEO Steve Jobs of Apple, Inc., actor Tom Hanks, Beatle Ringo Starr, and Lady Gaga.

2020 Major Medical Breakthroughs

In early 2019 I wrote this on my website on my Predictions page:

MS (Multiple Sclerosis)—Scientists will discover a gene that causes MS. It won't be a cure but will stop the progression of the illness that affects 2.3 million people worldwide (mostly women). On 11/20/19, I received an email today informing me that this prediction had come true. Scientists at Radboud University say they have discovered multiple DNA variants that indicate an increased risk of developing Muscular Sclerosis.

More medical breakthroughs will be made in 2020, especially for certain cancers like Hodgkin's, lung cancer and breast cancer.

Autism is now found in 1 out of 59 children, which is unconscionable. A scientific breakthrough for autism will come from the discovery of a gene that is inherited but sometimes lies dormant in one generation and then passed on to the next.

A vaccine will be created for the COVID-19 virus in early to mid- 2021.

More Alien Mummies

A huge discovery was made in the Chilean desert of a mummified child only six inches long, with a conical-shaped head and unusually hard bones for her size. The debate started in 2003 when the naturally mummified remains of Ata were discovered near a ghost town in Chile's Atacama Desert. A Spanish businessman, Ramón Navia-Osorio, purchased her mummy and in 2012 allowed a doctor named Steven Greer to use x-ray and computed tomography (CT) imaging to analyze her skeleton. The year was 2003. Some have claimed that she's an alien. But a new study published today in the journal Genome Research not only continues to disprove the alien theory but also reveals a scientific explanation for her allegedly extraterrestrial appearance. But the debate continues with Dr. Steven Greer. The bones of the mummified child indicate it was 6-years-old at the time of its death. How is that possible? There are stories and legends of "little people" all over the world, which may not be legend but fact. More of these discoveries will come to light in 2020.

The Year of Violence

Riots, demonstrations and angry youth worldwide will take to the streets. In China, protesters could be stopped by violence and death. Bloodshed will continue in the news around the world—school shootings and mass shooters. I foresee another Syrian chemical poisoning of men, women, and children. More Mexican cartel violence for Americans. Isis will continue to attack Europe and major cities there, and lone Isis followers attacking in the United States and Canada in 2020.

Where did all the Sunspots Go?

Our sun is behaving in a very strange way. As of December 12, 2019, the sun has been blank (no sunspots) for 266 days so far including the last 29 days in a row. If this continues for only 3 more days, 2019 will break the Space Age record for blank suns. The previous mark (268 spotless days) was set in 2008 during a historically deep Solar Minimum. The Solar Minimum of 2019 is shaping up to be even deeper. The current record-holder in the was blank for 268 days making the 2008-2009 solar minimum the deepest since 1913.

Could our sun have an evil twin out there, known as a brown dwarf or failed star that travels through our solar system every 3,600 years? There is speculation that Nibiru or Planet X, a brown dwarf, enters our solar system regularly and its size is huge, so much so that its magnetic pull affects our sun. Scientists say that most solar systems have two suns, and it would make sense that our solar system had two suns many eons ago. Brown dwarfs are objects which are too large to be called planets and too small to be stars. They have masses that range between twice the mass of Jupiter and the lower mass limit for nuclear reactions (0.08 times the mass of our sun).

How soon will our sun come alive again? As soon as Planet X starts to leave our solar systems. Right now we are feeling its presence on Earth with increased earthquakes and volcanic activity, mysterious booms, and extreme weather.

Atlantis Lessons Unlearned

Edgar Cayce, (1877-1945) known as the "Sleeping Prophet," gave thousands of trance readings on Atlantis, ancient Egypt, Earth changes and diagnosed illnesses for people, sometimes miles away. But the strangest is Cayce's description of Atlantis and how it became advanced in sciences, experimenting with DNA and genetics, produced half-human/half-animal creatures known as "Things". Now we believe such creatures were mythical, but they did exist and there were those compassionate humans in Atlantis that created temples to heal them and there were the mad scientists who kept creating them to be slaves. Cayce said that many of us alive today existed in those times before the continent of Atlantis began sinking into the ocean over 50,000 years ago. Fast forward to 2019: Chinese scientists have created pig monkey hybrids— paving the way to a future in which human organs could be custom-grown in animals for transplant. "This is the first report of full-term monkey-pig chimeras", Tang Hai at the State Key Laboratory of Stem Cell and Reproductive Biology in Beijing told New Scientist. Scientists are already experimenting with half-human/half-animal creations.

Genetics will change our world. Genetics can help health-care professionals to identify certain conditions in babies before they are born using techniques such as prenatal testing. Couples can pick the perfect baby—the color of their eyes, hair, and skin. Many of the genetic illnesses will vanish in the future. But like everything that has a positive side, there's also a dark side to genetics where humans can be altered to be super soldiers for future wars.

In the Year 2100

People will live in a far different world, a healed world, where most houses are round. Fewer people are living on the planet after a cataclysmic event years before. Children born in this century will have increased telepathic and psychic powers and will be honored for their gifts. Schools will be called Learning Centers and children will be taught to develop their psychic gifts. The climate will be more temperate and water will cover many lands now.

Mostly white robes and loose-fitting garments are worn in the future due to the warmer climate. People will be able to upload information to their brains and even download photographs from memories of events, just like a computer. Most will feel the need to eat a vegetarian diet and some fish, but no meat. Wars will be a thing of the past due to either a huge Earth pole shift or World War III. People of many colors gather and work in small communities, grow their vegetables and fruits, and everyone is treated equally. Money does not exist—only bartering. There will be temples of advanced healing, using music, resonance, herbs, crystals and some kind of triangle device to increase the vibration of the human body. Although there is an advanced technology, none of it is used for destruction or harming any living creature.

Some people are living on a space station orbiting Earth and there are people already living on Mars, where the planet is being terraformed into a place that will support life on the surface. A protective barrier has been put into place to protect the planet for harmful solar rays. People live in domes or underground.

Environmental Disasters (ED)
In 2015, Prince Ea, 31-years-old, activist, hip-hop artist and filmmaker, produced a YouTube video titled Dear Future Generations: Sorry.

"Sorry that we were too caught up in our doings to do something. Sorry that we listened to people who made excuses to do nothing. I hope you forgive us, but we just didn't realize how special the Earth was. We didn't know what we had until it was gone. You probably know it as the Amazon desert now but believe it or not, it was once called the Amazon Rainforest and there were billions of trees. They were gorgeous. You don't know much about trees, do you?

Trees are amazing. We literally breathe the air they are creating. THEY CLEAN UP OUR POLLUTION AND CARBON. They store and purify our water and give us medicine for diseases, give us food to feed us and that is why I am so sorry to tell you we burned them down, cut them with brutal machines, horrific at 40 footballs fields a minute. That is 50 percent of all trees gone in the last 100 years.

"Here's why... [Prince Ea holds up a hundred-dollar bill), if it wasn't for so many leaves on it. Sorry that we left you with a mess of a planet. When I was a child, I read how the Native Americans had such consideration for the planet for how they left the land for the next seven generations. This brings me great sorrow because most of us today don't care about tomorrow. I'm sorry that we put profit above people, greed above need, and the rule of gold above the golden rule. I am sorry that we used nature as a credit card with no spending limit, over-drafting animals to extinction before we could become friends with them. Sorry, we poisoned the oceans, so much you can't swim in them, but most of all I'm sorry about our mindset cause we have the nerve to call this destruction...PROGRESS."

Trees are dying worldwide from what scientists say is from "Climate Change." Most are afraid to use climate change or warming. Many of California's other tree species are already known to be at risk. The record-breaking drought that plagued the state from 2011-2016 killed an estimated 129 million trees, mostly in the state's mixed-conifer forests that include trees like white fir, only exist in California and they require 1000 gallons of water daily to survive.

Did you know that trees provide oxygen for our planet, they purify water, they clean up our pollution and carbon and they provide medicine? They need our love and prayers. If drought continues in California future generations will never see these sentient beings. Other tree species are already known to be at risk. The record-breaking drought that plagued the state from 2011- 2016 killed an estimated 129 million trees, mostly in the state's mixed-conifer forests that include trees like white fir, Douglas fir, ponderosa pine, sugar pine, and California black oak. The drought left entire swaths of the Sierra Nevada streaked with the sight of reddish-brown dying or dead trees.

Plastic and Our Oceans

How could an invention like plastic be so wonderful and yet so destructive to our environment? Every year, 8 million metric tons of plastics enter our ocean on top of the estimated 150 million metric tons that currently circulate our marine environments. Whether by errant plastic bags or plastic straws winding their way into gutters or large amounts of mismanaged plastic waste streaming from rapidly growing economies, that's like dumping one New York City garbage truck full of plastic into the ocean every minute of every day for an entire year! And that much plastic is bound to have an impact on the ocean ecosystem. Just think how all countries worldwide are also dumping garbage and plastic into the ocean and that plastic will not disappear—ever! Plastic production and consumption are predicted to double over the next 10 years. That means that if we don't do something now, we could be facing 250 million metric tons in the ocean in less than 10 years.

While plastic may break down into smaller and smaller pieces, these pieces are never truly biodegradable. Ocean fish and other sea creatures eat it and die and then we eat the fish and we die from various cancers. It's a vicious cycle. Birds, whales, dolphins and sea turtles get caught in plastic netting, and there are stories of a sea turtle with a plastic straw embedded in its nose or a whale entangled in a fishing net. Sometimes divers can release the animal from harm. Some of these incidents have a happy ending, but in reality, many more do not.

Nonprofit organizations like 4ocean.com are making a difference. Started by two surfer dudes, Alex and Andrew, from Florida, they had the vision to clean up the plastics in our oceans. To make the biggest impact on this global problem, they launched their efforts in places like Bali where a lot of plastic and other garbage regularly accumulates.

Inspired by successful lifestyle brands that built passionate followings, they decided to implement a business model that would allow them to grow quickly so they could pay workers, fund cleanups, and spread the word about the ocean plastic crisis.

So they created the 4ocean bracelet for $20.00 (a donation) and pledged to pull a pound of trash from the ocean for each one purchased, using the profits to scale cleanup operations, make donations to ocean-related nonprofits, and build an organizational infrastructure to support future growth.

I foresee other young people implementing ways of healing our planet. So how can we help with the plastics problem? First of all, buy glass or recyclable paper products whenever possible. Glass is from the Earth, and is a natural product that breaks down without any chemical residue. I know that most companies will not return to glass because of the expense, but we need to do it or find alternatives for plastic.

Polar Alert

Sea ice along Northern Alaska disappeared far earlier than normal in the spring of 2019, alarming coastal residents that rely on wildlife and fish. The ice melted as a result of exceptionally warm water temperatures extending far out into the ocean. The last five years have produced the warmest sea-surface temperatures on record in the region, contributing to record low sea ice levels. Polar bears are starving. In the Antarctic, krill are disappearing. They may be small, but krill—tiny, shrimp-like creatures—play a big role in the Antarctic food chain, especially for whales and penguins.

In the future, the warming waters of the Pacific will cause extreme storms and hurricanes. Last year, off the coast of San Diego, water temperature reached a record of 80 degrees. That's unheard of for these Pacific waters. It's the warmest it's ever been in the 102 years measurements have been recorded.

Our world is changing rapidly and many species will become endangered or extinct in a span of 10 years.

Goodbye Freedom of Speech

In the past year, I have noticed how hard it is to find conspiracy theories on YouTube videos. I was searching for conspiracy theories on chemtrails and 9-11 and all I could find was video after video debunking chemtrails and the 9-11 implosion bomb theories. Even on the internet, it's hard to find articles and videos on what is termed "conspiracy theories" with the naysayer's negativity that such things are fake news. If this continues at this rate, the new generations will never know the truth about chemtrails, 9-11 and other things that are being covered up.

More and more of your freedom will be taken from us in the coming years without many noticing. The ultimate tyranny in our society is not control by martial law, but by the psychological manipulation of consciousness.

The economy in the United States and World

Much has changed since the Coronavirus pandemic and the stock market has fallen to a new low. There have been some gains, but it will continue to be a roller-coaster with major downs and then up.

Unemployment is skyrocketing because of the Coronavirus shutdown of major businesses, restaurants, and hotels across the nation. People won't be able to pay their mortgages, their rent, their bills and thousands could be left homeless and penniless waiting for their stimulus check which won't be enough to cover all their bills. There will be massive home foreclosures and bankruptcies. People will be desperate.

I'd like to tell you that things will get better, but at this moment in time events look dire and the worst is yet to come. There will be people who will think outside the box and create new jobs and businesses on the internet. It will be a time for the strong.

*You're an interesting species. An interesting mix. You're
capable of such beautiful dreams, and such horrible nightmares.
You feel so lost, so cut off, so alone, only you're not. See, in all
our searching, the only thing we've found that makes the
emptiness bearable is each other. "
—Alien to Dr. Ellie Arroway
during her travel through a wormhole to an advanced distant
world—1997 movie CONTACT.*

AFTERWORD

Where are we going spiritually? I've asked this question for several decades and still, I find myself unable to get a clear answer. There are 7.8 billion of us divided as a people—we hate people for their religion, for their sexual preference, for the color of their skin, for their appearance, for their personality, for their obesity, for speaking their truth, for their political preferences, and we hate children that speak out about the environment. How can we ever get along as a species? Since the human species first walked on the Earth, we haven't gotten along. Will we destroy our planet and ourselves with our technology and our disconnect with Earth Mother? Or will we create a new world of peace and harmony? Will we look outside the parameters of our finely tuned perceptions or will we live in a bubble of ignorance, believing everything that we are told? Will those of you who are bringers of the truth today speak your truth without fear?

That does not mean demeaning or berating others in the process. As you rethink yourself, think about Earth and the destruction taking place everywhere today. Our biosphere, our lakes, our freshwater everywhere is becoming toxic, our oceans filled with oil, toxins, and plastics, and the planet's creatures are dying that hold the balance of the Earth.

The magic that once existed on Earth and its living library are no longer here. Rain forests are being destroyed that contain natural healing plants and the elements that protect them. Just think of all the creatures in the horrible wildfires set by arsonists in Australia that killed people and half a billion precious animals that were killed in the fires, burned alive.

A dark shroud has been cast over human consciousness, a darkness so vast that now many of us live in fear. Our bodies are filled today with cancer, stress, drugs, horrible food, and pollution because we have been primed for fear over the years and have drawn the negativity from other realms. Now we fear the monster Coronavirus. Lower vibration spirits feed off our fear. Reality mirrors itself. The marketing of fear has been massive and is growing each year. The problem is our system is corrupt, and it does not work and honor life, and it does not honor Earth. If something does not honor life and does not honor Earth as a living, sentient being, you can bet it is going to fall, and it is going to fall big time.

We are falling big time!

We are watched and monitored by higher beings. They observed us to see if we can save ourselves and this beautiful blue planet we call Earth. WE ARE THE ONES WE HAVE BEEN WAITING FOR—SO WHAT ARE WE WAITING FOR BEFORE WE CHANGE OUR REALITY?

Consciousness must change. When everything is taken from us, people will reprioritize what is important in their lives. Already people who have lost their homes by floods, wildfires and other natural disasters have learned the only important thing in life is each other and not material things. You can't replace a lost life! People are just beginning to awaken to their incredible potential.

If humans realized that our world is precious and can be destroyed like other worlds that have ended abruptly, the Earth wouldn't be in the predicament she's in now. Our innermost thoughts, our emotions, our feelings, and actions are recorded on the cosmic computer [Akashic Records] every second we exist or have existed. Nothing we do escapes the recorder. Perhaps each person would be kinder and more compassionate to all life on this planet and there would never be another war because each soul would understand that what they do as individuals determines their spiritual advancement.

We are standing on a precipice and any minute our world could cease to exist. For eons, we have been protected by the Star Elders, but there is only so much they can do. No one is coming to save us if we don't try to save ourselves from the mess we have created. But it goes much further than the destruction of our world, our home planet. What we do could compromise or even abort the Soul evolution of this world that we share with many life forms, and some of them are highly advanced beings. Unless our collective mass consciousness returns to a peaceful spiritual existence or Soul, we humans and our world will be one more long list of extinct species that have destroyed themselves or their planet.

Countless worlds have failed soul evolution experiments. Many people abducted by the gray alien Watchers have been told that they have our seed and DNA. They want to ensure that our DNA is not lost.

We often see ourselves as superior to all beings, but that is far from the truth. Many aliens species look like reptiles, ants, and even like the aliens in the *Star Wars* movie. Even the creature from the movie Star Wars known as Chewbacca "Chewie," a Wookie, which is a tall, furry, bipedal, and intelligent species from the planet Kashyyyk, really exists on our planet. Although most believe the Sasquatch, Yeti, Big Foot, Yowie, Almas, Skunk Ape, Misaabe, Bush Men, and Dooligah, are only legends, there is ample proof they do exist and are extremely intelligent. They are smart enough to have never been caught and put into a human zoo. Some say they are our Elders and although they have no written language, they have developed supernatural powers to escape human capture.

They existed long before humans walked on the Earth and they are in an intergalactic alliance with several dozen cosmic races that are observing us. They have made contact with those humans who are open psychically to them and they want to reach out to us, but they are truly frightened by what we are doing to the world we live in. They, like most indigenous races, understand that everything has a consciousness and is meant to be on the planet through evolution. It's a beautiful and perfect symbiotic relationship that humans just don't get. And some do get it but want to destroy the perfect harmony and relationship that all species have on the planet.

How can we change our thinking? Those of you, who are spiritually advanced, can come together, and intend a healed world. It takes visualization to see a new world that is healed and healthy again. Our thoughts are energy and that energy pulses into the Earth and can create miracles, but how many of you are willing to reach out to like-minded people and pray, intent and visualize a better world?

My wish is that everyone reading this book will reconnect to Mother Earth and Earth Wisdom like the Ancient Ones and indigenous people throughout the world. Each soul is made out of the dust of Stars, and we are all connected in ways we cannot imagine. We are One!

All living organisms store genetic information using the same molecules—DNA and RNA. Written in the genetic code of these molecules is compelling evidence of the shared ancestry with all living things. I know that everything has a consciousness, even rocks, and everything evolves toward the God Source. Plants, trees, and flowers have a living source, which ancient humans understood. It is only in our modern world that such Ancient Wisdom has been forgotten.

The Inca Wisdomkeepers say that once we step outside of time into infinity, the past and future disclose themselves to us—everything becomes clear.

Psychic Edgar Cayce said that 12 billion years ago, the energy gestalt we call God, existed in an unmanifested void, and so it decided to experience itself and produced the big bang, forming all matter in our universe and other universes. God continued to explore itself through all forms of matter—worlds, planets, stars, animals, insects, rocks, water, and all beings. It was both omnipresent and omniscient, and so were all its manifestations. If such a scenario is true, how can we deny our power and our connection to the Creator of all things?

It's time to say we've had enough of this insanity and disrespect for our Mother Earth. It's time to practice and live in *ayni,* and not only the Earth, but the universe will respond in kind to our actions. Time to walk in balance on the Earth and revere all things as divine, and created by Great Spirit or God. When we awaken to the unseen world, the spirit elements, and beings that surround our world and interact with us daily, we will have reached a perfect place of peace, grace, and understanding. But we will need to drop our egos like the purity of animals, and stop thinking that we are superior to all other life. We are equal to all.

We must teach our children a new way of living, to ensure future generations will have a beautiful Earth to enjoy and the abundance the Creator has given us. The Grandmothers tell us it is important to teach the children of the world how to humbly pray to the rocks, the trees, the sky, the mountains, the sacred waters, the birds, and all animals.

Like the Grandmothers, Ed McGaa and Corbin were deeply concerned about the younger generation, especially the Millennials (born between 1981 to 1997) and the future they are creating. Most younger people have become addicted to technology—their cell phones, video games, and texting. They have forgotten the natural world, the real world—it's sad for them and humanity and sad for Mother Earth. But the Millennials aren't the only ones. Most of us have become lost in technology and materialism and no have no idea what the natural world offers. Today the youth of the world seldom engage face to face with each other and instead they text each other. That isn't communication.

How will most of us survive if a great catastrophe should befall our planet? How will the young survive without Earth Wisdom? That's why we must teach them Ancient Wisdom.

Indigenous tribes who continue to practice the natural way will survive because this has been their way of life for eons. They understand the spiritual elements and the signs Mother Earth provides. They listen with open hearts—unlike most of us who have closed our hearts and have myopic minds.

Indigenous spiritual leader Corbin Harney believed it is very important to do the ceremonies and prayers. All of us need to get together again and again to honor Earth. He said, "Some of you go to church and pray together. That is very important, and it's what we must do. We also have to pray to the sun, the Earth, the water, and the air. I hope that we will all pick up this message that I'm putting out so that we can have a cleaner life, and so the younger generation can continue on."

We are connected to the Great Mystery. Through my own paranormal and spiritual experiences, I've learned there is so much more to life than what our normal senses perceive. There are other realities, parallel worlds, multiverses, and life forms that coexist with us in other realities. There are ghosts, spirits, angels, fairies, and deities that reside in our world—mostly unseen. Instead of having closed eyes, we need to open our eyes and minds to other possibilities, other realities, and realize that nothing is impossible, and everything is possible. We are fortunate to have taken on physical bodies to experience life at its fullest, to see with our physical eyes a sunset, a brilliant red sunrise, a rainbow arched across the sky, and an aurora borealis lighting up the night sky in vivid colors.

Life is a circle, as the ancients believed, and everything returns to the Oneness of life. As Earth changes increase, our bodies will feel the vibrational change. There are huge dynamics taking place within and on Mother Earth, and every living thing will be touched by those changes. If we believe the Hopi and that we are in the Purification Times, then the Prophecy Rock tell us that we have a choice. Will we save Mother Earth or watch her perish? Together, united, we can make a difference.

When we begin to understand the divinity, the cosmology of all life, we will no longer take our beautiful planet for granted, the Grandmothers tell us. They say in these times when the prophecies are being fulfilled, we are the ones who will determine whether or not we will destroy our Mother Earth and ourselves. Each of us should decide whether or not to live in harmony and with selfless love for the benefit of all. Not only do we have an obligation to ourselves but to the next seven generations still unborn.

Again, I ask, WHAT WILL OUR LEGACY BE FOR FUTURE GENERATIONS—DESTRUCTION OF MOTHER EARTH OR A WORLD OF BEAUTY AND BALANCE?

The Indigenous Grandmothers say it is important to create a more personal sense of connection by holding rituals, ceremonies, and festivals. It is then that we speak directly to the spiritual elements and Mother Earth. Ritual engages the spirit of a place, a circuit of energy in which the entire cosmos participates.

There was a time, the Grandmothers remind us when all of our ancestors revered Earth and used ceremonies to hold Earth's balance. Today, that balance no longer exists. "Prayer is the greatest thing I have as I walk upon this Earth," Grandmother Agnes of Oregon says. 'I am nothing without the Earth Energy. When you have the Creator with you, you have the force behind you, and negativity doesn't take over you, even in the dream time. You can't change even your children, except through prayer. Prayer is a duty that has been handed down from the Ancient Ones that went before us."

To be an Earthkeeper start with self-love and radiate that love outward—love Mother Earth, all her creation, and love all humanity. Eagle Man says, "Our survival is dependent on the realization that Mother Earth is a truly holy being, that all things in this world are holy and must not be violated, and that we must share and be generous with one another. Think of your fellow men and women as holy people who were put here by the Great Spirit.

Think of being related to all things! With this philosophy in mind as we go on with our environmental ecology efforts, our search for spirituality, and our quest for peace, we will be far more successful when we truly understand the Indians' respect for Mother Earth." In these times of great change, trust your intuition, trust what the creatures tell you, trust the sky, the ocean, the elements, the insects, the birds, the sea creatures to warn you when Earth starts to move in a big way. Speak to Mother Earth and ask her to guide you to safety areas—she hears your words. The most astonishing fact is that you are made up of stars, nebulas, galaxies, black holes—the very fabric of the universe. In other words—you are literally STARDUST, the atoms, and molecules of the universe. Now it's time to start acting like the remarkable spiritual beings we were created to be.

Astronomer, cosmologist, and astrophysicist Carl Sagan (1934-1996) left us with his beautiful words of wisdom in his book *The Pale Blue Dot,* "If you look at Earth from space you see a dot, that's here. That's home. That's us! It underscores the responsibility to deal more kindly and compassionately with one another and to preserve and cherish that pale blue dot, the only home we've ever known. Thank you all."

Healing Ceremonies
I recommend that all of you intend that the Native American teachings become a part of your life in some way. Begin to explore them through sweat lodge ceremonies, drumming, Pow Wow dancing, vision quests, and chanting. This will awaken many things in you and teach you about Mother Earth. Humans are coded to ritual; when you perform ritual, your body begins to remember who you are and what you know.

Prayers for Mother Earth take a few minutes each day. Sit down on Mother Earth and tell her you love and honor her. Give an offering of cornmeal (organic) or birdseed. Speak to her like you'd talk you're your own mother. Visualize her healthy, alive and vibrant. Visualize oceans teeming with life again, free of pollutants and trash. Visualize the rivers and lakes running clear again, see the animals, birds, finned ones and insects returning as they once did hundreds of years ago.

This exercise can be practiced alone or with other spiritually-minded people. Find a place where you can meditate away from phones and white noise. If you can escape to a river, mountain, lake or ocean, you'll find the energy much greater there (charged with negative ions). Draw a circle or create one with pebbles or stones. Step inside, relax, and still your body, while you visualize a pillar of light coming down from the heavens and filling your head. Although you can sit on the ground, Corbin Harney suggested that people stand up to pray, with the soles of their feet right next to Mother Earth. If you can take off your shoes, all the better to connect to Earth's energy.

As my mentor Corbin Harney saw it, all living things stand up, upwards. Energy can come from the bottom of your feet. Feel the pillar of light pulsating through your cells and your very essence. Bring the light through each of your chakra points—the Crown Chakra located at the top of the head, the Third Eye located on the forehead between the eyes, the Throat Chakra, the Heart Charka located at the center of the chest above the heart, the Solar Plexus located in the upper part of the stomach, the Sacral Chakra located at the lower part of the abdomen, and the Root Chakra at the tailbone. Allow the energy of light to enter the ground and into Earth Mother and visualize that pillar of pure white light traveling through Earth and around the planet, in the oceans, the land, the mountains, the rivers, the lakes and the people in those lands. See the light encompassing all creatures big and small.

Now speak to Mother Earth and tell her how much you love her. Tell her that you have come in a sacred way, and then give an offering of cornmeal or birdseed. Organic tobacco can be used as well. You can also burn sage or sweetgrass during your ceremony. Some prefer to chant or sing or even drum. Chanting Om or Oh is a great way to chant. If you have a rock or crystal you want to return to Mother Earth, this is a great way to show your reverence. It is a symbol of the value you have inside yourself and your gift to Earth. As you energize the planet, feel the pillar of light energizing you. Ask how you can make a difference for Earth now. Pray for the four directions, pray for truth, pray for healing, pray for knowledge, pray for everlasting love, pray for forgiveness and compassion.

Web of Life Prayer by Chief Seattle
Teach your children that the Earth is our Mother. Whatever befalls the Earth befalls the sons and daughters of the Earth. If men spit upon the ground, they spit upon themselves. This we know. The Earth does not belong to us, we belong to the Earth. This we know. All things are connected like the blood that unites one family. All things are connected. Whatever befalls the Earth befalls the sons and daughters of the Earth. We did not weave the web of life; we are merely a strand in it. Whatever we do to the Web, We do to ourselves.

Earth Prayer by Black Elk
Grandfather, Great Spirit, once more behold me on Earth and lean to hear my feeble voice. You lived first, and you are older than all need, older than all prayer. All things belong to you, the two-legged, the four-legged, the wings of the air, and all green things that live. You have set the powers of the four quarters of the Earth to cross each other. You have made me cross the good road and road of difficulties, and where they cross, the place is holy. Day in, day out, forevermore, you are the life of things. Hey! Learn-to hear my feeble

voice. At the center of the sacred hoop, you have said that I should make the tree to bloom. With tears running, O Great Spirit, my Grandfather, with running eyes I must say the tree has never bloomed. Here I stand, and the tree is withered. Again, I recall the great vision you gave me. It may be that some little root of the Earth Energy 195 sacred tree still lives. Nourish it then that it may leaf and bloom and fill with singing birds! Hear me, that the people may once again find the good road and the shielding tree.

Black Elk had many visions of the future and according to his cousin Benjamin, he was in the sweat lodge when a circular craft came out of the sky and hovered over it. Suddenly a stone penetrated the closed door and landed between Black Elk's feet. He picked up the stone but had to complete the sweat lodge ceremony before he could leave. By the time he was able to leave the lodge, the spacecraft was gone. Black Elk carried the stone with him the rest of his life with his vision of bringing together all people of the four directions—Red, White, Black, and Yellow.

Earth Healing Ceremony by Medicine Grizzly Bear – Spokane, Washington 1990 *O Great Creator*, I come before you in a humble manner and offer you this sacred pipe. With tears in my eyes and an ancient song from my heart I pray. To the four powers of Creation, To the Grandfather Sun, To the Grandmother Moon, To the Mother Earth, And to my ancestors. I pray for my relations in Nature, All those who walk, crawl, fly, and swim, Seen and unseen, To the good spirits that exist in every part of Creation. I ask that you bless our elders and children, families, and friends, and the brothers and sisters who are in prison. I pray for the ones who are sick on drugs and alcohol and for those who are now homeless and forlorn. I also pray for peace among the four races of humankind. May there be good health and healing for this Earth,

May there be Beauty above me, May there be Beauty below me, May there be Beauty in me, May there be Beauty all around me. I ask that this world be filled with Peace, Love, and Beauty.

Universal Meditation

This is the meditation for at least three people. Remove your shoes to feel Earth's energy. Draw a circle and within the circle, draw a hexagon, and step inside leaving a gap between each person. Standing inside the circle, stretch out your hands, arms and touch the person's palm next to you, so you are touching each other's hands with your fingers pointed upward.

This forms a triangle. Next, bow your head in reverence and begin to chant *Om* or *Oh* for several minutes! Clear your minds as you receive the universal energy—it's powerful!

I've been told that even beginners trying this meditation exercise experienced beams of light within the circle and around their heads. You may need to stop the exercise within minutes due to the incredible amount of energy created. As you continue this exercise, you'll build up to 10-minute meditations.

If you attempt this meditation, I suggest you allow only serious-minded people who want to create an energy ring for only the highest good. You can create a circle of six, but make sure that you connect palm to palm, with fingertips pointed upward, and then experience the energy.

BIBLIOGRAPHY

Felber, Ron, *Mojave Incident. Inspired by a Chilling Story of Alien Abduction,* Fort Lee, New Jersey, Barricade Books, 2015.

Fowler, Raymond E., *The Watchers. The Secret Design Behind UFO Abduction,* New York, NY: Bantam Books, 1990; *The Watchers II. Exploring UFOs and the Near-Death Experience,* Newberg, OR: Wild Flower Press, 1995.

Harney, Corbin, *The Way It Is,* Nevada City, CA: Blue Dolphin Publishing, 1995.

Lieder, Nancy, Zeta Talk. *Direct Answers From The Zeta Reticuli People,* Columbus, NC: Granite Publishing, 1991.

Lindsey, Hal, *There's a New World Coming,* Eugene, Oregon: Harvest House Publishers, 1973.

Marciniak, Barbara, *Bringers of the Dawn. Teachings from the Pleiadians,* Santa Fe, NM: Bear & Company, 1992; Earth. Pleiadian Keys to the Living Library, Santa Fe, NM: Bear & Company, 1995; Family of Light, Santa Fe, NM: Bear & Company, 1999.

Martin, Father Malachi, *The Keys of This Blood. Pope John Paul II Versus Russia and the West for Control of the New World Order,* New York, NY: Simon & Schuster, 1991.

McGaa, Ed "Eagle Man," *Mother Earth Spirituality—Native American Paths to Healing Ourselves and Our World,* New York, NY, Harper Collins Publishers, 1990.

Moosbrugger, Guido, *And Still They Fly,* Steelmark LLC; Revised edition 2004

Neihardt, John G., *Black Elk Speaks* – 1932.

Schaefer, Carol. *Grandmothers Counsel the World*, Boston, MA: Trumpeter Books 2006.

Stanford, Ray, F*atima Prophecy: Discover the Message and Meaning of Fatima,* Virginia Beach, VA, Inner Vision, 1987.
Summer Rain, Mary – Phoenix Rising: No-Eyes Vision of the Changes to Come, Charlottesville, VA, Hampton Roads Publishing, first publishing 1987.

ABOUT THE AUTHOR

At eight months of age, Betsey and her parents had a frightening UFO encounter late one night on a lonely Idaho highway as her parents drove from Northern Idaho to Southern Idaho to visit family. In 1981, Betsey and her mother were regressed through hypnosis by MUFON investigator and best-selling author Ann Druffel. They discovered that their UFO encounter involved two hours of missing time and alien abduction.

In 1981, Betsey and her mother were regressed through hypnosis by renowned author and MUFON investigator **Ann Druffel**. Both Betsey and her mother recalled an abduction by gray aliens with large heads who took them onboard a huge silver flying saucer. Paranormal events continued for Betsey since age three. She was communicating with two invisible beings who gave her secret messages. At the age of seven, she was followed home from her first-grade school by a giant silver disc in the sky, and shortly after the incident, Betsey began to have recurring dreams of massive Earth changes. These dreams were visions of the future taking place worldwide now.

Betsey inherited her psychic ability from several generations of women in her family. Throughout her life, Betsey experienced inexplicable events, UFO sightings, and visitations from Star Beings (benevolent ETs). She has always known that these paranormal experiences and premonitions of the future were given to her in order to prepare people for major Earth changes.

For over forty-five years, Betsey has investigated alien stories, UFOs sightings, ancient archaeological sites, explored ancient civilizations, and conducted field investigations into the bizarre cattle mutilations throughout the Northwest, and other paranormal mysteries. In the early 1980s, she collaborated with renowned cattle mutilation investigator Tom Adams to uncover the cattle mutilation mystery in the Northwest. She studied for ten years with two indigenous spiritual leaders—Western Shoshone Nation leader Corbin Harney and Ed McGaa "Eagle Man," Oglala Sioux Ceremonial Leader and Author during the 1990s.

Betsey has authored thirteen non-fiction books on spirit communication, life after death, healing Earth, UFO, aliens, Star Beings, Native American spirituality, reincarnation, and other paranormal topics. Just released *2020 Prophecies and Predictions* available on Amazon.

From 2009 to 2015, Betsey hosted the talk show Rainbow Vision Network, featuring best-selling authors and renowned investigators on paranormal/metaphysical subjects. She has been a frequent guest on Coast to Coast AM with George Noory, Ground Zero with Clyde Lewis, KTALK's The Fringe Paranormal Show in Salt Lake City, Fade to Black, Paranormal Central, New Orleans WGSO-AM Radio, and other popular talk radio shows. She was a keynote speaker at the UFO Conference in Alamo, Nevada in 2013 and was a speaker at the Stargate to the Cosmos Conference in Albuquerque, New Mexico in 2018.

Betsey's writing inspiration came from her step-uncle William "Bill" Peter Blatty, (1928-2017) director, producer, comedy screenplay writer, and author of the New York best-selling novel *The Exorcist.*

Betsey, her husband, and dog reside in the Southwest where she continues to provide psychic readings for an international clientele and experience premonitions. To learn more about Betsey, her psychic reading sessions and follow her Earth News blog visit https://www.betseylewis.com/

CPSIA information can be obtained
at www.ICGtesting.com
Printed in the USA
LVHW051512030121
675568LV00021B/3147